AIR POWER IN THE NUCLEAR

Also by R. A. Mason

AIR POWER IN THE NEXT GENERATION (*editor with E. J. Feuchtwanger*)
READINGS IN AIRPOWER
THE ROYAL AIR FORCE TODAY AND TOMORROW

AIR POWER IN THE NUCLEAR AGE, 1945–82

Theory and Practice

Air Marshal M. J. Armitage, CBE, RAF
Air Commodore R. A. Mason, CBE, MA, RAF

MACMILLAN

First edition 1983
Reprinted 1984

Published by
THE MACMILLAN PRESS LTD
London and Basingstoke
Companies and representatives
throughout the world

ISBN 978-1-349-04194-7   ISBN 978-1-349-04192-3 (eBook)
DOI 10.1007/978-1-349-04192-3

Contents

List of Maps

Foreword

Marshal of the Royal Air Force Lord Cameron, GCB, CBE, DSO, DFC

There has never been the same extent of strategic debate about the principles, effectiveness and uses of land or sea power as there has about air power. This is perhaps because it was the last arrival on the military scene and it used a little-understood third dimension. Its potential was greeted with much suspicion by a large percentage of so-called strategic thinkers. Churchill and Smuts, however, were in no doubt that one day it would dominate the battlefield and sea-lanes. Armies and navies saw the development of air power as a threat to their share of the limited financial cake and so tried hard to stifle its growth.

Unfortunately, the early air power advocates, perhaps in the nature of a precocious child, were inclined to overcall their hand on occasions and when put to the test could not entirely deliver the goods. Technology of the day did not move as quickly as doctrine. Seversky's dream that 'air power would be the key to survival' has not even yet been proved conclusively and there are still facets of modern warfare where its effectiveness can be limited.

The joint authors of this book are advanced and enlightened thinkers about the doctrine of air power as a vital and perhaps the most important element of modern and future warfare. This has not prevented them producing an objective study of what it can and cannot do, now and in the years ahead. My conclusion is that though air power may have been last on the scene in the military sphere, its potential in what is progressively a global scenario and coupled with the staggering developments in weapon and other technology may one day soon make it the 'key to survival'; if it is not that already.

Preface

In this study of air power, the authors have examined specific areas and campaigns which they believe to have had a particular significance for the evolution of theory and practice between 1945 and 1982. The result is that the survey is not a complete historical record, but rather a selective study ranging from the important role that air power plays in NATO strategy to the relatively minor contribution that it was able to make in, for example, the campaigns in Kenya or Aden.

The essential relationship between air power and ground and naval forces has not been underestimated, but because the emphasis in this study is on the role of air power the often parallel operations on land and at sea have not been dealt with in any detail. Nor has it been possible in such a brief study to pursue such vital considerations as those of manpower, or of the industrial base or the economic resources on which air power must ultimately depend. As to sources, some of them, for example, the French, but more important the Soviet, the Chinese, the Vietnamese and the North Korean, are still limited and restricted, and because of that the view taken by the authors has been not only limited to that of professional airmen but of British airmen, something that helps to explain at least the basis of the selectivity that has had to be applied.

In examining and analysing the theories and the practice of air power, the authors have been given a great deal of help from civilian and military friends in several countries, but the representation of facts and the conclusions that are drawn from them here are the sole responsibility of the authors, and they imply no endorsement from the United Kingdom Ministry of Defence or, indeed, from any other agency or individual.

The authors are very deeply indebted to the patient, unqualified co-operation of Mr John Andrews, Chief Librarian, The Ministry of Defence, London; Mr Chris Hobson and his staff at the Royal Air Force Staff College Library; Air Commodore Henry Probert, Head of the Air Historical Branch of the Ministry of Defence; and Mr Michael Root and his staff in the Staff College Drawing Office. Finally, the authors wish to acknowledge the unfailing good humour under stress of our typists Miss Glenys Evans, Mrs Daphne Stent, Mr John Hunter, BEM and Mr Geoff Blair.

M. J. A.
R. A. M.

Glossary

Some expressions which are used in the liturgy of air operations may be unfamiliar to the reader, while others are open to differing interpretations. They are used by the authors with the following meanings.

Air superiority. The ability to exercise sufficient control over a particular airspace at a particular time as to be able to carry out one's own air operations effectively with little or no enemy interference while, at the same time, denying the same opportunity to him.

Air supremacy. Usually indicates a broader and longer degree of control of airspace and would tend to be associated with a campaign and theatre of operations rather than a single or limited engagement.

Avionics. The generic term used to describe the electronic and electrical instruments in the cockpit of an aircraft, components in the aircraft and its weapons system.

Close air support. Used to describe air attack on enemy ground forces which may actually be in contact with friendly ground forces.

Combat air patrol. Describes the mounting of standing patrols by armed interceptors across the potential tracks of intruding enemy aircraft, or in the vicinity of a particular target area.

Combat radius. The combat radius of an aircraft is the distance which it can fly from its base, complete its operational activity and return to base. An alternative expression may be 'operational radius' and both expressions should be distinguished from 'range' which usually signifies a single journey between two separate points and may or may not include the carriage of weapons.

Command of the air. Denotes the absolute control of airspace, as opposed to the more limited concepts of air superiority or air supremacy.

Conventional. Used to denote operations, aircraft or weapons which are not nuclear, chemical or biological.

Counter-air operations. Designed to achieve air superiority or air supremacy by attacking the infrastructure of enemy air power,

notably his airfields, but including command, control, communication, radars and air defences.

Electronic countermeasures. The general term denoting methods of
degrading enemy radar or other sources of electronic activities. They
would include spoofing, jamming, decoying or, in certain circumstances, actual destruction.

Electronic counter-countermeasures. As the name implies, electronic
counter-countermeasures are the measures devised by the opposition
to neutralise electronic countermeasures.

Glacis. Defensive area.

Interceptor. Whereas traditionally some aircraft were classified as
'fighters', it is increasingly common now to distinguish between an
'interceptor' which will be designed for longer-range employment,
probably in combat air patrols, and air superiority 'fighters' which are
likely to be much more agile and suitable for close air-to-air combat.

Interdiction. The use of air power to sever supply links and to dislocate,
disrupt or destroy resources moving along them, between an enemy's
rear areas and the battlefield. Thus 'battlefield interdiction' would
imply air attack close to the actual combat area, while 'deeper
interdiction' would imply longer-range attacks on roads, railways,
bridges, etc.

Maritime operations. All air activities associated with naval forces are
referred to as 'maritime operations'.

POL. The usual military abbreviation for 'petrol, oil and lubricants'.

Stand-off. Refers to an aircraft's ability to launch air-to-surface
weapons some distance from the actual target instead of actually
over-flying the target to drop 'free-fall' weapons.

Stick. Used to describe a number of paratroops dropped in a group.

Strike. The use of the term 'strike', as applied to operations or roles or
aircraft, implies that nuclear weapons are involved.

Tactical. Has traditionally referred to aircraft or weapons of relatively
short range which would normally be employed in one theatre or
region. However, the traditional distinction between 'tactical' and
'strategic', which has usually referred to activities transcending
theatres or referring to the war as a whole, has latterly become
blurred.

Variable geometry. The expression used to describe an aircraft whose
wing, either whole or part, may be moved during flight to achieve
different degrees of sweep and thereby achieve improved effectiveness
in different flight conditions.

List of Abbreviations

AA	anti-aircraft
AAFCE	Allied Air Forces Central Europe
ABCCC	Airborne Battlefield Command and Control Centre
ACTS	Air Corps Tactical School
AOC	Air Officer Commanding-in-Chief
ASW	anti-submarine warfare
AWACS	airborne warning and control system
CAT	Civil Air Transport
COMAAFCE	Commander Allied Air Forces Central Europe
CP	Command Post
C-in-C	Commander-in-Chief
C^3	command, control and communication
DMZ	demilitarised zone
EAF	Egyptian Air Force
ECCM	electronic counter-counter-measures
ECM	electronic countermeasures
ESM	electronic support measures
EW	electronic warfare
FA	Frontal aviation
FAC	Forward Air Controller (Soviet)
FEAF	Far East Air Force
GATAC Nord	Northern Tactical Air Group
GATACs	Tactical Air Groups
GRU	Soviet General Staff
HE	high explosive
IAF	Israeli Air Force
ICBM	intercontinental ballistic missile
IDF	Israeli Defence Forces
IFF	Identification Friend or Foe
IISS	International Institute for Strategic Studies
IR	infra-red

IRBM	intermediate range ballistic missile
JCS	Joint Chiefs of Staff
JOC	Joint Operations Centre
KT	kilotons
LRA	Long-Range Aviation
MAC	Military Airlift Command
MACV	Military Assistance Command Vietnam
MRLA	Multi Role Large Aircraft
MT	megatons
NADGE	NATO Air Defence Ground Environment
NAF	Naval Air Force
NATO	North Atlantic Treaty Organisation
NKAF	North Korean Air Force
NKPA	North Korean People's Army
OASD	Office of Aerospace Systems and Development
OPEC	Organisation of Petroleum Exporting Countries
ORBAT	order of battle
POL	petrol, oil and lubricants
PVO	Soviet Air Defence
PVO-Strany	Soviet Air Defence Command
RAAF	Royal Australian Air Force
RECS	Radio Electronic Combat Support
RFC	Royal Flying Corps
RNZAF	Royal New Zealand Air Force
SAC	Strategic Air Command
SACEUR	Supreme Allied Commander, Europe
SAAF	South African Air Force
SAF	Soviet Air Force
SAM	surface-to-air missiles
SAS	Special Air Service
STAVKA	Supreme High Command (Soviet Union)
STOVL	short take-off and vertical landing
TAC	Tactical Air Command
TASMO	tactical air support of marine operations
2TAF	Second Tactical Air Force
UNC	United Nations Command
UNO	United Nations (Organisation)
USAAC	United States Army Air Corps
USAAF	United States Army Air Force
USAF	United States Air Force

USAFA	United States Air Force Academy
USAFE	United States Air Force Europe
USMC	United States Marine Corps
USN	United States Navy
VHF	very high frequency
VNAF	Vietnam Air Force
VTA	Military Transport Aviation (Soviet Union)
VSTOL	vertical, short take-off and landing
VTOL	vertical take-off and landing

1 The Dominant Factor

In August 1945 the longer-term implications of the devastation inflicted on Nagasaki and Hiroshima tended to be lost in more general feelings of relief as six years of worldwide bloodshed and misery came to an abrupt halt. Since then, however, it has been increasingly difficult to formulate any ideas about the present and future application of air power without ultimately taking into account the presence of nuclear weapons.[1] Indeed, the delivery of the weapons in 1945 seemed to mark the culmination of the pervasive impact of air power during the Second World War. So much so, that Marshal of the Royal Air Force Lord Tedder could quietly assert at the University of Cambridge in 1947:

> I am utterly convinced that the outstanding and vital lesson of the last war is that airpower is the dominant factor in this modern world and that, though the methods of exercising it will change, it will remain the dominant factor as long as power determines the fate of nations.[2]

Nor was such an assumption restricted to airmen who might have been accused of having a vested interest. The greatest statesman of his age, not always an unqualified devotee of air power, expressed his opinion in a famous address at the Massachusetts Institute of Technology in 1949. Mr Churchill said:

> For good or ill, air mastery is today the supreme expression of military power. And fleets and armies, however necessary and important, must accept subordinate rank. This is a memorable milestone in the march of man.[3]

Eminent soldiers were also convinced. In a widely reported address to the Royal United Services Institution in London in 1954, Field Marshal Viscount Montgomery, then Deputy Supreme Commander, Allied Forces in Europe, 'looked through a window at World War III'. After reflecting on the existence of a cold war, he predicted the likely progress

1

of a hot war: 'It is clear from the strategy I have outlined that the dominant factor in a future war will be airpower'.[4]

The gap between the theory and the practice, however, had taken a long time to close. As early as 1893, Major J. D. Fullerton of the Royal Engineers had presented a paper at a meeting of military engineers in Chicago in which he prophesied that the impact of aeronautics foreshadowed 'as great a revolution in the art of war as the discovery of gunpowder', that future wars might well start with a great air battle and that 'the arrival of the aerial fleet over the enemy capital will probably conclude the campaign'.[5]

In one man's lifetime, the aerial fleet had been reduced to one aeroplane and one bomb.

THE CONCEPT

The distinctive expression 'air power' was used in connection with manned aircraft very soon after the Wright Brothers' success and before Bleriot flew the English Channel in 1909. It was used by H. G. Wells in his *War in the Air* to describe the product of an 'immense aeronautic park'[6] and in 1909 F. T. Jane cautiously observed that 'airpower can hardly be more than one of many factors in deciding the issue of future wars'. Since that time there have been many attempts to define it, ranging from a simplistic but widely held view that air power is synonymous with strategic air bombardment to the extended definition of analysts such as Possony who, in 1949, identified a complex of at least fifteen elements including raw material, industrial potential, guided missiles, morale and intelligence as well as aircraft.[7]

In 1945 General Hap Arnold was more precise and more practical:

Airpower includes a nation's ability to deliver cargo, people, destructive missiles, and war-making potential through the air to a desired destination to accomplish a desired purpose.[8]

If one asks how does air power differ from military power on land and sea it is possible to move towards a working definition which is equally appropriate to 1908 or 1980. Air power is the ability to project military force by or from a platform in the third dimension above the surface of the earth. The element which distinguishes air power from land and sea power is the fact that the third dimension above the earth is actually exploited to advantage by the platform or vehicle; for example, for manoeuvre, deployment, concealment or surprise rather than simply traversed as by a bullet, a shell or ballistic projectile. The grey areas – for example, a ballistic surface-to-surface missile with independently targetable warheads, and the entire field of surface-to-air weapons – do not significantly detract from the central distinction. Moreover, such a definition recognises two other qualities of air power which are sometimes overlooked. In common with sea or land power, it has a latent impact; the influence of an aircraft still on an airfield, akin to the influence of a warship over the horizon. Second, air power may apply force directly, as in bombing or air-to-air fighting, or it may distribute it, by providing air mobility or rapid resupply to surface forces, or it may amplify it by providing reconnaissance or surveillance.

The earliest air power concept, as opposed to concepts of air power, seems to have been 'command of the air'. It is generally associated with Guilio Douhet's book of the same name published in 1921, but in fact the idea was well formed in the English language several years before. Major Fullerton, for example, in his Chicago address had considered it would be a prerequisite for all land and air warfare. In 1911 a British officer wrote the first article on air power to be published by the *Journal of the Royal United Services Institution*, first concentrating on the aeroplane as a reconnaissance vehicle, but then expressing the deeper concern of the islander: 'May not the command of the air be as important to us in the future as the command of the sea is at the present moment?'[9] while in France, General Frey asked 'May not the command of the air be of such importance that the power who loses it may be forced to sue for peace?'[10]

In reflecting on the enormous breadth of those speculations it is salutory to remember the actual capability of the aircraft at that time. In 1912 the first certificate of airworthiness was written at the British Army aircraft factory at Farnborough for the first Bleriot experimental aircraft to be handed over to the Air Battalion of the Royal Engineers of the British Army. It read:

BE1 Certificate

This is to certify that the aeroplane BE1 has been thoroughly tested by me, and the mean speed over a three-quarter mile course with a live load of three hundred and fifty pounds and sufficient petrol for one hour's flight is 58–59 miles per hour. The rate of rising loaded as above has been tested up to six hundred feet, and found to be at the rate of one hundred and fifty-five feet per minute. The machine has been inverted and suspended from the centre and the wings loaded to three times the normal loading. On examination after this test, the aeroplane showed no signs of defect.

14 March 1912   S. HECKSTALL-SMITH
                                      for Superintendent Army Aircraft Factory

Command of the air could not easily be won with machines like the BE1, for reasons which Major General Trenchard expressed when commanding the Royal Flying Corps in France in 1916:

> Owing to the unlimited space in the air, the difficulty one machine has in seeing another, the accidents of wind and cloud, it is impossible for aeroplanes, however skilful and vigilant their pilots, however numerous their formations, to prevent hostile aircraft from crossing the line if they have the initiative and determination to do so . . .[11]

Indeed, command of the air in the sense of denying all use of the air to a potential enemy, while retaining unimpeded use of it oneself, has very seldom been achieved. More often, it has meant 'air superiority' or 'air supremacy' in a given region for a given period. Trenchard sought air superiority over the area where he most wanted it, over the battlefield, by

> a policy of relentless and incessant offensive. Our machines have continually attacked the enemy on his side of the line, bombed his aerodromes, besides carrying out attacks on places of importance far behind the lines. It would seem probable that this has had the effect so far on the enemy of compelling him to keep back or to detail portions of his forces in the air for defensive purposes . . .[12]

After the First World War the emphasis on offensive air power increased. From Trenchard's initial belief in offensive air power in indirect support of the ground forces, he came to endorse the primacy of the strategic offensive against the enemy's heartland, albeit still expressed in defensive terms:

> It must be clearly realised that Home Defence does not mean only the process of keeping attacking aircraft from flying over this country. In its broadest sense it means the winning of an air war against any power which may decide to attack us. To win this war, it will be necessary to pursue a relentless offensive by bombing the enemy's

country, destroying his sources of supply of aircraft and engines and breaking the morale of his people.[13]

From there, it was but a short step to the unqualified tenets of air bombardment:

It is not, however, necessary for an air force, in order to defeat the enemy nation, to defeat its Armed Forces first. Airpower can dispense with the intermediate step, can pass over the enemy Navies and their Armies and penetrate the air defences and attack the centres of production, transportation and communication in which the enemy war effort is maintained . . .[14]

The Royal Air Force was in no need of a Douhet to formulate its concepts and, indeed, Marshals of the Royal Air Force Sir Arthur Harris and Sir John Slessor later denied all knowledge of Douhet as they contributed to the formulation of bomber doctrine before 1939.[15]

In the United States, Mitchell was strongly influenced in 1917 by both Trenchard and Italian thinking, possibly originating from Douhet, and there was a subsequent progression of doctrine in the USAAC similar to that in the Royal Air Force. In 1936 a hostile air force was still nominally a primary strategic air objective but only to enable 'unhampered pressure' to be brought against the enemy nation.[16] By 1938, the Air Corps Tactical School was teaching that:

The possibility for the application of military force against the vital structure of a nation directly and immediately upon the outbreak of hostilities is the most important and far-reaching development of modern times.[17]

These were the tenets of doctrine in the US and the UK which were to survive the Second World War and be reinforced by nuclear power.

Elsewhere, other air forces and air arms pursued different lines. Germany's Air Force was independent but, nevertheless, harnessed to the classical Clausewitzian concept that the primary objective in war was the destruction of the enemy's Armed Services and thus was equipped to contribute to *Blitzkrieg*. The Soviet Air Force, numerically the strongest in the world, was driven both doctrinally and organisationally by the purges of 1936–7. The Japanese Air Forces, on the other hand, subordinated to Army and Naval control, competed strenuously between each other to formulate doctrine credible enough to justify a greater share of defence resources. One result was Commander Genda's concept of the mass carrier strike force which was to have such a dramatic impact on the opening months of the war in the Pacific.[18]

Despite the initial and international acknowledgement of 'command of the air' little was done except in the US to provide for air defence until the years immediately before the Second World War. Support for 'pursuit aviation' was strenuously maintained by a strong but very junior minority at the Air Corps Tactical School but was faced with problems similar to those identified by Trenchard in the First World War. Without any way of early warning of air attack, defensive aircraft lacked the endurance to mount combat air patrols, the power to climb rapidly to intercept, and the speed to chase, catch and destroy bombers even in clear weather. Only with the advent of radar, greatly improved monoplane design and more powerful engines could 'fighter' aircraft be considered viable alternatives to the 'offensive-defence' based on the bomber.

It is therefore easy to see how, before 1939, air power did tend to become synonymous with strategic bombardment. It was even more significant to the Royal Air Force and the USAAC because it also epitomised their belief that air power should be applied by an organisation quite independent from Army and Navy control. The role concentration did not prohibit the allocation of resources to Army or Navy co-operation (in the UK), but it certainly afforded them a lower priority and thereby made more difficult an even-handed and progressive analysis of the contribution of air power to the statesman in peacetime and to the commander-in-chief in war.

On the one hand, air power had added a new dimension to existing strategies on land and sea. It had become possible to seek, locate and attack enemy surface forces before, during or after they closed with their immediate opponents. In addition, it could make an independent strategic contribution, either by carrying the war over the heads of the surface combatants to the enemy's heartland, or by defending one's own heartland against a similar offensive. Or, as adroit Nazi propaganda demonstrated, it could cast an independent shadow over diplomatic negotiations and foreign policy decisions. Sir John Slessor was not the only airman to be 'obsessed with the knock-out blow',[19] thought to be within the power of Hitler's Air Force in 1938. The following year the fears were proved to be groundless as the practical realities of war began to impinge upon the theories.

THE SECOND WORLD WAR

Between 1939 and 1945 Air Marshals and Air Force Generals who had learned their trade in aircraft little different from BE1, were called upon to organise and command the fleets of Lancasters, B-17s, Spitfires, Mustangs, Messerschmitts, Sturmoviks and the rest. They were supported by staffs who, for the most part, had been called to service on the outbreak of war or subsequently, and who frequently had no staff training, limited awareness of current operations and no first-hand knowledge of the capabilities of the new equipment which they were planning to commit to combat. Under such circumstances it is not surprising that pre-war theory and wartime practice were not always in harmony. Indeed, it was surprising that air power made the impact, in all theatres of war, that it actually did.

From the first day of the war it added the new dimension. In Poland, and subsequently in Western Europe, the Luftwaffe attacked airfields, communications, equipment parks and ground force combatant units in conjunction with the rapidly advancing German mechanised armies. Aircraft were used as flexible long-range artillery in close air support and battlefield interdiction roles. Regional air supremacy was established by technical superiority, concentration of force and counter air operations against airfields, especially in Poland. In France, for example, only 416 RAF aircraft and 1,200 French faced the 2,750 combat aircraft assigned to the campaign,[20] and no Allied fighter could match the performance of the ME-109. In the Russian campaigns, on the other hand, after the initial successes of 1941, German offensive air support was not so easy to provide. Quite apart from the problems posed by Russian winters, the areas of operation were many times greater than in the restricted campaigns of Poland and France. Aircraft designed for short-range support could not take the war more deeply into Soviet territory, could not disrupt Soviet aircraft production or training and therefore could not maintain command of the air. Nor could German aircraft production, prepared for a short war, make good increasingly heavy losses. By July 1943, in the region of Kursk, 2,000 Russian aircraft faced 400 German: the product of Soviet industry which the previous year had built 25,000 aircraft for one theatre while Germany had managed only 15,000 for three.[21] Such numerical disparity allowed the Soviet High Command to construct reserve air formations which could be used flexibly to achieve the required concentration of force, culminating in the final assault by 8,000 aircraft on the German Armies in Eastern Europe in 1945.[22]

Naturally, however, it was Western use of air power in support of armies which tended to establish post-war precedents. Despite the need to maintain the air defence of the UK, progressively more aircraft were released in 1941 to support the British ground forces in North Africa. Numerical and, ultimately, technical superiority was established over the Luftwaffe and slowly close air support tactics were developed which were to become a model first for Europe and then for the post-war Alliance. In a distinct geographical region it was possible to control all kinds of air power from one headquarters: fighters, reconnaissance, light attack and longer-range bombers. Once close and harmonious relations had been established with the Army Command, comprehensive tactics could be evolved which included offensive fighter sweeps against enemy aircraft, rather than defensive air superiority battles, and carefully co-ordinated short- and long-range interdiction of communications, supply routes and reinforcements. The whole was provided with constant armed air reconnaissance, mobile signal units and well-organised maintenance. Most important of all, the Royal Air Force enjoyed increasingly marked numerical superiority as the campaign developed and there was no industrial heartland behind Rommel, either constantly replenishing his aircraft and crews or drawing long-range bombers away from targets in obvious indirect support of ground forces.

Later, when the Desert Air Force principles had been successfully adopted by the dominant allies in Europe in 1944, the 'cab-rank' system of 'on-call' close air support was to give rise to a certain amount of post-war mythology. The fighter-bomber, typified by the British Typhoon, earned a high reputation for its ability to be summoned swiftly to the assistance of harassed land forces at a speed which enabled it to be switched from one threatened sector to another. A notable contribution was made in the Falaise Gap on 7 August 1944 when Typhoons of 83 Group of the Royal Air Force flew 294 sorties against the 47th Panzer Corps. Several Typhoons were damaged but only 3 lost, all to ground fire. The pilots claimed to have destroyed 119 tanks and 73 other vehicles, and damaged another 21 tanks and 39 vehicles. The Chief of Staff of the German 7th Army reported that his armoured attack had been brought to a standstill by 'the employment of fighter bombers by the enemy and the absence of our own air support'. Undoubtedly, the Typhoon attack was timely and decisive, but the subsequent report on the battle by AOC 2TAF was far from euphoric. Ground examination of the vehicles after the battle did not support the claims of the pilots. This did not provoke surprise because no combat film could be available to confirm kills, target identification and discrimination was frequently difficult and 'it had long been known that it was difficult to secure a large percentage of hits with rocket projectiles'. The report observed that the only definite conclusion that could be drawn from that operation was that air action was capable, in certain conditions, of breaking up a determined land attack. In that battle very favourable circumstances had combined to present an ideal target of a large number of tanks and motor vehicles head to tail in close country, opposition on the ground was negligible and in the air non-existent, and it had been possible to apply maximum air effort at a critical stage in the battle. Very seldom had circumstances such as these occurred together on the British Front.[23] Plausible theories could be developed about close air support which would not necessarily apply to a situation where the opposition had overwhelming air superiority, one's own ground forces were retreating, it was not bright sunlight and enemy armour was spread out rather than head to tail. The obvious danger was for air power to promise, and land forces to expect, too much. The essential point of the Typhoon attack was that it had caught the German armour still in column, but too close to the battlefield to be able to detour and still maintain its momentum. Further forward, it would have deployed to engage; further back, it would have had alternative routes. It was a classical example of battlefield interdiction.

Deeper interdiction could be more difficult. Unless the terrain restricts the number of possible reinforcement routes, the deeper the interdiction the more difficult it is to sever all links and the easier to circumvent what destruction has been achieved. Consequently, quite apart from additional range, such interdiction calls for much heavier bombardment over a much wider area. A considerable contribution to exercise 'Overlord' in June 1944 was, therefore, the interdiction of German reinforcement routes in Normandy. Railways, marshalling yards, bridges and highways were systematically destroyed by Allied heavy bombers so that German reserves had to make constant detours, were frequently delayed and consequently unable to mount counterattacks in sufficient force. Again, however, the interdiction campaign was centrally directed and co-ordinated with fighter activity which ensured almost complete air supremacy in the region.

It was that degree of air supremacy which not only allowed exercise 'Overlord' to proceed without interference from German air power, but also be spearheaded by airborne forces. Earlier in the war the spectacular success at Fort Eben Emael in Belgium and well co-ordinated drops in Norway had been followed by the Pyrrhic victory of German paratroop forces in Crete. Air mobility for ground forces was restricted not just by the need for local air superiority but by the size and quantity of transport aircraft generally available. Not surprisingly, therefore, it was the overwhelmingly superior Allied war industries which could afford to produce the number of vehicles used for 'Overlord' and for the subsequent Arnhem and Rhine crossing operations. There was little argument in 1945 that air supremacy was a prerequisite for such operations, that swift ground force support was essential and that, consequently, large-scale airborne operations might require more supporting resources than all but a very small number of very precise objectives could justify. Clandestine operations, however, well inside hostile territory, had been greatly facilitated by air power in occupied France, Yugoslavia and behind German lines in Russia.

Resupply by air eked out the defences of Stalingrad, maintained ground forces in Burma and gave a modicum of support to China. Generally, however, while only a small percentage of the total volume of supply to the armies was transported by air, in most cases these supplies were critical items requiring delivery at a critical time and place. One such example was the air delivery of 800,000 lb of supplies to the US 101st Division at Bastogne in December 1944. But without air supremacy, as for example at Stalingrad, and in the face of well-co-ordinated ground fire as at Arnhem, slow and cumbersome transport aircraft were very vulnerable.

Indeed, in operations in support of ground forces in all theatres two very important principles were established. First, at least localised command of the air was essential before positive assistance could be given to friendly forces, especially when slower aircraft were involved. Second, unless a region could be isolated from its industrial and training source, either by geography or by longer-range attack, the struggle for regional command of the air would be incessant.

AIR POWER IN MARITIME OPERATIONS

Although the provision of air support to land forces was ultimately on a larger scale than that required for maritime operations, the contribution of air power to the war at sea was frequently decisive and always dominant. At the outbreak of war, German and British maritime air power had been restricted by lack of naval enthusiasm and by low Air Force priority, but German aircraft exacted a heavy toll on Allied shipping in the Norwegian campaign and sank one million tons in the Atlantic, or almost half the total losses, in 1941. Thereafter, the provision of Allied escort carriers in September 1941 quickly ended the depredation of the long range Focke-Wulf Kondor.[24] Despite the provision of escort carriers and other naval protection, the German U-boat threat continued to grow until the beginning of 1943. From 17 boats on station in 1939 the U-boat strength in the Atlantic rose to over 100. In March 1943, 627,000 tons of Allied shipping were sunk but, thereafter, long-range air patrol rapidly reduced the areas where boats could confidently either transit or recharge batteries on the surface. The ring between North America, Iceland, the Azores, and the British Isles was slowly closed. In July, of 86 boats which tried to cross the Bay of Biscay, 55 were sighted, 16 sunk by aircraft and 1 by surface attack and 6 forced to return, for the loss of 14 aircraft.[25] Of the total U-boats lost in the war, nearly 60 per cent were destroyed by aircraft including losses from some of the 50,000 sea-mines laid by aircraft of Bomber Command.

The continuous submarine war was punctuated by spectacular demonstrations of the vulnerability of unprotected capital ships to air attack. The manner of the destruction of the *Prince of Wales* and *Repulse* by Japanese land-based aircraft, by *Bismarck* after carrier attack and *Tirpitz* trapped in a Norwegian fjord, closed the pre-war arguments about battleships and air power. In the Pacific, maritime operations were dominated by air power from the first attack on Pearl Harbor, which also resolved any doubts the US might have had about whether to develop a battleship or carrier strategy in the theatre. Within twelve months, at Midway, US naval air power had marked a turning point in the Pacific war. Four Japanese carriers, 322 aircraft, 100 experienced pilots and a lot of prestige were lost. The battle prepared the way for the later US carrier offensives into the Western Pacific, through the 1944 battle of the Philippine Sea, ultimately making possible the destruction of Japanese merchant shipping, the recapture of island territories, the construction of air strips for land-based aircraft and, ultimately, the assault on the Japanese mainland itself.

During the six years, a great deal was learned by air forces about maritime operations. The location of surface vessels was greatly helped by radar, but identification could still be a problem, as two German destroyers off Norway were the first to discover when sunk by the Luftwaffe. Closely co-ordinated control of both air and surface elements was essential to avoid duplication of effort and to reduce the risk of failure. The running of the English Channel by the *Scharnhorst*, *Gneisnau* and *Prinz Eugen* in 1942 provided a case history for both the Royal Air Force and the Royal Navy of poor communications, inadequate briefing, bad logistic support, indecisive leadership and poor tactical judgement which was still worthy of study thirty years later. The theoretical qualities of air power were, however, fully demonstrated in all aspects of maritime operations. Superior speed, extended combat radius, surprise and increasing ability to navigate through all weather by day or night reduced the old challenges and need for distinctive skills which had strengthened the pre-war naval claim to control its own land-based aircraft. But there was clearly a need for improved communications between ship, shore and aircraft, closely co-ordinated strategies and weapons designed for use in a maritime environment. Above all, as in operations in support of land forces, a favourable air situation had to be won before any other activity could successfully take place.

INDEPENDENT OPERATIONS

Air Marshal Harris, Commander-in-Chief of Royal Air Force Bomber Command, had strongly opposed the transfer of heavy bombers to contribute to maritime operations. In one sense he was correct, in that the weapons then available did not damage U-boat pens and high-level bombing was seldom effective against individual surface vessels. Nevertheless, his strong adherence to an undistracted strategic bomber offensive against Germany was, and remains, controversial. The offensives against Germany and Japan have been the subject of innumerable studies to attempt to analyse exactly what contribution they made to Allied victory, at what cost and whether the resources should have been allocated elsewhere.[26] Consequently, the development of the campaigns is well known. Bomber Command started the war with the intention of seeking specific targets by day and by night to destroy the industrial capacity of Germany. By day, the German fighter defences were too strong; by night the bombers carried neither the navigation, target acquisition, bomb-aiming nor destructive equipment capable of matching their intention. The reason for the gap between pre-war intention and wartime application with its roots in economic restriction, allocation of priorities and considerable difficulties involved in rapid expansion have been similarly examined. What has not received quite so much emphasis is the fact that the Royal Air Force was well aware of its shortcomings before the outbreak of war.

In a lecture to the Royal Air Force Staff College on 11 May 1939, Wing Commander F. J. W. Mellhuish explained the problems identified by No. 25 Armament Group. They included inadequate numbers and training for air observers (navigators), crews inexperienced on potential operational types of aircraft; infrequent opportunities for long-distance formation bombing practice; inadequate facilities for high-explosive bombing training; inadequate on-board basic facilities for aircrew; an expectation that results with higher-speed bombers would actually decline; difficulties in target identification, particularly in built-up areas; and even a doubt 'whether precision results will ever be achieved'. He concluded his address by identifying the fundamental problem of a small air force trying desperately to expand rapidly and re-equip to prepare for a war quite beyond the levels of its previous experience:

I want to end, however, with a word of warning. There seems to be a tendency to hitch our wagon to a very distant star, and for many of the important problems nearer at hand to be neglected. The equipment in our squadrons is by no means as efficient as it should be, and I feel sure that if part of the time now spent on long-range problems were devoted to the perfecting of our existing equipment, we should be very much better off. Many of our aircraft may be obsolescent but, if we go to war, they are the ones we shall have to fight with, and it is of vital importance to us to ensure that our weapons really do work efficiently. I fully realize the importance of long-range development work, but I contend that efficient functioning of existing weapons should come first and should not be neglected in favour of less pressing problems.[27]

The United States Army Air Corps had two extra years in which to prepare to join the war. It, then, also quickly discovered that precision bombing by daylight over practice targets in the US was one thing; fighting through European weather against a highly organised and determined German fighter force was something else again. The subsequent disasters after initial successes are also well documented. A combination of numerical superiority, technical advantage, long-range fighter escort and the degradation of German forward defences by Allied ground troops after 1944 was required before the German industrial heart could be ravaged as the theorists had prophesied. As the Allied bomber offensive had achieved one of its objectives, to divert more and more German resources to what Speer called Germany's biggest defeat, it inevitably made that objective more and more difficult to achieve as German resources were progressively re-allocated to thwart it. Hence the bitter struggle for air supremacy over the enemy's heartland itself. But in the arguments about the offensive's effectiveness, which usually include suggestions that air resources would have been better allocated to support of more traditional surface roles, it should be remembered that the air superiority upon which those tactical operations depended was itself ultimately dependent on the inability of Germany to replace the aircraft and train new pilots to make good the air power which it had lost. For example, there seems little recorded doubt that command of the air was an essential prerequisite for the preparation and mounting of exercise 'Overlord'. The fact that it had been won was attributable to the destruction of the Luftwaffe over Germany and northern France and the failure of the German war machine to make good the losses. That situation is readily compared with the one in the same area four years before. The inability of the Luftwaffe to destroy Fighter Command denied the German High Command the critical prerequisite for operation 'Sea Lion'. Aircraft designed solely for short-range army support could not cope with strategic demands. The problems of fighter escort range, muddled intelligence, poor leadership, unco-ordinated strategy and failure to appreciate the significance of British radar only compounded the basic problem. Upon strategic air defence depended the ability to maintain production of all other weapons systems. Until August 1945 it could only be broken down by strategic air offence. Only in August 1945 was a swifter way discovered to effect the necessary destruction, and even then only in the complete absence of air defence.

The impact of radar, jet engines, rocket technology and atomic power had combined to complicate the analysis and conclusions to be drawn about the actual extent and impact of air power on the Second World War. Unfortunately, the emergence of friction between Allies, and the almost immediate threat of another conflict, apparently with atomic weapons available from the start, meant that there would be little time for quiet reflection and the measured identification of lessons. Such activity, for the most part, would await the attention of historians absolved from pressures of responsibility but equipped with the advantages of hindsight. There would be no time for leisurely re-equipment, examination of campaigns and the unhurried reconstruction of doctrine and concepts appropriate to a future age. Lessons had to be drawn from personal experience, perception and hastily compiled combat records. It would not, therefore, be surprising if interpretations were all, in one way or the other, influenced not only by the fog of war but inevitably by national, organisational and personal preferences and prejudices.

THE INFLUENCE OF THE UNITED STATES

It is a truism of military history that it is not necessarily so much the quality of the lessons drawn as the influence of the analyst which determines the interaction between theory and practice. Consequently, when a considerable extent of quality and quantity in analysis was allied to political, military and industrial power, one could expect to see a very strong influence exerted on subsequent events. That was the situation of the US with regard to the development of air power in 1945.

At the end of the Second World War, the US had $11\frac{1}{2}$ million men under arms of whom $2\frac{1}{4}$ million were in the USAAF. She had over 31,000 combat warplanes, as opposed to the 9,000 of the Royal Air Force. The Soviet mobilisation was larger, and her air power numerically greater, but her influence would not match that of the US for many reasons. First, and most obviously, was the US possession of the atomic weapon. Second was the existence before August 1945 of a coherent if embryonic US concept of strategic air power. Disagreement in the US tended to concentrate not on the concept itself, but on which particular military organisation should discharge it. Third was the opportunity in the US to develop ideas publicly and to exchange them internationally. Fourth was the existence of a large and politically influential group of aerospace industries. For example, in 1944, the US produced 93,623 aircraft as opposed to 26,462 in the UK. Of the former, 14,861 were heavy bombers, compared to 5,507 in the UK.[28] The final reason was the swift awareness in the US that air power, particularly strategic air power, was a convenient instrument of military policy for a country which did not wish to maintain a large standing army and whose geographic circumstances were conducive to the projection of long-range offensive military power.

Conversely, little was known about the scale and details of either Soviet operations or doctrine. There had been little development in Soviet long-range bombardment capability during the war. What ideas did circulate were closely guarded military secrets and there was no residue of Soviet pre-war theory available to Western analysts. Indeed, there is little evidence of much Western search for it.

Nor was there much opportunity for the UK to wield any influence. The prestige of the Royal Air Force was extremely high in 1945, based not just on the total strength of 55,000 aircraft but on the accumulation of professionalism and success in all roles during six years of combat and a worldwide lead in jet-propulsion and electronic warfare. Yet, within

eighteen months the British Service had evaporated to 38,000 regular
personnel, supported by conscripts, and little more than 1,000 front-line
aircraft. Diminished resources restricted the re-equipment of fighter
squadrons with jets and postponed the entry into service of a jet bomber
until 1951. There had been no British anticipation of post-war air power
requirements, certainly no long-range concepts and, finally, no access to
atomic weapons. The dominant influence would, therefore, at least in
the early years, be unquestionably American.

As early as 1943 a Post War Division was established in the US War
Department to plan the size and structure of the post-war Army Air
Force. The staff officers were strongly influenced by belief in the
effectiveness of a strategic bombing offensive and by the associated need
to establish an autonomous Air Force, free from Army command and
control.[29] They were, of course, not privy to atomic weapon development and therefore force proposals were largely based on conventional
long-range heavy bombardment. General H. H. Arnold and other
leading airmen warned consistently of the vulnerability of the US to any
opponent who acquired a long-range bombing capability. The folk
memory of Pearl Harbor was very strong and frequently quoted. as by
General Spaatz to the Senate Military Affairs Committee in November
1945:

> The next war will be preponderantly an air war . . . attacks can now
> come across the Arctic Regions, as well as across oceans, and strike
> deep . . . into the heart of the country. No section will be immune.
> The Pearl Harbor of a future war might well be Chicago, or Detroit,
> or Pittsburgh, or even Washington.[30]

Earlier that year, before the attacks on Hiroshima and Nagasaki,
General Arnold had not only expressed his concern about vulnerability
but predicated the ingredients of strategic deterrence:

> It is clear that the only defence against such warfare is the ability to
> attack. We must, therefore, secure our nation by developing and
> maintaining those weapons, forces, and techniques required to pose a
> warning to aggressors in order to deter them from launching a
> modern devastating war.[31]

By November 1945 the atomic weapon had been included in the concept:

> While this country must employ all of its physical and moral force in

the cause of peace, it must recognise that real security against atomic weapons in the visible future will rest on our ability to take immediate offensive action with overwhelming force. It must be apparent to a potential aggressor that an attack on the United States would be immediately followed by an immensely devastating air atomic attack on him. The atomic weapon thus makes offensive and defensive airpower in a state of immediate readiness a primary requisite of national survival.[32]

That same very comprehensive report by General Arnold to the Secretary of War contained reflections on the lessons of the Second World War and forecasts of the future. With remarkable prescience it envisaged supersonic unmanned flight, intercontinental ballistic missiles, surface-to-air guided missiles, a 'netted' communication system linking individual aircraft and control centres, fully automated take-off and landing, navigation and target location, and the long-range projection of airborne task forces. In another paragraph it added to the distilled truths of air power:

National safety would be endangered by an air force whose doctrines and techniques are tied solely to the equipment and processes of the moment. Present equipment is but a step in progress, and any air force which does not keep its doctrines ahead of its equipment, and its vision far into the future, can only delude the nation in to a false sense of security.[33]

Not for the first time, however, the immediate difficulty was matching available equipment with current doctrine. In post-war Washington defence planning, the relationships between resource allocation, role responsibility and organisational control were complex and frequently acrimonious. Consequently, when the Air Force was presented in August 1945 by the War Department General Staff with a post-war plan for 70 Air Groups, and it was decided that they should include 25 very heavy bomber and 25 fighter groups, the Air Force

still saw strategic air operations – both offensive and defensive – as its principal mission and claim to autonomy. Everything else revolved round the strategic mission: doctrine, funds, aircraft, organisation, bases, personnel, strategic planning and technology.[34]

Yet there was little substance to support the atomic offensive postulated by General Arnold. Because the Air Force was not privy to details of the atomic bomb – at this stage, for example, assembly teams were still civilian – constraints were placed on the training of bomber commanders, weaponeers and flight crews. Planning staffs were further hampered by lack of target information about the Soviet Union, already designated by various euphemisms as the potential enemy. A member of the Office of Air Force History in 1978 summarised the situation:

> Even if an atomic plan had existed in late 1946, the nascent Strategic Force would have found its execution difficult, if not impossible. The 509th Bomb Group had 10 of 23 modified aircraft in commission, 20 trained crews, and few atomic bomb shapes – known as Fat Man 'Pumpkins' – for loading and bombing practice. Only 16 of 46 Silverplate B-29s modified during the war were available to operational units, while another 18 were stripped of equipment and in storage. Six of 16 very heavy bombardment groups were activated with aircraft; 3 had no aircraft; and the other 7 were not activated. The Air Force was far short of its goal of an all atomic strategic air arm to carry out its doctrines of atomic warfare and would have had serious trouble conducting even conventional operations.[35]

Not surprisingly, the infant Strategic Air Command, formed in 1946, did not develop the expertise which, even had the weapons been available, could have put the theory into practice. In October 1948, General Le May was appointed Commander-in-Chief and quickly decided to run a realistic test on the capability of his new charges.

He had learned that training missions were being flown at 15,000 feet, visually, in good weather, and over bright reflected targets on desert ranges. For the mission of 9 January 1949, things would be different. He would mount the entire force, require them to bomb by radar from 30,000 feet – the target would be Wright Field Outside Dayton, Ohio. A 1938 aerial photograph of Dayton would approximate in its relative accuracy the sorts of intelligence photos of Russia then available to SAC which were virtually all taken from German files in 1945.

The mission proved a complete failure. At 30,000 feet engine problems mounted, pressurisation systems failed, oxygen systems malfunctioned and inexperienced radar navigators had great difficulty reading (radar) scope returns. There were no 'shacks' (bullseyes) and innumerable 'boon dockers' (wide misses), the average displacement from the intended target running from five thousand to eleven thousand feet. Le May would later comment that 'you might call that just about the darkest night in American military aviation history. Not one aeroplane finished that mission as briefed. Not one.'[36]

Even allowing for the possible hyperbole of a forceful and extremely successful Commander-in-Chief, the reality of the actual strength which underlay the displays of force made by President Truman at the time of the Berlin Airlift,[37] when none of the deployed B-29s could have carried the atomic bomb,[38] seems to suggest either ignorance or a very strong nerve on the part of the President. At first, deployment to forward operating bases in Europe or the Pacific was required because of the range limitation of the B-29, and the bomber had to be accompanied by transports carrying unassembled atomic weapons, loading equipment and ground crews. The Command's capability was extended at the end of the decade by the intercontinental piston-engined B-36 carrying self-contained atomic weapons over a range of 10,000 miles. In 1953, the MIKE thermonuclear explosion at Eniewetok had a yield equivalent to 10,400,000 tons of TNT (10.4 MT) or 520 times the destructive capability of the weapons dropped on Hiroshima and Nagasaki. It became possible to produce weapons of 1–2 MT which would only weigh some 3,000 lb. When the B-52 entered service in 1955, able to carry thermonuclear weapons on intercontinental two-way missions, and SAC had reached a level of professionalism deemed satisfactory by its Commander-in-Chief, theory was finally substantiated by capability.

The theory of deterrence by the threat of strategic nuclear air bombardment was to dominate air power for the next twenty years. It was to prove translatable to Europe to underpin NATO strategy, but even five years before the advent of the B-52, it was to be challenged by events in the Far East. There, neither strategic offence nor strategic defence was to prove relevant, and some lessons from the Second World War had to be re-examined.

2 Air Power in Korea

Before Korea, all our military planning envisaged a war that
would involve the world and in which the defence of a distant
and indefensible peninsula would be folly.

General Ridgway[1]

In 1945 the Japanese occupation forces in Korea north of the 38th
Parallel had surrendered to the Soviet command, and those south of that
line had surrendered to the Americans. Five years later this convenient
division of responsibility had hardened to become part of the wider
global confrontation between East and West, and after a lengthy period
of local military and diplomatic skirmishing the North Koreans invaded
South Korea on 25 June 1950. The Security Council of the United
Nations called on the North Koreans to withdraw behind the 38th
Parallel, and when they failed to do so US forces were committed under
UN authority.

From the very beginning the US was faced with the problem of
whether to limit the war or to extend it, a subject on which there was
profound disagreement at the higher military levels. The fact was that
the US was ill-prepared for a war of any kind, and even the limited
conventional conflict that now began found the US forces seriously
short of resources.[2] It was a shortage that was aggravated for the USAF
by the need to preserve a strategic air capability, as well as by the need to
devote what little was available in the way of theatre or tactical air effort
to the first priority – which was Europe. As General Ridgway later said:

The industrial skills, the manpower, the technology, the mills and
factories, the quickly exploitable raw materials, and above all the
close ties of blood and culture – all these persuaded Washington that
Europe must come first and Asia second.[3]

As far as the USAF[4] was concerned, therefore, Korea took second place
among the second priorities.

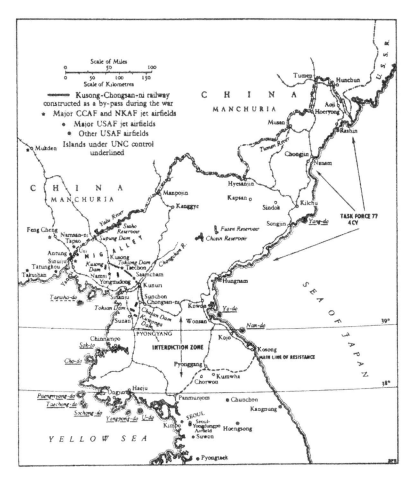

MAP 1 *Air War against North Korea*

When the war began there were actually no US combat forces at all in Korea; the last US Army units had been withdrawn in June 1949 leaving behind only about 500 military advisers. Far East Command as a whole, of which Far East Air Force was the air component, had only one minor mission in war that related to Korea and that was to provide for the safety of US nationals in the country. FEAF, with its extensive area of operations stretching from Japan to the Ryukus, the Marianas and Philippines, had under command on 25 June 1950, 30 USAF squadrons, the equivalent of 9 of the 48 combat wings in the whole of the USAF and a total force of 1,172 aircraft.

But it was an air force which, according to its commander General Stratemeyer, was totally inadequate for anything other than a limited defence of Japan, Okinawa and the Philippine Islands.[5] Only 553 aircraft were actually on operational units, and two-thirds of these were F-80 Shooting Stars, an aircraft designed for air defence and the oldest of the USAF operational jets. F-84 Thunderjets, an aircraft that had been adapted for the air-to-ground role, were to have joined FEAF in 1949 but could not be accepted because of a lack of suitable bases. In July 1950 there were only four airfields in Japan that had the 7,000-foot runways needed by combat-loaded jet fighters, and the means to build more was lacking. The FEAF engineer aviation units, or airfield construction units, were at this time poorly equipped, mal-deployed, grossly undertrained and 46 per cent under strength. Just as serious as this lack of combat aircraft and bases was the fact that, because the primary mission of FEAF was air defence, it had been training almost exclusively in that role. What little effort had been made towards joint operations with ground forces had gone into academic exercises that bore little resemblance to the demands of war.

Finally, there were the very important questions of the command and control of air power, and of its effective employment. Although in common with all theatre commanders MacArthur had been given a directive in December 1946 requiring him 'to establish a joint staff with appropriate members from the various components of the Services . . . in key positions of responsibility',[6] nothing had been done until August 1949 and even then only token measures had been taken. In spite of the obvious need to co-ordinate land-based air with ground operations and with carrier operations, the result, at least until the end of July 1950 – when improvised but still quite inadequate procedures were brought into use at Pusan, was what the official USAF history calls a 'fantastically confused command situation in the Far East'.[7]

As to naval aviation, at the start of the war the US Navy had one cruiser, four destroyers and six minesweepers in Japanese waters, but no aircraft carriers. Within a few days, however, the 7th Fleet had arrived in Formosan waters from Hong Kong and Subic Bay, and on 1 July Task Force 77 sailed for the West Coast of Korea with Pyongyang as its objective. Two assault carriers, the USS *Valley Forge* and HMS *Triumph*, made up the Carrier Group of the fourteen-ship force, and on 3 July the first sea-borne strike was launched by fifty-seven aircraft. It was the start of a contribution by carrier-borne air power that was to last throughout the war.

The strengths of the air forces in the Far East at the start of the war were thus very modest. Land-based aircraft in particular were short of equipment and other resources and they were inadequately trained for the roles that they were called on to perform. Not only that, but combat mobility as well as the chain of command and control for joint operations were all thoroughly unsatisfactory. As General Weyland, the Commander of FEAF from June 1951, would say in his report after the war: 'An astounding facet of the Korean War was the number of old lessons that had to be relearned'.[8]

The first lessons emerged very quickly; others were to follow throughout the four phases of the war that can be distinguished. The first of these phases lasted from June 1950 to the establishment of the Pusan perimeter two months later; the second was from Pusan to the defeat of the UN forces on the Chongchon River in November of that same year; the third lasted from the Chongchon to the stabilisation of the line in the spring of 1951, followed by the armistice in July 1951; and the fourth phase was the search for air target systems during the last twenty-four months of almost static ground warfare until the end of the war in July 1953.

RETREAT TO PUSAN

On 1 July 1950 the US Army began to move units into South Korea by air and a blockade of Korea by sea was implemented. On 2 July, B-29 Superfortresses from Okinawa attacked Yonpo airfield near Hungnam, where most of the North Korean force of 62 Ilyushin-10 aircraft was based,[9] and in the next few days carrier-borne aircraft joined in attacks on airfields and other targets in north-west Korea. By the end of July all but a handful of the enemy aircraft had been destroyed, mostly on the ground, and by the end of August it was estimated that the NKAF was capable of only 16 sorties per day.[10]

With that kind of air supremacy UN aircraft were now able to operate against targets well behind the enemy lines and to engage in close air support for the hard-pressed ground forces who were by now retreating towards the South. As the situation worsened, F-51 Mustangs[11] were taken out of storage in Japan and committed to the battle with considerable success both at this stage and at later stages of the campaign. They were the only UN aircraft that could operate from the poor airfields in South Korea, from whence they were nevertheless able to produce high sortie rates, and they could carry napalm which was highly effective against tanks and infantry. The jet aircraft on the other hand had no wing racks for bombs, and being based in Japan they could neither react quickly to tasking nor remain long in the battle area on cab-rank. In the words of General Timberlake at the time:

> One Squadron of Mustangs adequately supported (inside the Pusan perimeter) is equivalent to four F-80 squadrons based on Kyushu (Japan). Even Superfortresses were committed to support the battle-line, and from 10,000 feet they bombed targets of opportunity such as tanks, trucks and troops on the roads leading south towards Pusan.

General Ridgway was to write later of this phase of the war:

> As for our airmen, without them the war would have been over in 60 days with all Korea in Communist hands . . . the fliers of the Air Force, the Navy and the Marine Corps . . . managed to eliminate the North Korean Air Force early in the battle, destroyed much of the NKPA armour, and transported critically needed men and supplies to spots of greatest danger.[12]

By 4 August the Pusan perimeter was established, reinforcements were arriving in a steady stream and the battle to hold Pusan began. Air power was constantly used in support operations[13] and, for example, on 2 September at a critical stage of the battle, the US 2nd and 25th Divisions received 300 close support sorties from Navy and Air Force units.[14] Such operations were not, however, conducted without great difficulty. Timely intelligence was often lacking, techniques for effective air and ground co-operation had been forgotten, and most of the aircraft of FEAF were based in Japan, 150 miles and more away.

Sporadic interdiction attacks designed to prevent, delay or destroy the movement of enemy forces or their support to the battle area also had some effect during July, but the immediate needs of the battle absorbed most of the available air effort. In August it became possible to widen the scope of air operations and a modest strategic bombing campaign against industrial assets in North Korea was begun. A very small proportion of the FEAF B-29 effort was directed against arsenals, refineries and hydroelectric plants in the North, and in conditions of total air superiority a destruction rate of 55 per cent on those targets was claimed.[15]

Far more significant than the physical effect of these attacks, however, was the intrusion of a new reality into the equation of military effort and politico-military results. Although every effort was made to avoid international criticism of the attacks by forbidding the use of incendiary weapons, by carefully confining the raids to military and industrial targets and even by dropping leaflets giving pre-warning of the attacks, the Communists made capital from claims that the attacks were indiscriminate and barbarous.

If the air offensive had been decisively successful this reaction might have been unimportant; but the scale of the raids meant that even in terms of the North Korean target systems they were inconclusive. Worse than that, however, since the NKPA drew most of its supplies from sanctuaries beyond the borders of Korea, the overall military effect of the attacks was very small and on balance the raids probably did more harm than good at this stage of the war.

In parallel with that strategic bombing offensive, new efforts were put into interdiction, and Interdiction Campaign No. 1 was started on the 2nd of that month. On 25 August, 5th Air Force[16] for the first time flew more interdiction sorties than close support missions. Attacks were made on main transportation centres, key bridges and marshalling yards and the immediate results were very encouraging. On 4 September, for example, at the end of this particular interdiction campaign, all but seven of the forty-four bridges north of the 38th Parallel listed for destruction by Bomber Command had been put out of action.[17] About one-third of the total 5th Air Force effort at this time had been launched against interdiction targets that lay south of the 38th Parallel and among other successes they maintained forty-seven rail cuts on the main rail line between Seoul and Taejon.[18]

This level of destruction undoubtedly weakened the North Koreans' ability to maintain heavy equipment such as tanks and artillery in the front line, but the impact of the campaign was far less than had been hoped. As the USAF Historical Study admits:

In general the disruption of the already strained transportation network served to slow down the movement of supplies to an appreciable degree, but it never caused an abrupt halt . . . rarely, if ever, did the destruction of a road or rail line occasion more than two days' delay in the delivery of [North Korean] supplies.[19]

There were three reasons for this. First, the North Korean logistic demands were very modest; a division could fight with only 50 tons of resupply each day.[20] Second, the determination of the American forces to cut the NKPA supply routes was no match for the ingenuity and highly competent staff work with which the North Koreans sustained them. The North Koreans not only diversified their network of routes, they also showed a remarkable ability to improvise and to repair those bridges that were absolutely vital. And lastly, their columns were carefully dispersed and camouflaged by day, but reassembled and moved forward by night.

The air forces had no answer to this. No night intruder unit had existed in the USAF since 1948[21] and although local experiments with flares and with co-ordinated attacks were tried, they all failed.[22] The second reason revealed another forgotten lesson. Because the North Koreans held the initiative on the ground, their command could adjust its activity at the fighting front to match the level of supplies that were arriving. From time to time that level was high enough to permit heavy attacks on the Pusan perimeter, and in response to this pressure the USAF then switched back to extensive direct support missions, thus taking pressure off the enemy supply routes. In Korea, as in northern Italy and in Normandy in 1944, successful interdiction seemed to mean holding the initiative on the ground as well as in the air.

INCHON

With the Inchon landings by the 10th US Corps on 15 September, the pace of the war changed. The FEAF contribution to the landings was to provide general air support, to isolate the objective area – for which purpose Interdiction Campaign No. 2 was launched on 9 September – and to furnish air support for the 8th Army. FEAF would also provide cargo air support for the forces ashore and it would take an airborne Regimental Combat Team into battle.

This latter task was of particular interest. In order to lift simultaneously, as requested, all 3,500 paratroopers and the heavy equipment of the 187th Airborne Regimental Combat Team, no fewer than 140

C-119s or their equivalents were needed. In the event, the 187th could not reach the Far East until nearly a week after the Inchon landing, and the invasion went ahead without the airborne contribution. When the paratroopers were eventually committed, it was in an operation 30 miles north of Pyongyang designed to cut off as many retreating North Koreans as possible. In all, 2,860 paratroopers and 300 tons of supplies were dropped by 111 aircraft on the first day, and a further 1,093 troops and 106 tons on the second by 71 aircraft. It was an effort that, among other things, caused all other transport commitments in the theatre to be cancelled for the preceding two days so that essential aircraft maintenance could be carried out.

In so far as it caused the North Koreans to abandon some of their defences and inflicted casualties on the enemy that were claimed to be as high as 5,764 killed and captured out of an estimated force of 6,000 engaged, the drop was successful. But even if accurate, these claims scarcely justified the effort that was invested. Indeed the air drop was actually advanced one day because the ground forces were making such rapid progress in pursuit of the North Koreans. Many years later, General Tanner, the FEAF Combat Air Cargo Commander, said of this operation: 'The same result could have been achieved with a frontal infantry thrust combined with a tank encirclement. The drop was not worth the effort . . . it was unnecessary.'[23] Airborne forces had thus been used not because their unique qualities were essential to the success of the campaign, but simply because they existed.

As part of the general shift by UN forces to the offensive, on 9 September a rail interdiction campaign was mounted against the lines north of Seoul, with attacks on the marshalling yards and on the tracks that ran through thinly populated areas where, it was calculated, repairs would be more difficult. Other attacks were made against airfields to destroy the remaining handful of North Korean aircraft, and meanwhile the preparations for the breakout from the Pusan perimeter continued with heavy air attacks on enemy ground positions. On 11 September FEAF flew 683 sorties – the highest number so far in the war, and the breakout itself was preceded by attacks made with two groups of B-29s carrying out saturation bombing of areas indicated by ground forces, as well as by extensive air support further ahead of the advancing UN forces.

Enemy resistance collapsed within a few days, and the advance from Pusan became a pursuit with FEAF continuing its close air support work, and with B-29s making what amounted to harassing attacks by day as well as by night to prevent the escape of enemy ground units.

Interdiction Campaign No. 3 which had been planned to destroy 33 key enemy bridges at this time, was first cut back and then finally abandoned when it became clear that the remaining bridges would be of more use to the rapidly advancing UN command than to the retreating North Koreans. On 27 October the whole of the B-29 command was stood down from operations.[24]

The defeat of the NKPA had been so rapid and so decisive that on 29 September General MacArthur and South Korean President Rhee flew to Seoul for a victory parade. But what had caused the North Korean defeat was less clear. In his report to the UN dated 30 September, General MacArthur said: 'The seizure of the heart of the enemy's distribution system in the Seoul area has completely dislocated his logistical supply to his forces in South Korea and has quickly resulted in their disintegration'.[25]

But the Air Force view was somewhat different. According to the USAF Historical Division survey: 'Viewed in the light of prisoner of war reports, it was evident that the North Korean army was defeated by relentless air–ground action in South Korea – not by the opportune amphibious invasion at Inchon'.[26]

The truth was that each would have failed without the other. Air interdiction had proved ineffective so long as the North Koreans had dictated the tempo of the ground fighting. Once they lost that initiative, however, the combination of their losses at the front and their inability to replace them swiftly from the rear, brought about a collapse. The precipitate retreat of the NKPA was the result of the combined effects of ground and air action.

The advance of the ground forces towards the Yalu continued, heavily supported by airborne resupply,[27] but there were now clear signs that the Chinese were about to intervene in the war. On 15 October Chinese anti-aircraft (AA) guns fired across the Yalu for the first time and thereafter they engaged all aircraft that appeared along the river. Three days later more than 75 Communist fighters were seen on Antung airfield, and on 1 November Mig-15s were identified south of the Yalu for the first time. During these same two weeks at the end of October enemy ground resistance stiffened and by the end of the month the first Chinese troops had been taken prisoner by UN forces.

DEFEAT ON THE CHONGCHON

In the face of stiffening resistance, the 8th Army was now compelled to withdraw to the Chongchon River to regroup and to build up its supplies before resuming the advance. But meanwhile the South Korean 2nd Corps had collapsed under heavy Communist attack and the campaign took on an entirely new complexion when US troops found themselves engaged by Chinese forces on the night of 2 November. In the growing crisis there was renewed pressure from local commanders for heavier air attacks on North Korea, and on 5 November General MacArthur directed that two weeks of maximum air effort be launched against the Korean end of all the Yalu bridges, followed by a progressive move southward of the air attacks so as 'to destroy the enemy means of communication and every installation, factory, city and village'.[28]

At President Truman's direction the Joint Chiefs of Staff in Washington at once intervened to instruct that no bombing attacks should be made within five miles of the Korean border, but when MacArthur protested that 'men and material in large forces are pouring across all bridges over the Yalu from Manchuria', and that the only way to stop the flow was to destroy the international bridges and other installations supporting the enemy advance, the Joint Chiefs relaxed the ban on the Manchurian border though not on the frontier with Siberia.[29]

The seventeen major bridges over the Yalu proved to be very difficult targets. They were sited on a winding river, the far banks of which could not be over-flown, and enemy AA fire forced the B-29s to bomb from above 18,000 feet, a height at which real precision was impossible. About half the available Bomber Command sorties were directed against these bridges, while naval aircraft from USS *Valley Forge, Philippine Sea* and *Leyte*[30] flew an average of well over one hundred sorties a day against the six bridges that had been allocated to Task Force 77.[31]

By the end of November these combined attacks had put out half the bridges and damaged most of the rest, but it became increasingly clear that the expense of the attacks could not be justified by their results. There were three difficulties. First, the Communist engineers were again showing extraordinary powers of improvisation and adaptation. During the bombing campaign itself, for example, four new pontoon bridges were thrown across the Yalu at critical points. Second, Japanese railway engineers who were not only familiar with the Yalu but who had in many cases actually built the bridges across it, told FEAF that the winter ice on the Yalu could support rail tracks laid across it, and that trains had moved over the river in this way in the past. It would therefore be far easier for the enemy to replace destroyed bridges than the UN Commanders had calculated. Third, it was in any case too late to stop the Chinese invasion. Four Chinese armies, or very roughly 120,000 men[32] were already in Korea, and air reconnaissance had somehow failed to detect them.

It was true that the reconnaissance facilities of the USAF, including of course those of FEAF, had been severely constrained by defence economy programmes between 1945 and 1950, but the fact was that even the limited potential[33] that did exist in the theatre, and that was a daylight capability only, was being directed at the wrong targets, first on the Yalu crossings and second on the immediate battle area. The Chinese Army had shown considerable ingenuity in avoiding detection in the first area, and they had not yet deployed in the second. Finally, the few sightings of movement on the intervening area that had been made seem not to have been given the weight that they deserved.[34] These grave deficiencies were to have immediate consequences.

On 28 November General MacArthur reported that 'an aggregate strength of over 200,000 [Chinese] is now arrayed against the United Nations in Korea',[35] and he switched to a defensive posture. The 8th Army broke off combat north of the Chongchon, and to avoid threatened annihilation began a rapid retreat to the south. In Eastern Korea most of the exposed and over-extended troops withdrew as intended, but left two Marine regiments and one regiment of the 7th Infantry Division in danger of being cut off by six Chinese divisions.

While the 1st Marine Air Wing and Task Force 77 provided all the close air support needed,[36] FEAF's Combat Air Cargo Command dealt with the demands for air supply to the threatened units. For nearly two weeks a force roughly the size of a division was supplied entirely by air drop, and altogether 1,580 tons were delivered by this means. A crude airstrip was built by the beleaguered Marines into which another 274 tons were flown and perhaps even more important 4,689 sick and wounded were flown out.[37] A more unusual contribution by air transport was made on 7 December when eight spans of treadway bridge, each span weighing two tons, were dropped so that the Marines could replace a bridge destroyed by the Chinese, and thus bring out their transport, armour and artillery.[38]

Once these troops were back in the Hungnam–Hamhung perimeter on the coast of north-east Korea, a full-scale air evacuation of the bridgehead began. In four days over 4,000 men and more than 2,000 tons of supplies were flown out. As the perimeter shrank, the two airfields were abandoned and the rest of the US 10th Corps was withdrawn by sea.[39]

These unexpected reverses in North Korea raised again the whole question of extending the war. At a press conference on 30 November,

Truman remarked that the US would 'take whatever steps are necessary to meet the military situation'. He was then asked 'Will that include the atomic bomb?' and he replied 'That includes every weapon we have'. 'Does that mean that there is active consideration of the use of the atomic bomb?' 'There has always been active consideration of its use . . .'[40]

This exchange led British Prime Minister Attlee to fly to Washington to seek assurances about future US policy, and the general outcry provoked in the West by Truman's remarks made it clear that there was very little enthusiasm for extreme solutions.

The other possibility was that of a geographical extension of the war using conventional weapons. As MacArthur was later to say: 'If I had been permitted to bomb them before they crossed the Yalu, they would never have crossed.' But here too there were persuasive objections.

> It would be militarily foolhardy [said a JCS amendment to a State Department circular on 3 January] to embark on a course that would require full-scale hostilities against great land armies controlled by the Peking regime, while the heart of aggressive Communist power remains untouched.[41]

In other words, from a military point of view, even an air campaign against China would not be enough. The second difficulty was that any extension of the war by the US, particularly into China, ran the risk of destroying the unanimity with which the US and her allies had responded to North Korean aggression.

The final difficulty was referred to later by General Ridgway when he said:

> the Truman administration and the JCS were aware that an attack on the Manchurian bases or even on the Yalu bridges would put an end to the unspoken agreement that kept our South Korean and Japanese bases inviolate and had limited the war to the Korean Peninsula.[42]

Whether the Communists ever seriously considered an air offensive on UNC bases, particularly those in Japan, seems doubtful. It is more likely that the Americans were simply projecting their own air power doctrine into the minds of Chinese and North Korean planners; but even so the notion of sanctuaries on one or both sides was a new factor in the wars that air power was to fight in the nuclear age.

A NEW THREAT

At the same time that the November crisis in the ground campaign was developing, Communist air elements appeared in renewed strength and with growing aggressiveness over the Yalu. This potential air threat to the UN forces led to the hasty despatch of two wings of F-84E Thunderjets and F-86A Sabres from the US by sea.[43] With some difficulty, because only two airfields, Taegu and Kinpo, able to accept the new aircraft remained in UN hands, the six squadrons were eventually deployed to Korea and went into action in early December. Although their endurance over the Yalu was very limited, and although the Mig pilots learned to take advantage of that fact, the Sabre squadrons quickly developed tactics that enabled them to restore UN air superiority over north-west Korea. Nevertheless, Communist air strength continued to grow month by month until by June 1951 it was as high as 1,050 combat aircraft, 445 of them Mig-15s, and all of them operating from modern bases just north of the Yalu.

By early December 1950 UN ground forces had almost entirely broken contact with the enemy, leaving air power to continue the attrition against the advancing Communist forces and, for example, FEAF alone flew 7,654 armed reconnaissance and interdiction sorties during the month of December. At the same time, what was called Interdiction Campaign No. 4 was launched against 172 separate targets, of which 45 were railway bridges, 12 were road bridges, 13 tunnels, 39 marshalling yards and 63 supply centres. The plan for the offensive divided Korea north of the 37th Parallel into eleven zones stretching back to the Manchurian and Siberian borders. Three zones were allotted to Naval Forces Far East and the rest to land-based aircraft.

Some of these targets were in areas where strong enemy air reaction could be expected, and along many routes the enemy increasingly deployed AA batteries. These eventually grew to be so effective that armed reconnaissance missions were forced to operate at greater heights and speeds than circumstances demanded, with a consequent loss of effectiveness.

Far more telling, however, was the tenacity, the competence and above all the adaptability of the Communist supply system. Bridges proved once again to be particularly difficult targets. Although various tactics were tried, and although new weapons such as the six-ton radio-guided Tarzan bomb[44] and M83 cluster bombs were employed, the bridges all too often remained standing after attack. When the bridges were actually destroyed, the enemy built by-pass bridges and sometimes even multiple by-pass bridges. On 1 March, for example, a by-pass bridge next to the demolished bridge at Sinanju was put out of action, but on 12 March it was being repaired and a second by-pass was being built. By 26 March the first by-pass was back in use; it was put out again on 1 April and was back in use once more on 15 April. On 24 April it was hit again, but by now the second by-pass was almost ready for use again.[45]

Finally, the Communists showed once again their ability to operate the supply routes by night, and once again the UN Command had no means of countering this vital flexibility. By a process of what the USAF Historical Survey calls logistic osmosis, the movement of Communist reinforcements thus continued, usually at night and often on foot, leaving the vehicles free to carry supplies. Eventually an estimated total of seventy Chinese divisions had moved into Korea and was being successfully maintained there. Air interdiction campaign No. 4 had failed.

No better success attended the bombing attacks over north-west Korea that were re-started in February 1951. A lack of forward bases for escort fighters quickly led to serious attrition among the bombers, and on 1 March no fewer than ten B-29s were damaged by Migs, three of them so badly that they made emergency landings in South Korea. By 12 April Suwon airfield was available for the Sabre escorts, and seventy-two fighters accompanied forty-eight B-29s to attack the Autung and Sinuiju bridges across the Yalu.

But by now the Migs were both more aggressive and more numerous, and 80 of them engaged the attacking force. Nine of the B-29s aborted the mission and three Superfortresses were lost. In terms of the total force available these losses were very serious indeed, and they caused not only the withdrawal of the B-29s from operations in what had come to be called Mig Alley, but the new levels of enemy air activity also led to the F-80s, the F-84s and the Australian Meteors being restricted to operations south of the Chongchon, leaving air mastery over north-west Korea to be disputed between Migs and Sabres.

In the autumn and winter of 1950 it had become clear to the UN that the aim of unifying Korea by force was too ambitious in the face of Chinese intervention, and the UN objective became one of conducting operations that would maintain the security of its own forces, while inflicting maximum casualties on the Communists so as to force them to seek an armistice. In April 1951, at the time of General MacArthur's recall, President Truman explained publicly that the US military objective in Korea was to 'repel attack . . . to restore peace . . . and to avoid the spread of the conflict'.[46]

As for the Communists, in June, Malik, the Soviet delegate to the UN, accepted the idea of an armistice 'providing for mutual withdrawal from the 38th Parallel'.[47] Both sides were thus now seeking an end to the war, but each naturally hoped to extract as much as possible in the way of concessions from the other. There is no space here to deal with the protracted, intricate and frustrating progress of the armistice talks that started in July 1951, save to say that it became clear within the first few days that the fighting was by no means over and that a new kind of war was starting. It began with renewed efforts on both sides to seize the initiative in the air.

Already in June the enemy air force had begun to test new tactics, and on 1 September, a week after the truce talks had first broken down, the Chinese Air Force launched an all-out campaign. FEAF aircraft were drawn into full-scale air battles during September, and although US losses were only moderate, this activity seriously hampered attempts to continue the UN railway interdiction campaign. More ominously, it became clear that the increasing Communist air strength in Manchuria might eventually enable the enemy to establish air bases in Korea and then to threaten UNC air supremacy over the whole of the battle area.

Since no further UN air reinforcements were available for the Far Eastern theatre, the interdiction attacks on railways near the Yalu had to be halted in the face of this growing Communist air threat. At the same time the enemy began to repair old airfields south of the Yalu, and to build new ones. The struggle for air supremacy moved to a climax and during the first three weeks of October 1951 air-to-air battles were taking place each day between Migs and Sabres over the Yalu.

Attempts to disrupt the airfield construction work in North Korea using B-29s by night proved disappointing, and eventually, despite the obvious hazards, resort was again made to daylight raids. On 23 October eight Superfortresses, with an escort of fifty-five Thunderjets, attacked Namsi airfield and were intercepted by about fifty Migs. Three B-29s were lost, and all but one of the surviving bombers suffered major damage, including casualties among their crews. On the next day eight B-29s attacked a by-pass railway bridge at Sunchon and another bomber was lost. On 27 October eight B-29s set out to attack a railway by-pass bridge at Sinanju and four were damaged, one seriously.

Up until this time, Bomber Command had lost a total of only six aircraft in combat; but now five had been lost in one week, eight had suffered major damage and fifty-five B-29 crewmen were dead or missing. Moreover, this comparatively expensive effort had not neutralised the new airfields at Saamcham, Namsi or Taechon.

The bomber offensive had failed, and General Vandenberg told the press after a visit to the Far East at this time, 'Almost overnight, Communist China has become one of the major air powers of the world.'[48] The Chinese had now done what the Luftwaffe had been unable to do; they had called a halt to USAF daylight precision bombing.

Failure to destroy the Communist air bases was accompanied by new difficulties in the air over the Yalu. The Communist fighters had developed new techniques which involved, among other things, the dispatch of co-ordinated 'trains' of aircraft sixty to eighty strong, which crossed to the south of the Yalu at heights above 35,000 feet from where they detached flights or sections to attack USAF air patrols, returning UN attack aircraft, or any stragglers that they could find.

After December 1951 another change in Communist air techniques became apparent. Their efforts to maintain the airfields in North Korea in the face of renewed night attacks by B-29s were virtually abandoned, and the hitherto aggressive Mig pilots were replaced by a succession of 'classes' who went through a clearly defined cycle of training so as to improve their proficiency before they were replaced by another 'class' to start the whole process again. At the same time USAF activities were constrained by a severe shortage of F-86 spares, and the rate of kills in combat over the Yalu fell sharply.

On the ground the Communist forces launched their spring offensive in April 1951, but by the middle of May their attacks had failed and the enemy was being driven north by the 8th Army's counter-offensive. In support of that offensive, a new interdiction campaign against Communist roads was launched on 31 May with the codename Operation Strangle. For this operation the main road traffic routes within a one-degree strip of latitude across the neck of Korea, just above the battle line, eight routes in all, were selected for concentrated air attack. The three western-most routes were allocated to the 5th Air Force, the two central routes to the aircraft-carriers of Task Force 77, while the three eastern-most routes became the responsibility of the 1st Marine Air Wing. Selected defiles and passes along the highways were designated as 'strangle areas' or 'choke points' and bridges, tunnels and other constructions along the routes were also targeted. Delayed-action bombs were employed and aircraft equipped with searchlights and flares were used in an attempt to keep up the pressure on the enemy transport system by night as well as by day.

In spite of the effort expended on the campaign, it became clear almost at once that it was failing. The enemy very quickly filled in craters in the unpaved roads, or he simply by-passed them on newly-made tracks. Damaged bridges over rivers were rapidly repaired, and in any case the low summer level of the waters meant that the Communists could use makeshift fords. The delayed action bombs used were often simply ignored by the enemy and the risks of random explosion accepted, while the anti-personnel butterfly bombs that had been dropped were picked off by rifle fire.

The initial results of Operation Strangle were slender enough but they quickly became insignificant, while at the same time the effectiveness of the Communist AA weapons deployed along the highways became a serious threat to the attacking aircraft. In April and May, FEAF alone lost 59 aircraft to enemy ground fire, and in June another 22 were lost to the 275 AA guns and 600 automatic weapons that the Communists were estimated to have emplaced in Korea by 1 July.[49]

By early August 1951, yet another interdiction plan had been evolved, this time against railways. It had been calculated that each of the 60 Communist divisions south of Sariwon, below Pyongyang, needed 40 tons of supply each day for limited combat, i.e. a total of 2,400 tons. In the forward areas troops and pack animals could move these supplies, but further to the rear road and rail were employed, particularly for the longer hauls. The total of 2,400 tons would, it was estimated, tie up 6,000 trucks if road were used, but only 120 box-cars would be needed to move it by rail.

This greater load-hauling capacity, it was concluded, must mean that rail was the primary Communist transportation capability. Not only that, it was also his cheapest means of transport. Fuel for trucks had to be imported from China or Russia, but coal for the railways was available in North Korea. Finally, railways could not be concealed, and breaks in the tracks could not be by-passed. Rail was therefore the preferred target system from an airman's point of view, and it is difficult to avoid the impression that this assessment might have owed more to an appreciation of UN air capability than to the ability of the Communists to circumvent it.

It was of course realised that key points on the rail system such as bridges would be well defended by AA guns, and it was appreciated that when rail bridges had been destroyed in the past the Communists had resorted to shuttling trains between the breaks, transferring loads from one train to another, sometimes with distances of only eleven or twelve miles between transshipments. The most effective form of attack against a rail system with those point defences and that degree of resilience would therefore be one that was spread over as wide an area as possible.

The 5th Air Force calculated that 6 to 8 months would be needed to destroy the enemy's rail system using only its own aircraft, but that it could be done in 90 days with the help of Naval aviation and Bomber Command.[50] If the enemy switched his supplies to trucks, it had been planned that tactical aircraft of the 5th Air Force would concentrate on them and that the total attrition rate of Communist trucks would then be 7,500 a month. Since China and the Soviet Union together were estimated to be producing only 33,000 trucks each month, the UN air forces were, it was concluded, capable not only of destroying the Communist rail system but of 'hindering his highway transportation system to such an extent that he will not be capable of opposing the US 8th Army effectively'.[51] The operation was given the same name as the earlier road interdiction campaign, Operation Strangle. It was not a good omen.

From the very start of the new offensive on 18 August 1951, the Communists showed the same remarkable ability to repair the hundreds of cuts in their rail network as they had shown in maintaining the road system. Worse than that, as the raids continued the recuperative powers of the enemy increased until by November he seldom left cuts unrepaired for more than twenty-four hours, by December it was clear from reconnaissance photographs that rail cuts were being repaired within as little as eight hours, which meant that even after successful air attack the rail links could be reopened between midnight and dawn. Once that degree of resilience had been developed the lack of American night bombing capability meant that the last third of the enemy rail capacity was virtually invulnerable.

Although General Weyland was announcing on 26 December 1951 that Operation Strangle had shattered the North Korean rail transportation net, had destroyed or damaged 40,000 trucks and had prevented the Reds from building up for a future offensive,[52] FEAF intelligence had already admitted on 23 December that the Communists 'have broken our railroad blockade of Pyongyang and [have] won . . . the use of all key rail arteries'.[53] Another air interdiction campaign had failed, and what was more there was evidence of a serious fall in aircrew morale; but one more attempt was now to be made.[54]

Instead of attacks spread widely against the whole North Korean rail system, a round-the-clock concentration of effort against short segments of track would be mounted. The new offensive, known as Operation Saturate, was launched on 3 March 1951 and it continued throughout April and May against two-mile-long sections of the North Koreans' main rail routes. That the tactics could be effective was shown by the success of the 5th Air Force in keeping the line between Sinuiju and Sinanju closed, but combat losses and lack of replacements soon constrained the new offensive. By the end of April the Communists had deployed AA artillery along virtually all their rail routes, and soon the 5th Air Force had lost 243 fighter bombers – mainly in railway interdiction attacks – and 290 other tactical aircraft had sustained major damage. Only 131 replacements had been made available to replace these losses, and as a result some Wings were down almost to half-strength.[55] 'Saturate' could no longer be sustained, and although attacks on the Communist supply systems were to continue for the whole of the remainder of the war, from June 1952 interdiction was, in the words of the USN History 'de-emphasised'.

Ten months of comprehensive railway interdiction had not failed to isolate the battlefield, nor had it succeeded in putting enough pressure on the Communists to persuade them to accept the UN terms for an armistice. Indeed, General Ridgway was to tell the Senate Armed Services Committee in May 1952 that ' . . . the hostile forces opposing the Eighth Army . . . have a substantially greater offensive potential than at any time in the past'. General Shepherd, the Commandant of the Marine Corps, said publicly that Operation Strangle was 'recognised as a fizzle' while Admiral Clark, the Commander of the 7th Fleet, said 'the interdiction campaign was a failure. It did not interdict.'[56]

After the Korean War, General Weyland summed up the effectiveness of the railway interdiction campaign in more detail when he said:

Nothing is so bad in air campaigns as not having enough force to do a job completely. For example, all but 4 or 5 per cent of pre-war rail traffic in North Korea was stopped, but this was sufficient to form a solid base upon which to add enough truck and A-frame transportation to maintain a static supply line. Armed reconnaissance and highway interdiction require an even greater number of sorties. In all three tasks the effects accrue geometrically as the force is increased arithmetically. The last ten per cent of interdiction or armed reconnaissance gets the real pay-off.[57]

The facts were that even if the considerable effect of AA systems could be ignored, most of the resilience of the enemy transportation systems was provided by coolie labour, and that labour force was simply beyond the reach of air power. Particularly by night, the enemy transport system was able to elude the search by air power for the last critical proportion of effort, and whenever the military effort that was required approached that critical level of effort the enemy simply reduced his military consumption at the front.

THE SEARCH FOR TARGETS

Thus after nearly two years of war no target system had been identified for decisive attack by the air power that was available, and in April 1952 a new study into the possible future application of air power in Korea was made. The principal difficulty was that the Soviet Union and China were behind the negotiating intransigence of the North Koreans at Panmunjom, and there was no obvious way in which their interests could be put under direct pressure by the exercise of air power in Korea.

Nevertheless, as part of the concept of what was called 'air pressure through selective destruction', North Korean hydroelectric plants and the power transmission grid were identified as important elements in the wider Communist infrastructure, and they were made the next target for heavy air attacks at the end of June 1952. In a three-day series of raids using the co-ordinated efforts of USAF, USN and USMC aircraft, 90 per cent or more of North Korea's electric power potential was put out of action. Militarily the attacks were highly successful, but the pressure that they should have exerted on Communist decision-makers was greatly diminished by worldwide protests about bombing attacks on targets other than strictly military ones, the effect of which was to serve notice on the Communists that the war was likely to remain strictly limited.

Among the other targets that had meanwhile been selected for air pressure operations was the capital of North Korea itself, Pyongyang, which by now contained numerous military installations such as Command posts, barracks and supply depots.

In the biggest air attack so far made during the war, 1,254 sorties were flown against the city on 11 July 1952, and 'at least three of the 30 targets were completely destroyed and all but two of them were heavily damaged' according to USAF assessments. Radio Pyongyang, however, claimed that 1,500 buildings had been destroyed by the 'brutal' air attacks, and 7,000 casualties had resulted.[58] On 29 August an even larger raid was mounted, named 'All United Nations Air Effort', in which no fewer than 1,403 sorties were flown causing moderate to severe damage to 31 targets in the city.

Other attacks in the air pressure campaign included raids on mines, cement plants, factories, all types of military concentrations, and inevitably on the towns in which these targets were situated, all designed to bring the Communists to reach a peace settlement acceptable to the UN. Interdiction of a kind also formed a part of the offensive, but this time it was interdiction designed to destroy the Communist forces in rear areas, rather than merely to delay them or to disrupt their plans.

The tactic used was to create choke points that would expose enemy columns to follow-up air attacks, but once again the results were far from decisive. As far as road movement was concerned the 5th Air Force concluded that the 'Spring Thaw' operation in March 1953 had 'caused . . . a slow down of vehicular traffic',[59] but Bomber Command reported that the 'ability of the enemy to repair [rail] bridges was just short of miraculous'.[60]

Losses to attacking aircraft were kept down to a tolerable level only with great difficulty. Attacks could be made only in bad weather and with a tightly compressed bomber stream. ECM was employed, tactics were varied as widely as possible and crew protection was strengthened, but even so five B-29s were lost and five seriously damaged in the period 18 November 1952 to 30 January 1953, and the losses would certainly have been very much higher if the enemy interceptors had been equipped with airborne-intercept radar.[61]

As it was, total 5th Air Force losses were very high. No fewer than 771 aircraft were destroyed or damaged in the period 1 September 1952 to 30 April 1953, a rate of 11.1 per thousand missions.[62] Finally, there was still the unresolved problem of effective night attack. It was calculated by the 5th Air Force analysts that night-flying fighter–bombers were hitting only 0.262 vehicle targets per sortie, clearly a misuse of resources that bordered on the desperate.[63]

Air-to-air combats over the Yalu also continued throughout this stage of the war although UN pilots found that their opponents seemed reluctant to be drawn into engagements, and when they could be engaged their level of skill often proved low. As one example of the scale of effort involved at this time, between 8 and 31 May 1953, 1,507 Migs were sighted, 537 were engaged, and 56 destroyed for the loss of one Sabre. In looking at ratios of this kind, FEAF warned[64] that

> The phenomenon of a smaller Sabre force, flying planes with a performance not markedly better than the enemy force, winning and maintaining air superiority must recognise that the enemy consistently misused his capabilities and lacked skilled pilots.[65]

This was an interesting view of air superiority. The facts were that the strong Communist fighter screens near the Yalu had in the past inflicted unacceptable losses on USAF bombers and on their escorts. The continued presence of these same screens at this stage of the war was not only a clear warning to the UN planners that they did not have a free hand in their air attacks, but extensive UN air efforts were devoted to meeting what was seen as a challenge high above the Yalu. Valuable air resources were thus drawn into activities that had no perceptible connection either with the ground fighting or with the political aims of the war. Even if air superiority could be claimed, which is very doubtful, it was air superiority for its own sake, and the Communists seem to have had a clear grasp of how best to use their air power in these circumstances of limited war.

Task Force 77, meanwhile, had developed its own method of contributing to the air–ground campaign by developing what were called 'Cherokee' missions. These were pre-briefed strikes by concentrated air effort[66] delivered over a short period on targets beyond the bomb line. This line could be as much as 20 miles beyond the most forward ground positions, but it could be moved by the local ground commander to be as close to the battle line as he thought feasible.[67] After some difficulties, because they were not actually controlled from the ground and because bad weather led to counterproductive inaccuracies, Cherokee missions gained a new effectiveness from the spring of 1953 onwards and they were employed with success for the rest of the war.

Political pressure to end the war had, meanwhile, increased to a point when, in May 1953, President Eisenhower was willing to threaten an extension of hostilities to bring about an early end to the fighting. At the same time FEAF planners had identified what they saw as the last but possibly the most vulnerable of the many North Korean target systems that had so far been selected for attack. Examination had shown that twenty major irrigation dams, situated near important transport routes in north-west Korea, provided 75 per cent of the water for the country's rice production. After some hesitation both about the feasibility and about the desirability of destroying the rice irrigation system, a series of attacks was made on five of the twenty dams in early May 1953.

Tactically the strikes were a spectacular success. From one dam alone, that of Toksan, north of Pyongyang, the floodwaters washed out or damaged about six miles of embankment and five bridges on the important nearby railway line, destroyed two miles of the main North–South highway which ran parallel to it, flooded five square miles of rice crop, and inundated Sunan airfield.[68] General Clark gave as his opinion that this particular attack had been as effective as weeks of rail interdiction. Strategically, these same attacks not only threatened famine for the population, but they also raised the likelihood that China would have to supply rice from her own strained economy in order to sustain the war.

New pressures were thus put on the enemy in the theatre of war itself, but a new kind of threat was also being posed at the diplomatic level. General Mark Clark was authorised by Washington to make a final offer in the continuing armistice talks at Panmunjom, and if it was rejected he was to 'break off the talks rather than recess them, and to carry on the war in new ways never yet tried in Korea'.[69] The threat to widen the war and a threat if necessary to use atomic weapons seems to have been conveyed by Dulles during a visit to India at the end of May, and Sherman Adams relates that after the war, when he asked Eisenhower what it was that had led to the acceptance by the Communists of the armistice terms, he replied, 'We told them we could not hold it to a limited war any longer if the Communists welched on a treaty of truce. They didn't want a full-scale war, or an atomic attack.'[70]

A final Communist ground offensive was launched in early June 1953, but it was a limited attack probably designed to save face as well as to acquire some last-minute local terrain advantages. With the considerable assistance[71] of the 5th Air Force, Bomber Command and Task Force 77, it was beaten off. As both sides moved towards full agreement on the terms of the armistice, it was the turn of the UNC to gain an advantage. All but 6 of the 35 North Korean airfields had been kept under air attack since May,[72] but when General Clark intimated that the armistice agreement was about to be signed, a long-planned joint airfield neutralisation programme was launched that rendered every one of the airfields in North Korea unserviceable for jet-aircraft landings so as to prevent any last-minute arrival of Communist aircraft that would then have been 'frozen' in Korea under the terms of the armistice.[73]

On 27 July the armistice was finally signed, and the war was over. Fifteen nations had contributed combat forces to the UNC, and another five had sent medical units. An estimated 5 million men had travelled to Korea from all parts of the world. Total UN casualties were 159,351 including 70,452 dead, of whom 67,258 were Americans. FEAF lost 1,144 killed in air operations, and suffered an overall total of 1,841 casualties.

As for the scale of the air war, the USAF alone had seventeen wings deployed in direct support of the fighting during the last year of the war, a force that included three wings of B-29 Superfortresses, seven fighter wings, two B-26 wings, a reconnaissance wing and four troop-carrier wings. Over 1 million sorties had been flown by the UN air forces, and FEAF alone had expended 476,000 tons of ordnance. It was estimated that the USAF lost about 2,000 aircraft[74] to all causes during the war, less than half of them in combat, while the USN and USMC together lost another 1,200; 564 of them to enemy action.[75]

By any standards it had been a major war, and it held many lessons for air power in the nuclear age, not only technically and operationally, but also at the strategic level. At the technical level the war emphasised the unsurprising fact that aircraft alone are not enough. A lack of airfields and of the means to build new ones had been a seriously inhibiting factor at one critical stage of the war, while a shortage of trained photographic interpreters had led to crucial gaps in intelligence at another. Perhaps even more telling because of their pervasive effects throughout the campaign had been both a lack of precision weapons, and an almost total absence of any effective night attack capability.

These technical failings, and the general absence of technological innovation since the Second World War, were compounded by grave operational deficiencies, two of which were particularly telling. First, there was no comprehensive method of applying the available air power to the close support of ground forces. It was true that the USMC and USN air arms were highly effective in this role because a very sound level of expertise had been developed perforce in the amphibious campaigns of the Second World War. But although these maritime capabilities were extremely valuable, they were never fully integrated into a theatre-wide command and control system, and their value was therefore never fully exploited.[76]

As for land-based air, the art of close co-operation with ground forces had been lost altogether, and although ingenious *ad hoc* arrangements were often made, the potential of air power to redress critical imbalances in the land battle could only very rarely be applied.

Second, and even more telling given the circumstances of the war, was the almost total failure of all the interdiction campaigns. The logistic needs of Asian-style mass armies had been seriously over-estimated, while the resilience of a coolie-maintained logistic system was wildly under-assessed. These two misappreciations were then compounded by a failure to realise that successful interdiction must imply at least some degree of initiative on the ground as well as in the air. If the enemy being interdicted is free to determine the intensity of the combat at the front, then he will adjust the level of that combat to match the logistic effort that is escaping the air interdiction blockade. Since in Korea the logistic system could never be completely closed, and since the Communist armies had such modest logistic demands, they were able with very few exceptions to maintain an adequate level of frontal activity at all times.

The only collapse in the enemy front occurred on the Pusan area at the time of the Inchon landing, and although as we have seen there was disagreement about the precise causes of that collapse, it cannot be denied that Inchon threatened to cut off all the invading North Koreans and that this must have been a principal factor in the decision to withdraw northwards. Thus even when the North Korean logistic system was stretched to its greatest extent, as it was during Inchon, it could not be claimed that air interdiction on its own produced any decisive results.

But all these technical and operational aspects of the air war were, after all, merely variations on lessons that had been learned before and all too often forgotten. It was at the strategic level that the war in Korea made its greatest impact. Until Korea three strategic convictions were widely held in the West: first, that modern war was about the absolutes of unconditional surrender and of total victory; second, that the key to total victory lay in strategic air bombardment; and third, that strategic air bombardment meant manned strategic bombers.

Korea changed everything. Not only did manned bombers prove to be far more vulnerable than had been thought, but even if the strategic air bombardment of key enemy centres had been militarily feasible, which it was not at the time of Korea, it was politically unacceptable. More fundamentally, however, the scale of the Korean fighting, which was considerable, and its effect on the global balance of power, which was minimal, made it clear that the idea of total victory in war had receded a very long way since the German and Japanese surrenders only eight years before. Korea was thus a watershed in the history of air power.

At the time, however, there was a great deal of reluctance to accept that things might have changed. Thomas K. Finletter, Secretary of the Air Force from 1950 to 1953, wrote in 1955 that 'the Korean War was a special case, and air power can learn little from there about its future role in United States foreign policy in the East';[77] and 'certainly', said the FEAF Report[78] at the end of the Korean War, 'any attempt to build an air force from the model of the Korean requirements could be fatal to the United States'.

Other military thinkers saw the way ahead more clearly. General Otto P. Weyland, who commanded FEAF from June 1951 to July 1955, said in 1956: 'I feel rather strongly that the most likely conflict in the immediate future will be the peripheral type. In this event it will be primarily a tactical air war.'[79] Air Chief Marshal Sir John Slessor went further:

> We must expect to be faced with other Koreas . . . The idea that superior air power can in some way be a substitute for hard slogging and professional skill on the ground in this sort of war is beguiling but illusory . . . all this is cold comfort for anyone who hopes that air power will provide some kind of short cut to victory. We are in World War III now.[80]

3 Air Power in Colonial Wars

Even before the Second World War ended, the lines were being drawn for a number of less intense conflicts of a kind that were to become all too familiar in the nuclear age. Some of these campaigns were large scale civil wars like that in Greece from 1945–57: others were local rebellions on a smaller scale, such as the Huk campaign in the Philippines. But as far as air power was concerned, the most significant conflicts were to be found among those fought by the European powers as they sought to resist or to delay the process of decolonisation in their overseas territories.

Most of the leaders of the nationalist movements in those territories had naturally been attracted in their struggle for independence to allies as far removed from their colonial masters as possible, and that meant the Communists, who drew aid and comfort from the Soviet Union or from China, or from both of those powers.

For their part, all the European colonial powers except Portugal were either recovering from devastating occupation during the Second World War, like France and Holland, or, like Britain, they were simply on the verge of national bankruptcy. Yet somehow they had to re-arm against what was seen to be a clear Soviet military threat in Europe and at the same time they had to reimpose their control in their overseas possessions. Extensive aid from the US helped to meet the first of these demands, and although this assistance was largely directed towards European defence, it clearly enabled military resources to be released for use in colonial wars.

Thus the blurring of distinctions between nationalism and communism in the overseas territories affected by insurgencies was matched by a general Western reaction that combined anti-communism with efforts to maintain the colonial status quo. Weapons produced for a possible global war between the superpowers were often diverted for use in conflicts of a quite different kind.

MAP 2   *North and Central Indo-China*

FRENCH INDO-CHINA

One of the first and, as it turned out, one of the most important of these counter-insurgency campaigns in which air power was engaged, was that fought by the French in Indo-China from 1945 until 1954. Its importance springs from two things. First, the eventual victory by the Viet Minh insurgents became a model as well as an encouragement to similar movements in other parts of the world. Second, because the success of the insurgents left the political problems of Vietnam unsettled, the French defeat led to an even more disastrous setback for the West when the US was in turn compelled to disengage from Indo-China nearly two decades later.

The campaign had its roots in the Japanese surrender in 1945, when British troops moved in to occupy Vietnam south of the 16th Parallel, while Chiang Kai-shek's forces took over control north of that line. By the time both these groups of forces arrived, however, local nationalist movements in the South and in the North had already established provisional governments. That formed by Ho Chi-Minh in Hanoi was recognised by Chiang Kai-shek, who then refused to re-arm French troops in the area, and instead left law and order as well as administration in the hands of the Viet Minh government. In the South, the British took the opposite line, and retained control[1] until late December 1945 when a French force of 50,000 troops under General Leclerc arrived from Europe. The French air element at this time was very modest and seems to have been made up of 18 Dakotas, 4 Catalinas, 12 ex-RAF Spitfires and a handful of ex-Japanese Oscar III fighters. More Spitfires, some Toucan transports,[2] and some Criquets[3] arrived at about this time, and took part in what was then thought to be little more than a mopping-up operation against small groups of guerillas.

Nationalist sentiment was, however, running more strongly than the French had realised, and although negotiations were opened with Ho Chi-Minh which eventually allowed 15,000 French troops into the North to replace the Chinese and to train a Viet Minh army, guerrilla activity in the South was spreading. Attempts at compromise failed, and as one writer has said:

> The French forces sent to Indo-China were too strong for France to resist the temptation of using them; yet not strong enough to keep the Viet Minh from trying to solve the whole political problem by throwing the French into the Sea.[4]

The growing tension led to skirmishes and to reprisals in Haiphong, and finally the French demanded that Ho Chi-Minh surrender his forces in Hanoi. When this was answered on 19 December 1946 by Viet Minh attacks on a number of French garrisons, the Indo-China war had begun.[5]

The Viet Minh had about 60,000 troops, but only two-thirds of them were armed and they quickly scattered to fall back into sanctuary areas when pressed by French ground forces supported by air attacks. During 1947 the French forces took the offensive and managed to retain most of the main centres in the country. These operations included the use of parachutists both in direct assaults and as a means of dispatching reinforcements to beleaguered outposts. Operation Papillon in the spring of 1947, for example, involved a drop of 500 parachutists over Hoa Binh to take the town and link up with Moroccan troops advancing from Hanoi.[6] Communications between the various French-held areas were not easy, and although they could be kept open in daylight hours, most of the countryside was still controlled by the Viet Minh, especially at night.

In October the French launched an all-out attack, Operation Lea, against Ho Chi-Minh and the main body of guerrillas in the Viet Bac region north-west of Hanoi. Fifteen thousand troops, more than a third of the whole French expeditionary force, were engaged in an effort to encircle a vast area of mountainous jungle, an operation in which several parachute drops were again made involving 200–300 troops in each.[7] Although the French claimed to have killed 8,000 guerrillas and to have captured large quantities of arms and supplies, the Viet Minh avoided a large-scale action and by the end of the year the main French force had returned to the lowlands, leaving behind a network of outlying forts mainly along the key lines of communication. But this meant that the Viet Minh could still carry out their guerrilla attacks from bases in the mountains, and the war continued.

By the start of 1948 the French air strength in Indo-China had grown to about one-tenth of the whole of the French Air Force, itself of course not very strong at this time. In Tonkin there was a squadron of 8 Spitfires, another of liaison aircraft and a wing of JU-52 transports. In Annam there were 6 fighter aircraft while in Cochin there was one group plus a squadron of fighters, one wing of JU-52s and one of Dakotas.[8]

During 1948 and 1949 the French attempts at pacification, interrupted by sporadic fighting, were maintained, while the overall French military effort expanded until the force numbered about 150,000 including some local units, and the war was absorbing over half the total

French military budget.[9] On the Viet Minh side, the continuing guerrilla activity led the French to believe that they were still involved in mopping-up operations, when in fact the Viet Minh were building up a regular army[10] behind these low-key activities, and mobilising large sections of the population to support it.

In late 1949 the US administration had begun to supply economic aid direct to the three states of Indo-China as well as military equipment to the French overseas forces, but when the Korean War began in June 1950 the Americans began to see the fighting in Indo-China as part of a wider ideological struggle and direct military aid to the French was accelerated. At the same time, however, the Communist victory of 1949 in the Chinese civil war opened the way for military aid to the Viet Minh from the North, and the Ho Chi-Minh government was confident enough to be able to proclaim a 'national mobilisation' at the end of that year. With their new-found strength, the Viet Minh now began to launch bolder attacks against the French outposts in the North, which continued until February 1950 when Giap declared that the guerrilla phase of the war was over and that mobile warfare could begin.

The first of the new Viet Minh offensives was staged against a string of small French outposts in the Black River Valley, and when this was successful a series of effective assaults throughout Tonkin left the French forces in the north-east holding only a line of forts along Route Colonial 4, between Cao Bang and the sea.

Occasionally French offensive air power was able to intervene in this kind of fighting, though at other times bad weather, and particularly the persistent low cloud, prevented them from doing so. That air power was, however, able to play some part in these operations is shown by their description at the time as 'Operation Combinées Air-Terre', and by the fact that ground unit commanders acknowledged the contribution that the air was making, notably in re-supply and in transport operations.[11]

But the French effort was no match for the growing strength of the Viet Minh offensive and eventually Cao Bang itself was cut off by strong enemy forces. When the garrison marched south to meet a relief force fighting its way north it met such fierce resistance that despite being reinforced by a drop of three battalions of paratroops, the whole French force was practically wiped out outside Dong Khe. Following this, the southernmost French fort at Lang Son was evacuated, and by October 1950 control of nearly the whole of the North of Vietnam had been given up. The French had lost 6,000 men as well as enough arms and supplies to fit out a whole Viet Minh division. It was a major defeat, and the worst French colonial disaster since Quebec.[12]

By this stage of the campaign the French air strength had grown to about 190 machines, including 48 P-63 Kingcobras, 19 Spitfires, 43 Toucans, 25 Dakotas and three groups of Criquets, which were used not only for liaison and casualty evacuation but also as air control posts.[13] In offensive air support operations bombs, cannon and napalm were all being used by this stage of the war.[14] Some idea of the extent of the air effort employed is shown by the fact that, for example, in the month of October 1950 the French Air Forces flew 391 fighter sorties, 78 recce, 326 transport and 49 bombing sorties totalling 5,480 hours.[15] Small numbers of US-built aircraft had been arriving in the theatre for some time, but now reinforcements of US aircraft provided under the new aid programme began to arrive, starting on 26 October when 40 F-6F5 Hellcats were delivered in Saigon.

Encouraged by their successes so far, the Viet Minh next attacked the outpost of Vinh Yen as a prelude to an advance on Hanoi itself. Massed assaults were launched, but the French were not only well prepared, they were also well supported both by artillery and by air. Forty P-63s, 8 Hellcats, 29 JU-52s, 5 Dakota transports[16] and 24 observation aircraft[17] were committed in transport sorties, in strafing and in napalm attacks during a four-day battle that cost Giap an estimated 6,000 killed, 500 prisoners and thousands of wounded.[18] On the Viet Minh side, the Communists' logistics were simply not up to fighting of this intensity, while on the French side the ability to drop ammunition to their garrison made a very significant contribution to the Viet Minh defeat.

Giap launched his next major attack just before the rainy season[19] in March at Mao Khe, aiming to cut off the whole of the delta area from Haiphong, but the small garrison, supported by 138 ground-attack sorties, was able to hold out until reinforcements arrived.[20] A force of transports stood by to take in a force of paratroops, but they were not needed.

Blocked to the north, to the north-east and to the north-west, at the end of May Giap attacked from the south at Ninh Binh, and a series of battles on the River Day began. In the most important engagement, that at Thai Binh between 28 May and 8 June, 8 26s, 48 Bearcats, 23 Kingcobras, 29 JU-52s and 11 Dakotas took part in attacks against a force of about three Viet Minh divisions. The French ground attack aircraft flew 381 sorties, dropping 55 tons of bombs and 216 napalm tanks as well as firing rockets, while the bombers put down 130 tons of bombs, the transports delivered 31 tons of ammunition and the liaison aircraft evacuated 117 wounded. These attacks and parallel action by French river craft succeeded in cutting Giap's lines of communication, and he was forced to break off the attack. The battles had cost the Viet Minh about a third of their committed force and in June they retired to the mountains to rebuild their badly mauled units.[21]

While Giap now maintained a degree of pressure on the French by smaller-scale actions, General de Lattre, the French Commander-in-Chief, was planning to attack key Viet Minh installations in the hope of bringing Giap to combat on French terms. Instead of giving up the Red River delta rice-growing area as Giap had hoped, de Lattre built a complex network of 2,200 forts and pillboxes, both large and small, across an area of 7,500 square miles of countryside,[22] and at the same time he formed 7 mobile groups made up of crack infantry, armour and artillery units backed by 8 parachute battalions, special river patrols of landing craft and the units of the air force. Ranged against this French effort were by now some 6 or 7 Viet Minh divisions.[23]

THE FIRST AIRHEADS – HOA BINH

With his new mobile capability, de Lattre now tried to draw Giap into another 'meatgrinder' like that of Thai Binh five months earlier, and he chose Hoa Binh, a major road link between the Viet Minh forces in the north-east and those in Annam. In the first move, on 14 November, three battalions of paratroops[24] secured the area, meeting very little resistance. At the same time, fifteen infantry battalions, seven artillery battalions together with two armoured groups, two naval assault units and engineer support moved up the Black River to open up the 25 miles of water route between what had become known as the de Lattre Line and the new outposts. Giap's answer was to draw back until his units could infiltrate the area in strength, and then attack the French lines of communication.

The fighting that resulted at the strongpoints along the river continued throughout December with the French being compelled to commit three of their mobile groups as well as an airborne group in order to hold on. The main difficulty the French faced was that whenever Giap found himself outnumbered at any particular point he could withdraw into the nearby hills, identify new areas of French weakness, and then return to strike again. During this month of December the French air contribution was to fly about 500 offensive support and 400 transport sorties in the Black River area. Some 700 parachutists were dropped, and 1,600 passengers were flown into Hoa Binh as well as 550 tons of ammunition and supplies.[25] The final outcome of all this effort was, however, that instead of a French meatgrinder at Hoa Binh, the offensive produced a Viet Minh meatgrinder along the French lines of communication leading up to it.

After bitter fighting the French finally abandoned the Black River route and the emphasis moved to the shorter but more difficult road link to Hoa Binh, Colonial Route 6 from Hanoi. Meanwhile the enemy had occupied the hills around Hoa Binh itself and brought the airfield under artillery fire. This, together with increasingly accurate Viet Minh anti-aircraft fire, caused the loss of half a dozen aircraft either on the ground at Hoa Binh or on the confined approaches. At the same time Viet Minh activity along Colonial Route 6 intensified to such an extent that the French were obliged not only to clear the underbush from the roadside along the whole of its 25-mile length, but also to station no less than twelve battalions of infantry and three artillery groups along it. All these resources were tied down merely to maintain five battalions of infantry at Hoa Binh, a force that had no offensive value whatever. But worse than that, the operation was absorbing a third of all the mobile forces in the Red River area, a zone into which the Viet Minh were meanwhile infiltrating growing numbers of troops.

Finally it became clear to the French command that Hoa Binh had to be given up, and the troops began to pull out on 22 February 1952. By the end of the retreat, which became one continuous defensive battle along the Black River and along Colonial Route 6, the French had suffered heavy losses. The affair had cost the French almost as much as had the battles for the border forts in 1950, and nearly as much as Dien Bien Phu was to cost two years later. It was true that the Viet Minh had also suffered heavy losses, but the difference was that the Viet Minh had gained invaluable experience for any future conventional battle, while the French had failed to draw the right lessons from their first attempt to create what they called 'une ile aero-terrestre',[26] a device that they would use again later at Na San, Xieng-Khouang and finally at Dien Bien Phu.

SUCCESS AT NA SAN

During all the campaigns so far the Viet Minh had been weighing the capabilities as well as the limitations of the heavy equipment used by the French, and they now decided on a campaign across the top of the Indo-China peninsula. This was an area in which it was calculated that the French would be unable to deploy their heavy equipment, and over which their air force would be operating at maximum range[27] against troops concealed by thick rain forest so that the Viet Minh could swiftly concentrate their light forces for attacks and just as swiftly disperse for survival.

In October 1952 Giap sent three divisions across the Red River on a 40 mile front with the aim of taking the Tai hill country and reaching the Laos border. Within a week a series of French outposts had been overrun including the key position of Ngia Lo, a loss that opened up the possibility of a disaster on the scale of that in 1950, and isolated the positions of Lai Chau and Na San.

The French moved to reinforce these outposts, and within four days four infantry battalions, one artillery group and supporting combat engineers were airlifted into Na San. But when, after initial assaults by two divisions the Viet Minh realised that the destruction of Na San would be an expensive operation without offering any significant strategic gain, they left a small covering force and by-passed the position. For the French, their success in holding this Ile Aero-Terrestre against apparent attempts upon it by 'human wave' assaults was to have a profound effect on later thinking. Na San became the symbol of French ability to withstand a massive Viet Minh attack on an organised position.[28]

In a further effort to threaten the Viet Minh lines of communication along the Red River and to draw the enemy into a set-piece battle, the French command launched Operation Lorraine at the end of October 1952, a venture that involved the largest force committed during the entire war. It consisted of 4 complete mobile groups, 1 airborne group with 3 parachute battalions, 2 infantry battalions, 5 Commando units, 2 armoured sub-groups, 2 reconnaissance squadrons, 2 naval assault units, 2 artillery battalions and 3 battalions of combat engineers; all told a total of more than 30,000 troops.[29]

During this offensive considerable quantities of enemy arms, ammunition, supplies and even a few recently supplied Soviet trucks were captured, but although the columns advanced as much as 100 miles beyond the de Lattre Line, the Viet Minh were already across the Black River and into north-west Tonkin. This removed the strategic justification for the offensive, and since the vast logistic burden entailed could not be sustained on any other grounds the force withdrew again. This last deep penetration by the French into Communist-held territory had cost the equivalent of a battalion in casualties, it had tied up a sizeable part of all the mobile forces available to the French command, and it had put an intolerable strain on the available air resources, all without producing the set-piece battle for which the French had hoped.

In his next offensive, in the spring of 1953, Giap invaded Laos with three divisions supported by 4,000 Pathet-Lao already in that country, a move that compelled a rapid retreat by the Laotian army of 10,000 men and their supporting force of 3,000 French troops. The French command reacted by forming yet another major outpost, this time on the Plaine des Jarres, 500 air miles from the French airfields in the Hanoi area. Ten battalions were flown into the airhead and a continuous airlift was mounted to support them. On 21 April forward Viet Minh elements attacked the French garrison on the Plaine des Jarres in the hope of taking the position before it could be properly organised, but the attack failed as did an assault at the same time against the capital of Laos, Luang-Prabang, and Giap was compelled to fall back on his major supply depots before the rainy season began in May.

Once again a French airhead had survived, but only at the cost of a further deterioration of the French hold in other areas, and, more ominously, only because the whole of the available French air effort had been committed to the operation.[30]

In July 1953 the arrival of a new French Commander-in-Chief, Navarre, together with promises of more extensive American aid, led to a new spirit of optimism about the outcome of the war. There was much talk of the Navarre Plan, which was essentially to 'break the organised body of Communist aggression by the end of the 1955 fighting season', although even at that time Navarre was convinced that the most that could be hoped for was a 'coup nul', in other words a draw.[31]

Navarre set about rebuilding an operational reserve, and he first of all evacuated the airhead at Na San. The move began covertly on 15 July when troops and supplies were flown out and back to Hanoi in aircraft that were being used at the normal rate to fly in essential supplies. Preparations were next made to deceive the Viet Minh into believing that an attack was to be made on Hoa Binh, and meanwhile the rate of withdrawal from Na San was increased until on 7, 8 and 9 August the flow of transport aircraft had reached seventy-five movements a day. On 10 August the last civil aircraft took part in the airlift and by 13 August the evacuation of the 9,000 man garrison was completed without the Viet Minh having realised what had happened.[32] Faith in the concept of airheads was thus now reinforced by satisfaction at the ease with which an airhead could be withdrawn if the need arose.

Giap had realised that he must defeat the French before post-Korean American aid could permit the French to build a stronger indigenous force, and he now drew together an army with which to conquer Laos and perhaps Cambodia too. This amounted to four infantry divisions together with a heavy division made up of two artillery regiments and a combat engineer regiment. Meanwhile the 60,000 Viet Minh guerillas and five regular regiments (i.e. battalions) operating behind the de Lattre Line would paralyse French logistics and inhibit their ability to react to the offensive further West.

Giap launched a series of attacks in December 1953 and January 1954, in one case compelling the reinforcement by air of yet another airhead – that of the important airfield at Seno in Southern Laos. By this stage of the campaign the confidence of the French command in the viability of these airheads had led to the creation of a dozen or so of them stretching from Muong-Sai, North of Luang Prabang, to Anke on the southern mountain plateau more than 600 miles further south.

DIEN BIEN PHU

One of the airheads was to be at Dien Bien Phu on the Laos–Vietnam border and 300 km by air from Hanoi. Dien Bien Phu was the largest valley in the whole of Indo-China's northern mountain area, and indeed its size was one of the main reasons why it had been chosen as a Base Aero-Terrestre.

The tasks assigned to the base were to 'guarantee at the very least the free usage of the airfield' and to inflict heavy losses on the enemy and to delay his laying a tight siege ring around the valley, as well as to link up with a column advancing from the south-west.[33]

It was planned that the French garrison would build up to a force of nine battalions, five batteries (twenty guns) of 105 mm howitzers, and two batteries (eight guns) of 75 mm recoilless rifles as well as a company of heavy mortars and ten Chaffee tanks – which were to be dismantled, flown in and assembled on the spot. Six Bearcat fighters, five Criquets and a helicopter were stationed on the airstrip itself[34] and by March 1954 when the Viet Minh began their assault phase on Dien Bien Phu, the French garrison totalled 10,814 men.[35]

This confident projection of so large a ground force into an unprepared site so far removed from its logistic support in the Hanoi area still remains something of a puzzle. Some light is shed on the matter by Jules Roy, according to whom the French Chief of Air Staff, General Fay, dissented from the otherwise unanimous local opinion that the airhead could be held. According to Roy, when Defence Minister Pleven and the Chiefs of Staff visited Dien Bien Phu on 19 February 1954, Fay said:

I cannot join in today's concert [of views]. What I have seen has only confirmed me in an opinion which I shall express bluntly, in full awareness of my responsibilities. This is it; I shall advise General Navarre to take advantage of the respite available to him and the fact that he can still use his two airfields[36] to evacuate all the men he can, for he is done for.[37]

This opinion apparently made no impression on the others present, but it was a remarkable comment on so vast an undertaking. It was also a prescient forecast of what was to come.

Unfortunately the French had not had enough time to burn down the tens of square miles of jungle on the slopes overlooking their outposts, and Communist assault groups could therefore approach to within a few hundred yards of the defensive positions practically unobserved. Once these outposts were lost, and they fell within twenty-four hours of the start of the main battle, the French were left with only their artillery and their air power to suppress any Viet Minh guns that might be emplaced around the valley.

With very great skill, and to the total surprise of the French, the Viet Minh had not only dismantled and transported guns of up to 105 mm calibre to Dien Bien Phu, and not only did they carry an estimated 30,000 shells for these guns as well as over 100,000 shells for other artillery pieces, but they dug the artillery in on the forward slopes above the fortress without being observed.[38]

The uncleared jungle had concealed the construction work, and when the bombardment began the cover of vegetation on the hills made French attempts to spot the positions almost universally unsuccessful. Indeed the failure of the French counter-battery fire was so comprehensive that the artillery commander in the garrison committed suicide at an early stage of the fighting.

A great deal was thus to depend on French air efforts, and this was planned to be employed in three ways at Dien Bien Phu. First, it would interdict enemy supply routes from the north; second, it would provide direct offensive air support for the garrison, notably by taking out Viet Minh assault formations and artillery positions; and third, it would maintain the base at Dien Bien Phu by parachute drop, by air landing and by flying out the casualties.

For the total air effort in the north at this time GATAC Nord had at its disposal a theoretical 107 aircraft out of about 128 in Indo-China as a whole, including French Navy aircraft. They were made up of thirty B-26 Marauders, two groups (augmented by detachments from a third group) of F-8F Bearcats, one squadron of French Naval Hellcats and one of Helldivers from the aircraft carriers *Arromanches* and *Bois Belleau* as well as six Privateers, which were naval versions of the Second World War Liberators, carrying eight tons of bombs. This made a total of thirty-six bombers, forty-five fighter-bombers, and thirty-two fighters. Allowing for combat losses, maintenance and so on the effective strength was, however, likely to be closer to seventy-five aircraft, a very small force for the tasks that now faced them.[39]

The French High Command appreciated the importance of interdicting the Viet Minh supply routes, but despite the experience of Korea, the belief was still widely held that Asian-style lines of communications could be severed by air action.[40] But just as in Korea, once the main roads were cut the Communists reverted to a coolie system of transport, a kind of supply by osmosis.

Two interdiction techniques were attempted: first, the opening of a single major road cut maintained by repeated raids on the same area; and second, the creation of multiple cuts all along the roads being used by the Viet Minh supply columns. Major cuts were made possible by a reasonable concentration of air effort, but the Viet Minh met the technique by a matching concentration of repair effort. The second technique forced the Viet Minh to disperse their repair capacity, but, taken together with a lack of precision in French attacks, the scattered nature of the raids meant that they had little impact. A compromise solution was eventually decided upon. A handful of choke points such as the crossings over the Black and Red Rivers was selected, and a number of smaller cuts were made up and down the road routes, but the French air effort available was simply inadequate, the campaign failed and eventually all available air effort would be drawn into the immediate battle in the valley.

On top of this there was an entirely new factor that distinguished the battle for Dien Bien Phu from any other war that had so far been fought against a guerrilla army, and that was the deployment by the insurgents of substantial AA defences. Isolated enemy machine-gunners taking aim at attacking aircraft was something to be expected in a campaign of this kind; but even as early as December 1952, French air reconnaissance had located 170 flak positions in Northern Vietnam and ten aircraft had been shot down.

Since then the situation had grown much worse, and during the two weeks beginning 24 November 1953 forty-five French aircraft out of the fifty-one that had been bombing and strafing the Communists along Roads 13 and 41 had been hit by flak, and three of them had been shot down. During December, as the French extended their interdiction campaign towards the Chinese border and away from their own bases, for a total of 367 sorties forty-nine aircraft were hit, eventually compelling the French from the end of December onwards to devote more air effort to flak suppression.

At Dien Bien Phu itself the Viet Minh mounted for the first time since the beginning of the war an air defence 'tegere et moyenne comparable a celle que nous avons recontrée en Allemagne au course de la compagne 1944–45'.[41] This was a major surprise to the French. They had earlier made an assessment of the threat likely to be posed by Viet Minh AA fire over the valley, and they had even sought the advice of the USAF. On 23 January a party of three US officers from HQ FEAF, Tokyo, travelled to Dien Bien Phu accompanied by seven French Air Force and Naval officers to make a study of the likely effectiveness of the locally deployed Viet Minh AA artillery. The conclusions they reached were that the enemy would have great difficulty in bringing his 37 mm guns to bear on aircraft in the circuit at Dien Bien Phu and that his gun-sites would be vulnerable to counter-battery fire. In any case, they reported, night re-supply would be possible and the maintenance of Dien Bien Phu was, they decided, assured.[42]

Giap fully realised the vital role that air power was likely to play in the battle, and he did not content himself only with measures at Dien Bien Phu itself. In an attack of great daring on 7 March, his guerrillas penetrated the fortified airfield of Haiphong Cat-Bi through the sewers and destroyed no fewer than thirty-eight aircraft on the ground; a similarly successful attack was made on Hanoi Gia Lam.[43]

On 12 March, the day before the main assault began, Viet Minh 105 mm guns opened up in strength on the airstrip, and by late afternoon on the next day the airfield had to be closed to all traffic. From the 14 March, offensive air support could be provided only from airfields in the Hanoi area, and the ability of air power to intervene directly and in response to local air tasking had practically disappeared. Meanwhile, the Viet Minh determination to keep the airstrip closed was matched by their efforts to dominate the airspace above it. The battle to maintain Dien Bien Phu from the air began, and the build-up of the base continued.

By 18 March the re-supply problem was further complicated by 37 mm AA guns which the Viet Minh had installed to fire directly into the circuit pattern from two outlying strong points, Gabrielle and Anne-Marie, that were by now in enemy hands. On that same day repairs were made to the severely battered runway and from then until 27 March it was possible to make night flights into the strip under cover of decoy airdrop flights, and 223 wounded were evacuated by this means.[44]

About 200 aircraft were now flying transport and close air support missions over Dien Bien Phu, but because of the north – south orientation of the valley and the prevailing winds, there was only one approach path and the aircraft had no choice but to run the gauntlet of Viet Minh AA fire. The risk was heightened in many cases because obsolete transport aircraft such as the C-47 were obliged to make up to twelve runs on each mission in order to drop supplies through their narrow side-doors. Their losses were correspondingly high, but the supply missions continued, as did the sporadic and often hazardous evacuation of some of the wounded, in spite of the fact that by 21 March Viet Minh patrols were making occasional forays on to Dien Bien Phu airstrip itself.

On the afternoon of 23 March another technique to clear the Viet Minh from their commanding positions was launched when the French Air Force made a massive napalm bombardment of the enemy siegeworks. But the impressive sheets of flame and the clouds of dense black smoke concealed the fact that the napalm burned up in the rain-soaked jungle without setting any fires, and without causing any appreciable loss to the Viet Minh. The French watchers in Dien Bien Phu reported that the attack had 'not yielded observable results'.[45]

The meagre French transport resources had for some time been augmented by those of various civilian concerns[46] and in particular by Civil Air Transport (CAT), the Taiwan-based airline. By now twenty-four of the twenty-nine C-119s being operated over Dien Bien Phu by this airline were crewed by Americans, including some military pilots who had been attached to CAT to familiarise themselves with the area in case of American intervention.[47] All this led to certain language difficulties and to considerable air traffic confusion when thirty or forty aircraft were operating over or near the valley at the same time.

By mid-April the viability of the air supply system for the garrison, never adequate, had become dangerously tenuous, and nothing could now be done to restore matters. The Viet Minh AA artillery could not be suppressed from the air or captured on the ground, and any attempt even to expand the dropping zone, still less to try to capture the surrounding hills, would have called for a military effort that was simply not available to the garrison. Even had that effort been available, it would have had the effect of increasing the already insupportable air supply bill. There was no way out of this spiral and the trap was complete.

On the last day of the siege none of the sixteen C-119s available made the supply run but twenty-two C-47 Dakotas did, and they kept flying until the end at about 1700 hours. It was, however, by now far too late and when eventually it was found that the direct air support effort by sixteen French Naval fighter-bombers, twenty-five B-26s and thirty fighters was hitting friend and foe alike because of the congestion on the ground, the air effort to maintain the garrison ceased. Finally, at 1730 hours on 7 May the main position at Dien Bien Phu surrendered and the battle was over. In the days that followed, the French aircraft rendered their last service to the garrison by flying out the very seriously wounded in return for an understanding with the Viet Minh that their columns pulling out of the valley to the north would not be molested from the air.

Dien Bien Phu had fallen essentially because the French had allowed themselves to be drawn into a battle on what they thought was their terms, but which in the event turned out to be more favourable to the Viet Minh. There were several elements in this reversal of advantage. First, the Viet Minth proved to be astonishingly adept at transporting weapons and supplies to their besieging force, and the limited French air interdiction efforts were no answer to the forward flow of Viet Minh resources.

Second, unknown to French intelligence and undetected by the modest French air reconnaissance effort, the Viet Minh were able to position and conceal a far larger besieging force, including powerful artillery, than the French had anticipated. Third, when the French command did realise the extent of the threat to Dien Bien Phu it was too late to construct defences able to withstand the heavy artillery bombardment that followed, even had the combat engineering equipment and the means to transport it from the Hanoi area been available.[48]

This left the French with only three options. One was to rely on counter-battery fire, a response that failed as early as 12 March. The second was to extend the perimeter and deny the artillery sites to the Viet Minh; but this would have called for a massive increase in the size of the garrison and it would have meant a demand for air-transported support that could not be met, even if the necessary troops could have been found. The third and final option would have been to take out the Viet Minth artillery with air power. But the Viet Minh had not only brought up heavy artillery, they had also deployed and concealed a dense array of AA weapons. These weapons proved to be extremely difficult to locate, and meanwhile they caused such heavy losses to French combat and transport aircraft that the air bridge was severed on many occasions.

So the French faced a set-piece battle, 300 km from their main base area and with inadequate resources on the ground or in the air to deal with the situation in which they found themselves. Speculation about the results had the US intervened in French Indo-China can be endless, but two things seem clear. The first is that the kind of air power available to the US at the time could almost certainly have saved Dien Bien Phu; but the second is that neither a success at Dien Bien Phu nor the continued application or massive air power could, on their own, have saved the French from ultimate defeat in Indo-China. Indeed it is just possible that the use of US air power might have produced the very thing that the French planners all along feared – the intervention of the Chinese Air Force.

The French forces had fought throughout the campaign with great tenacity and determination; their losses alone testify to that.[49] The fact was, however, that conventional forces were being pitted against Marxist style guerrillas, and as later campaigns were to confirm, the advantage is too easily seized and held by local insurgents. That the French defeat came where and when it did, at Dien Bien Phu, can be put down to the fact that the missions attempted by the French outstripped the resources available to perform them, and this was particularly true of the resources that were available to French air power.

MALAYA, 1948–60

The campaign in Malaya was won on the ground by small-unit tactics. But since a fairly comprehensive air power was also employed against the guerrillas, including bombers, modern jet aircraft and for the first time in a colonial campaign, helicopters, it will bear a somewhat closer examination. The brief account of the campaign given here will serve as a background to a description of the air contribution.

The war began with the murder of planters in isolated areas in 1948 by Communist terrorists who had been equipped and organised to fight the Japanese occupation forces after 1941. A state of emergency was declared on 16 June 1948, and the insurgency reached its height in 1951, by which time the British had taken special measures to deal with it. These included the deployment of about 67,000 police, 300,000 Home Guards and 23 Infantry Battalions or their equivalents.[50] British, Gurkha, Malayan, Fijian, African, Australian and New Zealand units all at one time or another took part in the campaign.

The terrorists' field army was made up of ten regiments, each of between 200 and 500 terrorists divided into four or five companies each

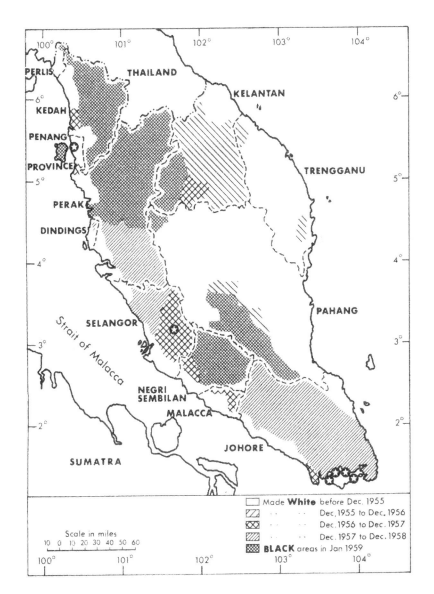

MAP 3   *'White Areas' in Malaya, 1955–9*

of ten or twelve platoons. Each regiment also had an Independent Platoon, 60–70 strong. At the start of the Emergency the total insurgent force numbered about 2,500, with a further 600 organised into highly mobile killer squads that were to lead the initial wave of terrorism.[51] By 1951, these bands, 95 per cent Chinese in racial origin, were living in well-camouflaged and usually inaccessible training areas in the jungle. Because of the blockade imposed by the Security Forces, little in the way of resupply reached the insurgents throughout the war, and their inability to replace captured weapons and supplies was one of the factors that led to their ultimate defeat.

The terrorists were, however, able to draw on the passive local support of over one million Chinese at the height of the campaign, and it was one of the features of the successful Briggs Plan of 1950 to combat the insurrection that the Administration was able to cut off the terrorists from the population and to protect vulnerable elements of the community, especially in isolated areas. By the end of 1952, nearly 462,000 Chinese had been moved into 509 settlements enclosed by barbed wire perimeter fences and lights, and protected by the Malay Police and by the Chinese Home Guard. Once the terrorists had been isolated in this way, military operations against them in the jungle began in earnest.

These operations included a plan under which a minimum number of troops were deployed to protect populated areas, and the rest were used to dominate as much jungle as possible. Using this strategy, it was planned to clear Malaya area by area starting with Johore in the South. The tactics were to launch a pre-planned combined operation with constant patrolling and full air support so as to keep the enemy on the move and split him into small parties that could be more easily ambushed.

This approach met with considerable success, but it also led to an all-out terrorist offensive to disrupt the Briggs Plan and to seize the initiative. The number of incidents rose to 606 in the month of June 1951 and fell below 580 only in one month in the rest of that year. The security forces suffered casualties of 505 killed and 603 wounded during 1951 but claimed 1,021 killed, 650 wounded and 121 captured terrorists in return.

With their dependence on the civilian population seriously inhibited, many of the terrorists were forced to withdraw to bases deeper in the jungle where they could cultivate their own food. The security forces now launched several operations in areas where the terrorists were weakest, mainly the Central States, and during 1953 numerous camps were discovered and at least 75 terrorists were killed. These activities so weakened the MRLA that Emergency restrictions could be lifted from a large part of Malacca, which became the first 'white', i.e. cleared, area in Malaya.

By the middle of 1954, over 7,500 terrorists had been eliminated, only 3,500 were still operating in the jungle and the average number of military and civilian fatal casualties had dropped from 188 a month to 35. The remaining terrorists were, however, the hard core and the final phase of the Emergency, which opened in July 1954, was one of sustained attrition with ground forces occupying and dominating areas of the jungle for protracted periods.

At the end of 1954, some 3,000 terrorists were still at large, but against that nearly one-third of the population then lived in areas declared 'white' and the number of terrorist incidents was down to an average of only 65 per month. The terrorists continued to avoid contact with the security forces where they could, but intensive food denial operations in some areas and successful attacks on terrorist sanctuaries in others combined to create a split in the large 'white' area in Central Malaya that cut off the main concentrations of terrorists from those remaining in the border area of Thailand.

Meanwhile the first Federal elections on the road to eventual independence were being held, and the Communists tried to negotiate an armistice whose terms would have allowed them to continue their subversive activities virtually unchecked. When this approach failed at the end of 1955, the campaign continued. A total of 473 terrorists were eliminated in 1956, leaving some 2,000 in the jungle, and major operations, some lasting as much as 9 months and more, continued against the rest. During 1957 over 200 terrorists were accounted for, and in July of that year for the first time since 1948 there were no terrorist incidents and no fatalities among the military or the civil population. By Independence Day, 31 August 1957, about 1,830 terrorists were still at large, 450 in Thailand, 500 in North West Malaya and a further 500 in the far South. The number of Commonwealth troops engaged in the campaign was now reduced, and at the same time increasing numbers of terrorists began to accept the surrender terms of the new government. Of 650 terrorists eliminated in 1958, 478 gave themselves up including 130 in the North of Johore alone, which was then declared 'white'. Operations against the remaining terrorists continued, particularly against 500 or so terrorists on the Thai border, but after final mopping-up operations in the remaining parts of Malaya still harbouring terrorists, the state of Emergency was ended on 31 July 1960.

Through the twelve-year campaign, the Royal Air Force and the associated Commonwealth Air Forces carried out sorties that included bombing, close air support, supply dropping, troop lifting and casualty evacuation. Visual and photographic reconnaissance made an important contribution to the intelligence base on which the success of the campaign depended, while leaflet-dropping and voice-hailing missions sought to undermine the morale of the isolated terrorists.

This work was undertaken by part of the Far East Air Force of the Royal Air Force. In the offensive support role there were two fighter squadrons, one light bomber squadron and a misemployed flying boat squadron. The total force grew to a maximum strength of two medium bomber, two light bomber, two fighter and two flying boat squadrons in 1950, and fell again to one medium bomber, one light bomber and three fighter squadrons by 1953. In addition, occasional detachments from the United Kingdom-based Bomber Command took part in operations. During the final stages of the campaign there were three light bomber squadrons and three fighter squadrons in Malaya, but most of them belonged to the Commonwealth Strategic Reserve and were not engaged in Emergency operations. The medium bomber force included the Lincolns of No. 1 (RAAF) Sqn from July 1950 to June 1958, aircraft which carried 14 × 1,000 lb bombs.

The primary role of FEAF was the defence of Malaya, Singapore, North Borneo and Sarawak against external attack. Even the small[52] but invaluable transport force had as its main responsibility the maintenance of scheduled services throughout the Far East Command, which stretched from Ceylon to Japan and from Hong Kong to North Borneo. As far as air effort was concerned, therefore, the campaign was fought on a shoestring, but it seems clear that the local circumstances of the anti-terrorist campaign called for little more, at least so far as offensive air support was concerned.

Air attack as a means of eliminating terrorists had definite limitations.[53] In dense jungle covering more than three-quarters of a country the size of England and Wales, fewer than 10,000 terrorists were operating in gangs of less than 100 strong and it is hardly surprising that casualties among them caused by air attack were at best fortuitous[54] and that the destruction of their camps was often no more than an inconvenience.

The aims of the offensive air operations were to kill terrorists, destroy their camps and disrupt their organisation. At the start of the campaign the terrorists occupied camps holding as many as 300 men, but the poor air maps of Malaya, the general lack of features and the cover[55] afforded by the jungle canopy made it extremely difficult to locate and attack these important concentrations. As the efficiency of air attacks improved with better mapping and with accumulating experience, the terrorists reacted by camouflaging the camps and by splitting into smaller groups.

Air attacks were therefore made on specified areas of jungle, about 1,000 yards square, and on line targets stretching across as much as 6,000 yards of jungle. These techniques were used from 1949 until the end of 1952, sometimes with the aim of flushing terrorists out of concealment and into waiting ground force ambushes, but at other times to 'keep the terrorists awake and to make life generally difficult for them'.[56] This was clearly a very wasteful application of air power, but by this stage of the war it was becoming clear to the civilian population that the security forces were gaining the upper hand and the intelligence information flowing to those forces consequently improved.

This improvement in the political climate led to an attempt to concentrate air strikes on to pinpoint targets, but it coincided with a sharp decline in the number of terrorist surrenders, and large-scale air harassment was resumed interspersed with occasional precision attacks.

By 1954 the doubtful effectiveness of air attack together with the impending arrival of new aircraft types and the need for squadrons to concentrate on their primary roles, which were still those of conventional air power, caused offensive air operations to be restricted almost entirely to harassing the terrorists. During 1955 and 1956, improved target location methods combined with the need to economise in war stocks to produce another change back to precision attacks – but only when high grade intelligence made success probable. But as the number of terrorists was whittled down even these targets became more scarce and the campaign ended with the aircraft again taking up the harassing role.

Almost throughout the whole campaign the use of offensive air support had progressively decreased[57] so that in the last six months the bids for air strike fell to as little as one a week[58] and in August 1959 it ceased altogether. The tangible results of the air attacks had been insignificant, but they certainly exerted pressure on the terrorists throughout the campaign. It is also true that once the terrorists retired to deep jungle area, air attack was the only kind of action that could be taken against them.

But since it was precisely in those circumstances that direct air attack was likely to be less accurate and harassment less likely to produce operational results, it is questionable whether the effort was justified. A total of 35,000 tons[59] of bombs was dropped during the course of 4,067 air strikes throughout the campaign, while 74,159 RP and 9.8 million rounds of cannon and MG ammunition were expended.[60] Expenditure on air armament alone had been more than £1.5m per year at the height of the Emergency. The results in terms of terrorist casualty figures will never be exactly known, but for example by the end of 1950, 126 terrorists had been confirmed as killed by air action with a further 141 unconfirmed out of a total of 1,641 claimed by the security forces as a whole. This was less than 10 per cent of the total, and it seems very likely that even this claim is exaggerated.[61]

General Clutterbuck, one of the leading authorities on counter-insurgency and a soldier who served in Malaya from 1956–8, gives as his opinion that:

except for occasional successes with pinpoint bombing, offensive air strikes were almost wholly unsuccessful in Malaya; they probably did more harm than good. Hundreds of tons of bombs were dropped on the jungle every month; they probably killed fewer than half a dozen guerrillas a year – more by accident than design. Such senseless dropping induced a feeling of contempt for the power of modern weapons and the enemy made full use of this contempt in their propaganda among the villagers and aborigines who had heard all the noise. Worse still, if bombs were dropped in or near inhabited areas, the people's means of livelihood, rubber trees or cultivation, would be destroyed and innocent people might be killed. It has been argued that the people would, in fact, turn against the communists for bringing them (such attacks) down on their heads. Fortunately . . . these arguments never prevailed in Malaya.[62]

Supply dropping on the other hand, made a very significant contribution in the campaign. The total supplies dropped exceeded 25,000 tons and called for up to eight transport aircraft sorties per day at periods of greatest activity. Troop-lifting was unquestionably the next most important air contribution to the campaign. A relatively small[63] force of helicopters also gave valuable assistance to the ground forces from 1953 until the end of the fighting, lifting small parties of troops into clearings from which they could then advance on suspected terrorist positions. To give an example of the scale of effort involved in this type of operation, in May 1953, 1,623 troops and 36,500 lbs of equipment were lifted into jungle landing zones during a ten-day offensive that killed 9 terrorists and destroyed 12 camps.[64] In 1956, at the height of helicopter activity, 25,700 troops were lifted by helicopter, an effort that equated to moving every soldier in Malaya at least once during the year.

Casualty evacuation was a major role for the light helicopter, while paratrooping, general communications work, crop spraying to deny food to terrorists in the jungle as well as aerial broadcasting and leaflet-dropping were all subsidiary air activities that played a part in the often subtle character of the activities of the security forces.

In summary, the most important contribution of the limited air power that was deployed in Malaya was the mobility it brought to other arms and activities. In terms of firepower delivered by air on to terrorist targets, and that meant either the terrorists themselves, their training camps or their cultivated plots, the meagre results were out of all proportion to the extensive effort engaged. It must be remembered, however, that the aircraft of FEAF took part in the campaign because they were there.[65] Air power did what it could with the resources that could be spared from the primary roles of the Far East Air Force, but the campaign was won essentially by the long, painstaking and tenacious operations of the forces on the ground in Malaya.

ALGERIA, 1954–62

Only three months after the end of the war in Indo-China, France was faced by the start of another colonial crisis, this time in Algeria. On 1 November 1954, some thirty small and poorly-armed bands made attacks at a series of points across the country, but mainly against gendarmerie posts in the Aures Mountains of Eastern Algeria, while a simultaneous announcement was made on Radio Cairo that a National Liberation Front had been formed. The French garrison in Algeria numbered about fifty thousand, and to deal with what was at first thought to be a minor local uprising of a kind that the French had seen before during their 130 years of rule, reinforcements in the form of three battalions of paratroops were moved in from France.

For fifteen months the French tried to deal with the rebellion using traditional methods. Several battalions would cordon the area in which rebel activity had taken place; the whole area would then be searched for political activists and all arms seized. Finally, heavy air attacks with bombs and cannon would be made on any suspected hiding places.

Not only were these techniques singularly ineffective, since the guerrillas had enough warning of French intentions to be able to escape into the wild and almost impenetrable terrain outside the towns and cities, but the removal of self-protection from the now unarmed villagers made them more vulnerable to guerrilla pressures and thus worked against French interests. Worse than that, however, the rebellion spread within a few months to the coastal area and then west across the country until French resources were stretched beyond the point at which traditional pacification measures were effective.

By 1956 the French had recognised the nature of the revolution and a second stage of the war began with three measures being taken to counter the rebel initiatives. First the rebels were to be separated from their sources of supply by closing the borders. An elaborate system of barriers with a total length of about 3,000 km was built along the Tunisian and Moroccan borders using complexes of minefields, electrified fences and alarm systems patrolled both in the air and on the ground.[66] Together with active patrols at sea this imposed a reasonably tight blockade on the whole country.

The second measure was to isolate the rebels from the Moslem population by improving education and living standards and by offering physical protection. By mid-1957 a system of local defence had developed into 270 armed villages protected by some 11,000 auxiliaries, linked to the main system of 'quadrillage' defence, which was a comprehensive network of garrisoned cities, towns and villages covering the whole country on a regular grid basis.

The third measure was to increase the capacity of the main French forces to react to guerrilla initiatives, and this was achieved almost entirely by air power. At the start of the rebellion there were three main air bases in Algeria, with a total strength of one fighter-bomber wing in Oran, a transport squadron in Blida, several light aircraft of various kinds and a naval coastal reconnaissance flight at Lautigue.[67] These slender air resources were expanded, the command structure re-organised so as to provide the ground forces with the air support that they needed and an infrastructure of airfields developed.[68] Joint Operation Centres were set up at corps and divisional level, while commanders of specific operations were given Air Directing Posts through which the immediate air support could be made available.[69] This provided a decentralised system for most of Algeria, but in the Sahara the particular characteristics of the region called for even lower decentralisation, and co-ordinated air/ground operations were conducted at brigade rather than at divisional level. As to the build-up of air resources, the end of the war in Indo-China released some aircraft and the expansion of the French Air Force in Europe during the early 1950s made others available. By January 1959, there were 130 Mistral (Vampire) fighter-bombers, 24 P-47 Corsairs, 5 old night-fighters,

22 B-26 Invaders and 8 RB-26, the reconnaissance version, as well as 242 Texans on which the French principally relied for their air firepower.[70]

There were 48 Noratlas transports in the theatre as well as 23 C-47s, 65 Broussard six-seat light transports, 20 old, but useful, Junkers 52s, 10 French Naval Neptunes and 35 MD 315 Flamants. All told, this was a force of 801 aircraft, not counting light helicopters of which there were about 100, as well as 36 French naval helicopters.[71] It was one of the features of the Algerian war that helicopters were used in large numbers for the first time in any conflict.[72]

By early 1959, although the French efforts to hold down the rebellion were effective in many areas, there was still an active rebel army of 40,000 men. Nor were these untrained guerrillas. The profession of arms was one of high prestige in Algeria and Moslem French Army veterans, many of whom had served in Indo-China, formed the backbone of the guerrilla movement. The military skills of these men and the classic tactics of the guerrilla, that of massing to strike with a superior force and then disappearing into the countryside, meant that by early 1959 the ALN was tying up no less than half of the total French Armed Forces and the campaign was costing the French treasury over three million dollars a day. By that stage the war had cost the lives of 7,200 soldiers, 77,000 rebels, 1,500 European civilians and 10,000 Moslems.[73]

In January, 1959, General Challe of the French Air Force became Commander-in-Chief of the French forces in Algeria. He took a new approach to the problem of countering guerrilla activity over such a wide area and used the French Foreign Legion as well as three divisions of paratroops to form the core of small and highly mobile forces totalling some 20,000 men. He used primarily air-gathered intelligence[74] to make an accurate assessment of a local situation, and then without making any obvious concentration or preparation he spread a net and closed it at once, striking usually at dawn. Cluster bombs and 'daisy cutting' weapons were launched by fighters and bombers, and within two minutes a force of troops up to 480 strong, supported by armed helicopters, would land on the rebel concentration. Other attack aircraft, accompanied by spotting planes and helicopters, would patrol the perimeters of the operation area to prevent escape. At the same time, regular ground forces moved forward to converge on the guerrilla area, and by sundown the whole operation was usually complete and the French forces withdrawn. Using these methods, General Challe's mobile forces broke the ALN into even smaller groups until by May 1960 their strength was estimated at less than 12,000 and groups of rebels larger than a dozen or so were not to be found.

The technique was summed up by Lt General Ezanno of the French
Air Force, who commanded the 2nd Tactical Air Command in Algeria
for two years in this way:

> Obviously the role of the Air Force in Algeria was very different from
> its traditional role in conventional warfare. Instead of powerful
> concentrations of force and manoeuvres conducted at a very high
> level of command, the Algerian war called for dispersion of forces and
> manoeuvre at low levels of command . . . The organisation was
> established to permit great flexibility. Operations ranged from a well-
> prepared, combined attack to action initiated by an air report and
> performed by aircraft diverted from routine missions.[75]

Without the benefit of complex hardware, or perhaps even because of it,
an efficient and effective counter-guerrilla air/ground force was, thus, in
existence by 1959.

Command and control was particularly crucial in these dispersed
operations. Air power was assigned or 'leased', subject to reassignment.
Each ground – air echelon availed itself of the air power resources it
normally required, and each was also able to call on additional means
through joint channels. Of particular importance were the communications and, in particular, the VHF network that was developed across
the country. General Enzano, for example, sited his aerials for VHF
automatic repeater stations on the hilltops that had been used for visual
telegraphy in the 1830s, and within eighteen months he had complete
coverage of his whole area of responsibility down to about 1,000 feet.
This meant that if a patrolling aircraft saw anything unusual on the
ground, it could call up support. Similarly, troops on the ground
could call for assistance and the request was usually received simultaneously at Army division, Air Force Advanced Air Command Post
and at the Tactical Air Command Post. Aircraft on airborne alert could
react at once, and the Joint Operations Centre could, if necessary,
devote extra air resources to the task, though normally the JOC was
concerned only with pre-planned missions. All air activity was controlled ultimately under one authority. the appropriate Tactical Air
Group, of which there were three on a geographical basis, and these
Groups also had responsibility for air defence identification against
intruders.

The air defence aircraft themselves were retained by the theatre air
HQ, the 5th Air Region, which also had the responsibility for a
transport, but 5th Air Region leased most of the jets and a few

transports to the GATACs. Aid could sometimes be given from one GATAC to another within as little as fifteen minutes depending on operational circumstances.[76]

Most of the T-6 Texans and other attack aircraft were reassigned down to the next level of control, the Zones,[77] while the Broussards and helicopters in detachments of six to eight aircraft were almost continuously on lease to zone and to lower level. Each GATAC, Zone and Sector was told in advance that a certain number of aircraft, by type, would be available for so many days, or, conversely, that a large-scale operation would utilise a given number of their assigned aircraft for a specified period. The weapons used were high-fragmentation rockets and bombs, but 500 lb and 1,000 lb bombs were occasionally used against dug-in rebels and against caves. The use of napalm was restricted on political grounds, but on one occasion it was used to kill 300 guerrillas in a valley of the Kabyle Mountains.[78] Air planning and the direction of joint operations were carried out by the joint commanders in fixed JOCs/Command Posts. In the field, airborne, air-transported, truck-mounted or truck-transported CPs were used. Although not particularly original or exotic, the command and control system played a major role by providing the most valuable tool in the inventory of counter-guerrilla warfare – the ability to direct an instant reaction.

As the campaign developed the French refined their air-to-ground operations to a high level of effectiveness, and once the enemy quickly learned that the gap between firepower and occupation was critical the techniques were further improved. Armed helicopters were developed, armed with rockets and cannon to give cover to the deploying infantry, while additional attack aircraft were kept immediately available to give further support.

Although military operations destroyed three-quarters of the force of 40,000 organised rebels within Algeria by late 1959, guerrilla action continued in the countryside, and urban terrorism was actually on the increase. General de Gaulle was unable to share the optimism of his military commanders about the progress that the counter-guerrilla campaign was making, and took steps to end a war that was by now costing France over a billion dollars a year. This prompted a military rebellion in which, among other things, French troops fired on French civilians in Algiers, two hundred French officers including five Generals were arrested and disloyal units were disbanded wholesale. De Gaulle took special powers for a year to contain what threatened to be a collapse of the State and opened secret negotiations with the leaders of the Algerian revolt. The guerrillas, in turn, reduced the intensity of their campaign and agreement was reached on Algerian Independence, which was eventually proclaimed in July 1962.

The French military claimed a victory against the rebels operating in the country areas, and a victory in sealing off Algeria from the thirty battalions or so of armed rebels who were in sanctuaries in Morocco and Tunisia. But it was a level of success that had been achieved only by the presence of 550,000 French troops in Algeria and by the employment of something like 1,000 aircraft, not including 200 or so helicopters.[79]

To sustain a long-term effort of this kind against the 10,000 armed rebels remaining and to do so in the face of, at best, a passive and, at worst, an actively hostile local population, would have been an impossible drain on French resources. Even had the burden been acceptable, the problem of urban terrorism remained and the mobile air and ground tactics were no answer to that kind of threat. De Gaulle realised that the solution must eventually be a political one, and he said as much in his 'self-determination' speech of September 1959.

The French had taken a long time to recognise the rebellion for what it was, and they had not been swift to develop concepts to deal with it. Within certain limits their concepts became highly effective and the security forces scored notable tactical victories. They did so, however, only by deploying forces on a huge scale, and even then they had no answer to all aspects of the rebels' activities. Above all, however, their military successes were being achieved at a pace that was overtaken by a growing hostility to the French among the Moslem population, and, indeed, the effect of intensified military operations was often a further acceleration of local disaffection.

As to the employment of air power, it had certainly played a decisive part in the military successes that had been won. The high mobility of air transport, as well as the firepower provided by air, could lessen the impact of initiative and surprise, which was always on the side of the rebels, to a point where locally at least the imbalance was redressed. One interesting thing is that the French developed an effective system of centralised command and control but delegated operations to deal with the huge areas for which the security forces were responsible. It was, of course, a use of air power that was very much in the supportive role, and when the ground forces found their operations inhibited, as they did in the urban areas, then air power became irrelevant. No amount of air power could have changed the final pattern of events in Algeria, but air power had shown that, properly employed and given favourable terrain, it could provide an equaliser even in anti-guerrilla warfare.

ARABIA AND EAST AFRICA

British air power had taken on a permanent role in the Middle East in 1921, when the Royal Air Force was given responsibility for the control of the mandated territory of Iraq (then Mesopotamia). Supported by a record of considerable success scored by aircraft against tribesmen in Somaliland and in Mesopotamia, in 1920 the Royal Air Force argued that air control would be a very economical method of controlling undeveloped tribal territory. Instead of slow-moving columns of troops that had hitherto been used, local levies would be raised which could be supported by armoured cars on the ground and by aircraft that would stage 'demonstrations' or, if that failed, make selective air attacks on dissident tribesmen.

These air control operations were later judged to have been so successful that the concept of air control was extended to the Northwest Frontier of India, to Transjordan and, in 1928, to the Aden protectorate.[80] In practice, and once the tribesmen had got used to the sight of aircraft, air control meant the destruction of villages and the dispersal by air attack of flocks of livestock, which drove the tribesmen away from their settlements in what was sometimes called a 'reverse blockade'; that is to say instead of populations having their supplies cut off, they were prevented from reaching their supplies.

One of the first of these campaigns after 1945 was a frontier dispute between Saudi Arabia and the Trucial States at the Buraimi Oasis in 1953, in which Lancaster and Lincoln bombers, Vampires and Anson aircraft were used for demonstrations and reconnaissance, and there were also minor operations in Central Oman in 1957. These latter involved attacks on fortified towers in six villages occupied by rebels seeking to overthrow the Sultan of Muscat, in which warning leaflets were dropped before the walls of the towers themselves were breached by rockets fired by Venoms in what were officially referred to as 'firepower demonstrations'.

The attacks were followed up by units of infantry, brought in by transport aircraft, who completed the destruction of the forts with demolition charges. The mobility that the transports gave the ground forces made one indispensible contribution to the success of this small campaign, and the use of offensive aircraft made another. It was, however, air power designed to intimidate rather than destroy the enemy and as such it was very close to the use of air power that the region had seen in the 1920s and 1930s.

Further operations in south-east Arabia followed until February

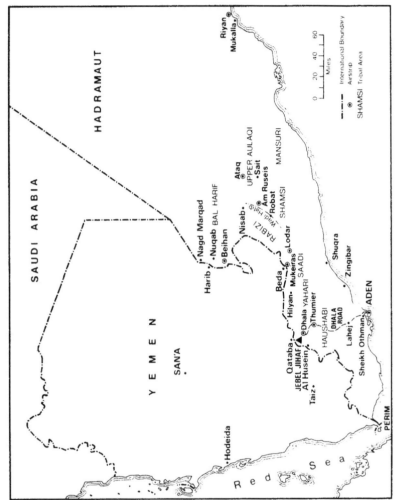

MAP 4   *The Radfan*

1959, when heavy air attacks[81] combined with a skilful assault by two squadrons of SAS on the rebel stronghold of Jebel Akhadar, led to the collapse of a local revolt. Although border disputes in the area had not been resolved and the leaders of the rebellion were still at large, the politico-military situation in this volatile area was, at least temporarily, stabilised.

Aden had also seen sporadic outbreaks of fighting from 1947 onwards, but they were well within the capabilities of the Aden levies and the single squadron of ground attack aircraft available at Khormaksar. When air demonstrations were called for, leaflets were first dropped giving 48 hours warning so that the villagers and their flocks could move out of their huts, which were then attacked with bombs and rockets. In one such attack, that on Thumier in November 1947, Tempests and Lincolns dropped 66.7 tons of bombs and fired 247 rockets, destroying the rebel village and a number of forts without causing a single casualty.

After a period of relative quiet, incursions into the Aden protectorate from neighbouring Yemen in 1954 provoked an air and ground reaction by forces from Aden that involved the Vampires of No.8 Squadron in 220 operational sorties during which 316×500 lb bombs, 350×60 lb rockets and 9,000 rounds of 20 mm ammunition were expended.[82] These operations must qualify as demonstrations rather than as effective military answers to the incursions from the Yemen, since no fewer than 54 attacks were made on government forces during the month of July 1954 alone, a level of activity that diminished only after the Governor of Aden had received a 'most unexpected invitation'[83] to meet the Imam of Yemen and was able to conclude a limited agreement with him on frontier observance.

A lull in operations then followed until March 1955 when activities by Shamsi tribesmen led to another small punitive expedition. Stocks of food and flocks of animals were confiscated, which no doubt inflicted punishment on the villagers, but it did nothing to subdue the militant tribesmen whose depredations eventually led the Aden government to launch an expedition to relieve the garrison at Robat using a strong battalion group supported by Lincolns, Venoms and Vampires. As part of this operation an intensive bombing programme was carried out on preselected targets, and when it was complete the column withdrew at the end of July leaving the fort at Robat to the rebels. Whether tribesmen were mollified by the fact that the garrison at Robat withdrew, or whether they were impressed by the show of force remains uncertain, but no further operations were necessary during the rest of that year.

The Suez crisis of 1956 had two results on these low intensity operations in Arabia. First, anti-British feeling was intensified in some areas and awakened in others. Second, the centre of gravity of the British military presence in the Middle East had to be shifted from the Mediterranean to Aden, and the strength of the RAF there was increased by 1959 from one fighter squadron and a handful of communications aircraft to nine squadrons, including two of fighter-bombers. The potential for intensified operations on both sides was thus stepped up.

Further minor incidents continued throughout this period and into 1962, when in September of that year there was an Egyptian-inspired republican revolution in Yemen that brought the new forces of Arab nationalism right up to the borders of Aden. Confronting these forces were the twelve members of the Aden Federation, including Aden State itself, which represented the traditional autocratic arab rulers of the area. The lines were thus drawn for the last phase of British operations in South Arabia.

Subversion had been growing in the area for some years, and the murder of the Assistant High Commissioner[84] finally led to the declaration of a state of emergency in December 1963. A punitive expedition of three infantry battalions of the Federal Regular Army with an armoured car squadron, British tanks, artillery and engineers was launched into the Radfan to provide a show of force in the Wadi Misrah, the main stronghold of the dissident Quteibi tribe. The Royal Air Force, which by now had the equivalent of ten squadrons at Khormaksar, including three squadrons of Hunter day-fighter/ground attack aircraft, provided close support, air transport and air resupply. Operation 'Nutcracker', as it was called, proved to be a difficult though not a costly undertaking, but it proved impossible to sustain the force in the Radfan and, in any case, the political justification for doing so was far from clear. The column, therefore, withdrew and Egypt was able to proclaim a victory over the 'puppet imperialist forces' in the first battle for 'occupied South Yemen'. The result was a sharp increase in rebel activity.

A further operation, this time using a light scale brigade group of British and local troops[85] was now launched to 'end the operations of dissidents in the defined area'. But the defined area was a series of map squares thought to contain the main rebel centres, and the difficulties of movement in the harsh terrain as well as the unexpectedly strong resistance of the tribesmen, made it clear that settling the Radfan was going to be a long and arduous business.

Reinforcements of troops were moved into South Arabia from the UK and regular air patrols were maintained round the clock in a harassing form of air control. Hunter aircraft provided accurate close air support to the army units as they moved up to the main enemy position on the Jebel Huriyah, and eventually the dissident force of fifty tribesmen was compelled to fight a pitched battle in which they suffered heavy losses, mainly from the concentrated air attacks. This operation brought the level of activity down in the Radfan, but by now the general tide of unrest in South Arabia as a whole was leading to an entirely new situation.

Policing operations continued in the Radfan right through until 1966 by which time the British Government had announced its intention[86] to withdraw its defence forces from Aden when independence was granted in 1968, a move that encouraged the Yemen and dismayed the local rulers, who had always assumed that they could count on a continuing British presence. Authority began to collapse, the police became unreliable and finally mutinied and although air operations continued with varying intensity until the final withdrawal, the limited part that air support was playing had little influence on the course of events. Air transport was able to render a final service to the garrison by flying out the last 3,700 members of the British security forces in November 1967. A modest air force had shown its worth in low-key operations against very small forces in terrain that almost entirely negated other forms of mobility.

KENYA, 1952–5

An even more modest use of air power was seen in Kenya between 1952 and 1955, but it was none the less a campaign of some interest because it again involved land – air operations against dissidents, though this time in bush country rather than in jungle or desert terrain. The campaign began when a state of emergency was declared in Kenya in October 1952 during a growing wave of terror and violence by the Mau Mau, a Kikuyu secret society.[87]

Four battalions of the King's African Rifles had, by this time, been concentrated in Kenya at the expense of the other East African territories, the Kenya Regiment was in Nairobi and a British infantry battalion was flown down from Egypt to coincide with the government declaration. At the same time, 83 of the known Mau Mau leaders were arrested and the security forces prepared to mop up the remaining terrorists using police supported by army units.

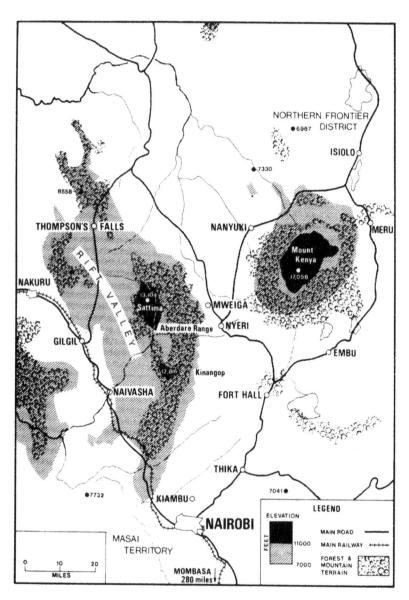

MAP 5   *Central Kenya*

New leaders soon took the place of those who had been arrested, however, and Mau Mau gangs made their way into the dense cover of forest and jungle, particularly on the lower slopes of Mount Kenya and in the Aberdare range of hills, from whence they continued their highly disruptive and destructive attacks. The operational area covered some 17,000 square miles to the North and North East of Nairobi. The two mountain areas themselves were declared prohibited areas covering about 820 and 780 square miles.

Further murders, this time of white settlers as well as loyal Kikuyu in early 1953, led to the setting up of a military command and to the arrival of two more British battalions, which gave the security forces enough strength to carry the campaign into the jungle.

Light aircraft from the Kenya Police Air Wing and eight RAF Harvards carried out reconnaissance flights, while Valettas and Dakotas were used for supply drops during this build-up phase. A campaign of attrition against the terrorists was well under way by mid-1953 which involved, among other things, the use of Harvards in the attack role. In a typical week of air operations, that of 22–9 July, fifty-six strikes were flown, twenty-one in direct support of ground forces and thirty-five against suspected terrorist hideouts in the Aberdares. Although 232 fragmentation bombs were used and 18,950 rounds of ammunition fired, there was no evidence of enemy casualties and the most that could be claimed was that the attacks harassed the gangs and kept them on the move.

In September, two more British battalions were flown in so that the networks of small units could be extended to more forest areas and the net on the gangs thus closed more tightly. The security forces now totalled eleven infantry battalions, the Kenya Regiment, 21,000 police, a Kikuyu Home Guard and the aircraft of the Police Air Wing and the Royal Air Force. September saw the Harvard Unit, No 1340 Flight, fly 332 offensive sorties, fire 97,760 rounds of ammunition and drop 2,555 bombs. But these weapons were only 20 lb anti-personnel bombs and their effect was almost totally absorbed by the dense vegetation, so that eventually a detachment of six Lincoln bombers was brought out and maintained in Kenya from the UK Bomber Command.[88]

Air attacks continued through to the next year and in March 1954 a particularly large-scale effort was made during the handover of one detachment to another. In this operation, 81 sorties were flown during which 612 × 500 lbs bombs, 171 × 1,000 lb bombs and 18,000 rounds of 0.5 inch ammunition were directed into suspected terrorist areas.[89] These raids were held to be so successful that from August 1954 air attacks were given priority over ground operations in predetermined areas of the Aberdares, and their intensity increased. In September, they reached a peak when 159 day and 17 night sorties were flown during which 2,025 × 500 lb bombs were dropped and 77,850 rounds were fired from the turrets of the Lincolns. Later, these attacks were switched to the Mount Kenya area, and by the end of the year the inevitability of the constant air attacks was having its effect. More and more terrorists were either being driven out into the arms of the cordon of waiting troops, or they surrendered when their food supplies from the main Kikuyu Reserve were cut off.

The success of the security forces' efforts reduced the need for heavy air attacks from May onwards, and they were then replaced largely by aircraft broadcasting psychological warfare messages. The Lincoln detachments ended in July, and 1340 Flight was disbanded in September.

Finally, the Army withdrew from operational control and police again took over to carry out what little mopping-up was necessary until on 12 January 1960 the state of emergency ended. The campaign had cost the Mau Mau 10,527 killed and 2,633 captured, whilst another 38,500 were under detention at its end. Losses to the security forces were 600 dead, including 63 Europeans, and 1,884 loyal civilians had lost their lives.

It had been a long campaign of attrition in which extensive ground operations had been conducted, not only by regular army units and police, but also by small teams of skilled gang-fighters[90] who penetrated the bush and met the terrorists on their own terms. The air weapon had been able to make a contribution in the campaign, but it was once again a contribution mainly in terms of mobility for other arms. The results of direct air attacks were again best seen as exerting general pressure on dissidents rather than as an efficient means of eliminating them, and although General Erskine, the Commander-in-Chief gave as his opinion that had the bombing campaign not been pursued, an additional infantry brigade or three regiments of artillery would have been essential, this was almost certainly an exaggeration.[91]

4 The Air War in South-East Asia

The history of US involvement in Vietnam presents a complex picture, and one that is still the subject of extensive research and analysis. The air aspect of the conflict, for example, involved not only several air interdiction campaigns in Laos and North Vietnam, but a running battle for air supremacy, strategic bombing efforts in key areas of the North, very extensive air support of ground forces in South Vietnam and massive efforts in the employment of helicopter, tactical and strategic transport.

Above all, perhaps, the war was fought against a variety of threats, in a very variable climate and, even more important, in conditions of shifting American politico-military perceptions. The air analyst is therefore presented with many difficulties, not the least being that of the danger of over-simplification; nevertheless it is possible to offer at least a tentative assessment of the place of air power in the eight-year war from 1965 to 1973. A brief chronology of the war is given, leading into a more detailed analysis of some of the principal features of the air war.

CHRONOLOGY OF THE WAR

The end of the French War in Indo-China had left Vietnam divided by a DMZ that ran roughly along the 17th Parallel, and when the elections promised in the Geneva Accord of 1954 were not held, the division of Vietnam hardened. The Viet Minh regrouped in the North – aided by China, the Soviet Union and certain Communist states of Eastern Europe, while the US increasingly supported South Vietnam. By 1957 the Communists had consolidated their hold on the North and before the year was out guerrilla warfare against the government of South Vietnam had begun.

In December 1960 Ho Chi-Minh announced the formation of the Viet

83

Cong, a National Front for the Liberation of South Vietnam, and by the end of 1961 the Viet Cong had a strength of about 17,000 and were threatening the approaches of Saigon itself. These events brought the first US forces to Vietnam in the shape of Special Forces, and as early as 1962 the members of the 'Farm Gate' training detachment, flying T-28s and B-26s found themselves drawn into combat in response to emergency calls which their Vietnamese students could not fly.[1]

Meanwhile, Laos and Cambodia had been given their independence at Geneva; but whilst Cambodia managed to maintain a kind of neutrality, Laos was the scene of continuing struggle between rival factions, and in these unsettled conditions the Viet Cong were able to establish their main line of supply to South Vietnam, the Ho Chi-Minh Trail, through southern Laos. By March 1964 the situation had so deteriorated that President Johnson directed the Joint Chiefs of Staff to begin planning for US retaliatory air strikes against North Vietnam.

Throughout 1963 and 1964 reinforcements and supplies for the Viet Cong insurgents continued to flow in from the North, and it took only a comparatively minor incident to accelerate the whole tempo of the conflict. This came on 2 August 1964 when North Vietnamese torpedo boats attacked the US destroyer *Maddox* in the Gulf of Tonkin, and on 5 August US carrier-borne aircraft from the 7th Fleet retaliated against North Vietnam by attacking four harbours and an oil storage depot in what the Americans saw as a measured response to North Vietnam aggression.

For a time President Johnson resisted suggestions for further retaliatory raids, even when, on 2 November 1964 a Viet Cong attack on the USAF base at Bien Hoa, near Saigon, killed five Americans, wounded another seventy-six, and destroyed six B-57 Canberras on the ground. By early December, however, President Johnson was under political pressure at home to contain the worsening situation and air attacks were authorised against enemy lines of communication in Laos as well as on targets in North Vietnam, just above the DMZ.

This expansion of the air war over Laos began on 14 December with Operation Barrel Roll, and it was followed by Operation Flaming Dart against North Vietnam in February 1965 as a reprisal for a series of Viet Cong attacks on US installations at Pleiku and Qui Nhon. With the deployment at about this time of more modern aircraft such as USAF B-57s, extensive engineering work was begun to refurbish and to extend the airfields at Da Nang, Bien Hoa and Tan Son Nhut, as well as to build bases at Cam Ranh Bay, Phan Rang, Phu Cat, Tuy Hoa and Chu Lai. Pleiku was extended to act as an emergency strip only, but each of the other major airfields would by 1967 have two parallel 10,000-foot runways.[2]

On 1 March 1965 the first attacks of a limited and measured air campaign against North Vietnam with the codename Rolling Thunder were started; but when it seemed by early April that these strikes had had the effect of hardening the attitude of Hanoi, the attacks were limited almost entirely to Viet Cong lines of communication below the 19th Parallel, although it was understood that some targets in the Hanoi area would also be designated from time to time.[3] One result of this offensive, however, was that instead of dissuading Hanoi from further action against South Vietnam, it prompted them to start work on a comprehensive and efficient air defence system that would eventually come to include Migs, SAMs and AA artillery, all linked into a centralised warning and control system.

On 8 March 1965 the first US Marines landed at Da Nang, Task Force 77 in the Gulf of Tonkin was expanded to include three aircraft-carriers, and priority for air activity was given to missions in South Vietnam, including the first use of B-52s, which in June 1965 in Operation Arc Light began attacks on Communist bases in that country.

A proposal by the Joint Chiefs of Staff that an air offensive should be launched against ninety-four key targets in the North was turned down, but when on 24 July an F-4C was lost to the new North Vietnamese air defences and three more were damaged, clearance was given for wider reprisals. Fears about a possible confrontation with China, as well as doubts about the likely effectiveness of an air campaign against the North, still meant that severe restrictions were placed on these attacks, and, for example, only those SAM sites actually firing at US aircraft could be attacked, and even then only if they were below the 20th Parallel and outside the main air defence systems of Hanoi and Haiphong.

This very gradual escalation of the air offensive was, however, only one element of a four-part strategy designed to impose the American will on Hanoi. It was believed that the air attacks would warn of worse to come, while at the same time ground operations in South Vietnam were intensified, civil government in the country was consolidated and offers of negotiation and post-war reconstruction were extended to Hanoi. From 1965 onwards, US air activity against the North was progressively stepped up, a process marked by intermittent bombing pauses and diplomatic contacts in efforts to force or to persuade Hanoi to negotiate. By late 1966, a total of 12,000 sorties were being flown each month, double the rate in 1965, and by 1967 North Vietnamese airfields, power stations and certain industries as well as the rail routes from China were included in US air activity.

By mid-1965 there was still no improvement in the overall military situation, and President Johnson decided that only a major build-up of US forces could save the South Vietnamese Army from defeat and protect the US base areas, some of which had come under costly attack.

At this stage of the war the US ground forces operated mainly from fortified bases, and devoted their efforts to search and destroy missions against Communist units and their bases in the Central Highlands and in the provinces around Saigon. No attempt could be made to occupy and to hold large areas of the country, and most of the many scattered combat engagements that took place from this time on in the war were at only platoon or at the most, battalion, strength. The difficulty was that as soon as the Viet Cong found the local military pressure to be unsupportable, they were generally able to break off contact and to melt into the familiar countryside.

Gradually the US commitment grew from a strength of about 181,000 men at the end of 1965, to 215,000 in March 1966 and 385,000 at the end of that year. By the end of 1967, US strength had risen to 436,000 and there seemed to be signs of military progress.

The new strength of the US commitment was one of the factors that made it possible to launch two large-scale operations, Cedar Falls and Junction City in January and February 1967 respectively; but the Communists were again able to break off, re-group, and later to continue their operations both along the border with Cambodia and south of the DMZ. Viet Cong activity then spread again across the country culminating in the Tet offensive of early 1968 and the siege of Khe San. At the tactical level, the outcome was a victory for the US and South Vietnamese forces; but strategically the Viet Cong had shown that US optimism about the progress of the war was badly misplaced.

After intense public and governmental debate in the US, President Johnson halted all bombing north of the 20th Parallel on 21 March and offered Hanoi peace talks, which began in Paris on 18 May 1968. But the fighting and the assassinations in the South continued undiminished, and the North Vietnamese not only repaired with great dispatch the communications that had so far been damaged by air attack, but they sent along those routes as much material to the South as the transportation system could bear. When the US called a total halt to all bombing above the DMZ, on 31 October 1968, the North Vietnamese accelerated their efforts and the build-up of their forces in the South greatly expanded.

By November 1968, after the Presidential election which saw Richard Nixon the winner, the US was committed to a gradual withdrawal from Vietnam, although the North Vietnamese were still moving war stocks south ready for what they planned to be a final offensive. One apparently critical area that had meanwhile been identified in the North Vietnamese logistic system was the area of south-eastern Cambodia, from which the Viet Cong and the North Vietnamese were launching attacks in Military Region III, and on 19 March 1969, with the secret agreement of Prince Sihanouk, B-52s began bombing these enemy bases.[4]

The withdrawal of US ground forces was by now under way, and air power was employed not only to fill with firepower some of the gaps left by US troops, but to support the South Vietnamese forces who, without that air power, would not have been able to hold the widespread North Vietnamese pressure. Realising the importance of US air power during this stage of the war, the North Vietnamese extended their own air defences further south including an airfield construction programme south of the 20th Parallel.

As a partial counter, fighter escorts for the US reconnaissance flights were authorised in November 1968, and although at first these escorts were permitted to attack only air defence sites that were actually engaging the US formations, by the end of 1970 the size of the formations had grown and the quality of the weapons they used had greatly improved so that they emerged as a much more powerful factor in the air battle.

Meanwhile, the North Vietnamese air defences continued to improve until they had a considerable umbrella of SAMs north of the DMZ, and Mig air defence missions were intercepting US strike forces attacking the mountain passes leading from North Vietnam to Laos as well as the B-52s that were attacking supply lines in Laos itself.

During 1971 the limited defence suppression attacks that had been authorised were augmented by strikes on focal points of the North Vietnamese supply routes, but these attacks were no substitute for a comprehensive campaign of interdiction, and on 30 March 1972 their insignificant effect was exposed when North Vietnam launched a major conventional attack across the DMZ using a force of 400 armoured vehicles, anti-tank missiles and medium artillery.

The offensive was brought to a halt only after the northern half of Military Region I had been lost to the enemy, and that it was halted even then was largely due to the effectiveness of the US air power that was committed. Tactical aircraft based in Thailand, together with Marine aircraft, units from Task Force 77 and B-52s were all engaged in stabilising the battle and preventing any deeper enemy advance.

On 7 May Operation Pocket Money, the mining of Haiphong and other major coastal ports, was launched; and on 10 May most of the original 94 targets in North Vietnam were finally released for attack, in an operation codenamed Linebacker I.

For the first time since the campaign began, air power was employed with something like the determination that had all along been advocated by the air commanders. The objectives of Linebacker I were threefold: to restrict the external resupply of North Vietnam; to destroy stockpiles of military supplies and equipment; and to restrict the flow of forces and supplies to the battlefield.[5] On 23 October 1972 bombing was again halted above the 20th Parallel in the expectation that more progress would be induced in the Paris negotiations, but once again it became clear that the North Vietnamese were not anxious for a negotiated settlement. On 18 December an all-out air offensive against the heartland of North Vietnam was therefore launched.

Air power was at last to be used to concentrate its firepower at the vital centres of the enemy, to cause maximum disruption and to force the North Vietnamese to settle. This campaign was given the codename Linebacker II and it embraced the neutralisation of area targets by B-52s, tactical strikes against point targets and a comprehensive campaign against the whole North Vietnamese air defence infrastructure. After eleven days of Linebacker II, the North Vietnamese asked for a cease-fire and eighteen years after the end of the first Indo-China War, the United States war in Vietnam at last drew to a close.

OPERATIONS IN SOUTH VIETNAM

Air transport

One of the earliest US contributions to the war had been that made by transport aircraft. Even before the intensification of the conflict in 1965, they had linked a network of airstrips across the country, each able to take twin-engined transport types; and transport aircraft were the means by which, for example, the scattered units of US Special Forces were resupplied. Later in the war the use of transports was extended to include work as flare-ships in support of isolated garrisons under attack, as vehicles to defoliate Viet Cong logistic routes and as gunships carrying heavy machine guns mounted to fire down on to ground targets from beam positions.

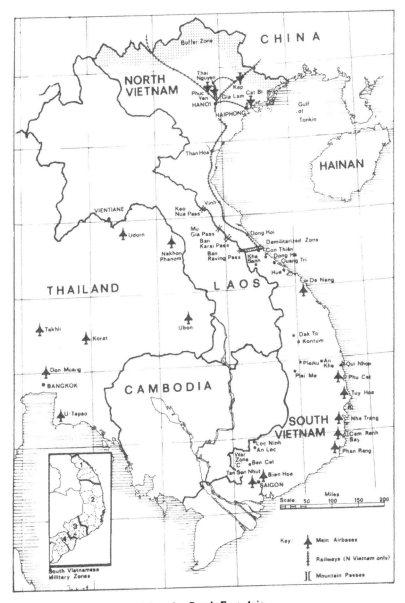

MAP 6   *South-East Asia*

In 1961 the US air transport effort had consisted of a mere four C-47s, but these were later joined by numbers of C-123s until by late 1964 there were four squadrons each of sixteen aircraft.[6] Together with two Vietnamese squadrons of C-47s, this force was used to airlift Vietnamese infantry units around the country, and occasionally to launch combat parachute assaults which, however, in most cases failed to bring the enemy to battle.

Air mobility

The first US Army helicopters arrived in late 1961, and together with US Marine helicopters and a company of US Army Caribous they were employed mainly in giving tactical mobility to Vietnamese Army units. With the arrival of the US 1st Cavalry Division (Airmobile) in the summer of 1965, however, mobility on an entirely different scale became available. The division was based at An Khe, bringing with it eight infantry battalions, three of them parachute-trained, and over 400 aircraft, nearly all of them helicopters and most of them equipped for the troop-lift role. For general support the Division depended on Chinook helicopters and Caribous, but they did not have the capacity to meet the whole of the task, and in order to simplify the logistics problems the division was based reasonably close to the coast.

The test of the concept of air mobility came in October 1965 when the Viet Cong attacked the camp at Plei Me, 25 miles south of Pleiku. USAF C-123 and Army Caribous resupplied the garrison by air, and three weeks of combat by the Air Cavalry Division then followed.[7] This first action exposed the inadequacy of the organic airlift capacity of the force. Combat units and supplies had to be airlifted the thirty-five miles from their base at An Khe to Pleiku, from where elements were moved forward by helicopters to sites chosen for the artillery support of the relief force. Fuel supplies at Pleiku were soon exhausted and the force of Caribous and Chinooks was badly overstrained by the huge effort demanded by the air activity. USAF C-130s were then brought in to replenish fuel stocks, while C-123s flew between An Khe and the area of operations to relieve the pressure on the Army air units.

Eventually, roads into the battle area from An Khe were cleared, and in late November the enemy broke off the action and retired into Cambodia. His losses were estimated as the equivalent of a full brigade.

A good indication of the air effort implied in an operation of this kind is shown by the fact that, in the 29 days starting on 27 October, the USAF delivered a total of 5,400 tons, a daily average of 186 tons; 58 per cent of all this was POL. Meanwhile forward distribution by Army organic aircraft amounted to 5,048 tons over a period of 35 days.[8] It was true that the Airmobile Division had shown its ability to engage the enemy in areas where no other forces could do so, but the scale of air effort needed both from Army organic aircraft and from Air Force support, made it clear that the technique could have only a limited application in the future.

At various times in the campaign parachute troops were employed on operations, but because the helicopters were clearly superior for short-range lifts, paratroops were only very rarely used in their primary role. When a full battalion made a parachute assault in the 1967 Operation Junction City, for example, it was with the modest aim of supplementing the force that could be lifted by helicopter.

Air supply

A far more common use of airlift capability was the air supply of conventional ground forces. During the four-week invasion of Tay Ninh province in April 1966, for instance, three full brigades of US infantry were moved by air the thirty or so miles from their bases north of Saigon, and maintained there by a day and night airlift that averaged 424 tons per day over the first six days of the operation. It was an operation that was to last twenty-three days, during which time the USAF had flown 945 C-130 and C-123 sorties, lifting 9,500 troops and 9,700 tons of cargo.[9] This huge effort brought to battle only a single enemy battalion, and although enemy supply dumps along the Cambodian border were destroyed, like many other operations of this type it had been a costly affair in terms of the resources engaged.

Airborne assault

Actual airborne assault against a well-armed and determined enemy revealed more fundamental problems in the whole concept of air-landed forces. In the March 1971 Operation Lam Son 719, the South Vietnamese army launched an offensive against a force of about 25,000 hard-core North Vietnamese troops holding the Laotian panhandle area, with the object of troops using US air and other support seizing and straddling the main junction of Highways 9 and 92 just below the DMZ, the centre of the Viet Cong logistic system in Central Vietnam. No US ground forces were involved, but extensive air and other support was provided by the Americans for the South Vietnamese. That support included a certain amount of close air support, and eight B-52s also made a strike to suppress the enemy air defences, but most of the air firepower for the operation was planned to be laid down by helicopter gunships.

The strength of the enemy air defences had, however, been seriously underestimated and in the assault against Lolo for example, no fewer than 20 helicopters out of the 40 employed were shot down, and 7 more were totally destroyed. The total number of helicopters lost in the whole operation is more difficult to establish, but the USAF estimated that 200 out of the 600 employed were lost.[10] Because of language difficulties and because of weak planning that did not guarantee adequate close air support, air intervention was slow in being applied, and although all the air-lifted troops were finally put on the ground, Lolo and the later similar landings showed the essential need for air power to create a favourable environment for the use of assault helicopters.[11]

As it was, more than 8,000 tactical air sorties were eventually flown in support of the landings in Lam Son 719, with a loss of only seven aircraft; but seen as a helicopter assault landing the operation was a costly affair not justified by the meagre success that was achieved on the ground.

Strategic airlift

The airlift capacity of the USAF was backed by the global support of Military Airlift Command (MAC). Its extent varied during the campaign, but an idea of the resources engaged can be gained from the effort involved during the North Vietnamese invasion in 1972. Within Vietnam itself the USAF tactical airlift forces were moving, at the height of that invasion, more than 1,000 tons of supplies per day. Meanwhile MAC, which had up till then been flying about 134 tons a day into the country, increased its daily effort to 1,875 tons. When necessary, C-5s of the Command were employed to carry tanks, helicopters, artillery pieces, trucks and other large items of equipment, and at one stage during the North Vietnamese invasion, a fleet of E-5s and C-141s airlifted an entire USAF wing, the 49th Tactical Fighter Wing, from New Mexico to Takhli Air Base in Thailand. In 9 days these transports, supplemented by charter aircraft to lift passengers, airlifted 8 million lb of equipment.[12] This was a clear demonstration, not only of the sheer lifting power of a mature air transport organisation, but a striking example of how such a force can wield enough flexibility to be able to expand from routine operations to sustained emergency rates.

Tactical air power

The Farm Gate detachment at Bien Hoa in 1961 was the beginning of a growing US combat air power commitment which, by the end of 1964 had slowly grown to a total force of 117 aircraft, 50 of them combat types, in the 2nd Air Division. At this time the US Army held 47 per cent of all the aircraft in Vietnam, most of them helicopters, while the VNAF had about 170 machines of all types.

After the Viet Cong attack on the US base at Pleiku in February 1965, and when the retaliatory US air operations against North Vietnam failed to produce any reduction in the scale of fighting in South Vietnam, the US ground forces were committed to offensive rather than purely defensive missions, and the US military build-up began in earnest. By the end of 1965 US strength was more than 184,000 men, and USAF strength in 2nd Air Division was about 500 combat aircraft.[13] It was the start of tactical air warfare on a very large scale.

As far as air power over South Vietnam was concerned, from 1965 to 1968 up to 70 per cent of the 7th Air Force effort was employed on pre-planned missions, and particularly on those in support of search-and-destroy operations conducted by the ground forces. Ground attack aircraft were allocated to specific targets such as suspected enemy positions, and his routes to and from the battle area.

Fighter-bombers were also allocated to the operations against targets of opportunity that could not be accepted by artillery or army organic weapons. Two categories of Forward Air Controllers were developed for use in these and other ground support missions. First, there were fighter-bomber pilots who spent their first six months in Vietnam in fighter units before joining US, Korean or Vietnamese ground force units. The second category consisted of pilots from a variety of backgrounds who were given FAC training in the US before being assigned to a Tactical Air Support Squadron. These airborne FACs proved to be the only way to ensure rapid reaction by air strikes and, because the FAC pilots were able to familiarise themselves with particular areas of the country, they were able to bring local knowledge to bear in identifying targets, marking them and in directing strikes onto the enemy positions. FACs in Vietnam proved to be a key factor in directing air power against the elusive enemy troops.[14]

Thirty per cent of the available air effort was used for 'immediate' or troops-in-contact situations. Once ground forces made contact, air-borne aircraft could be diverted into the area, a process that took only 15–20 minutes, whilst others scrambled from airfield readiness.

Meanwhile, the ground forces pulled back to a safe distance and marked their positions for the FAC with smoke.

On an average, 40 aircraft would be held on ground alert for these tasks and they would sometimes be scrambled up to 4 times a day. By this means weapons could be delivered on the targets within 35 or 40 minutes. About 300 sorties a day were pre-planned by the 7th Air Force, while the Marines in I Corps flew an average of another 200 and the VNAF about 100. On a typical day, a total of 750 to 800 sorties would be flown in support of ground forces, and in periods of intensive activity such as the Tet offensive in 1968, surge operations could be flown which raised aircraft sortie rates from 1.2 per day to 1.8.[15]

In all these operations air power was essentially used to complement or to replace artillery in support of ground forces. Tactical air could switch its effort rapidly from one scene of combat to another, and it could concentrate massive firepower within a short period over a limited geographical area. In many cases the ground operations by US and Allied forces were carried out primarily to find and to fix enemy units against which air power and sometimes artillery fire could then be directed.

In daylight, fighter-bombers usually operated in flights of two or four aircraft, and on those occasions when more than four aircraft were required, further flights, separated by ten or fifteen minutes, would usually be scheduled on to the target. Most of the enemy AA fire came from automatic weapons, but by flying to a minimum pull-out height of 3,500 feet, loss rates were kept very low and the attacking aircraft were normally able to make several runs over the target.

For night attack, special techniques using AC-47s to illuminate the targets with flares were developed. These aircraft were held on patrol ready to respond to calls for support. In late 1968, AC-130s with advanced sensor systems joined the 7th Air Force, and by using low-light television and infra-red detectors the aircraft could locate targets, direct firepower on to them and also mark the target accurately for follow-up attacks by tactical aircraft. Later, laser designators were added to the equipment carried, and by this means fighter-bombers could make highly accurate laser-guided bombing attacks.

Strategic air in the tactical role

One of the major innovations of the air war in South Vietnam was the extensive use of B-52 bombers in the close support of ground forces. There had been examples of the use of strategic bombers in tactical situations before, for example at Caen in 1944. But in South Vietnam

B-52s were employed on a continuing basis in what were known as 'Arc Light' operations. These aircraft, originally built in the 1950s as part of the US nuclear deterrent, were still under the control of Strategic Air Command and were based on Guam and at Kadena Air Force Base in Japan.[16] Eighty-two of them had been modified in 1965 to carry eighty-four 500 lb bombs on wing pylons, a total bombload of 60,000 lb, or about the equivalent of five fighter-bombers.[17]

B-52 attacks were begun on 18 June 1965 and the number of sorties flown grew steadily to thirty a day in 1966 and reached sixty a day at the time of the Tet offensive in 1966. Over most of South Vietnam the B-52s could attack with impunity, but near the DMZ there was always the possibility that the Viet Cong might fire SAMs at them, and even that Migs could be launched to intercept them. The loss of a B-52 at that stage of the war would have been a considerable propaganda coup for the Viet Cong, and the highest tactical air force priority was therefore given to the protection of the bomber force.

Marine and Navy Air

Apart from the 7th Air Force and the B-52s from the 8th Air Force on Guam, Marine and Navy Air was heavily employed in the war in Vietnam. Until July 1966 the US Navy maintained an aircraft carrier on station Dixie, off the coast held by IV Corps, and its aircraft came under the tactical control of the 7th Air Force. In August 1966, when operations against North Vietnam were stepped up, the carrier on Dixie station was moved up to Yankee station in the Gulf of Tonkin, and from then on most of the Naval Air missions were employed against targets in North Vietnam, or in the interdiction campaign in Laos,[18] described later in the discussion of the interdiction campaign.

Marine aircraft had arrived in Vietnam with the Marine infantry in March 1965 and by the time the Third Marine Amphibious Force (III MAF) reached full strength in early 1966, the First Marine Air Wing was in a position to provide direct air support for its two divisions. Until control of all fixed-wing air power was centralised in February 1968, Marine air power was used almost entirely for the direct support of the 1st and 3rd Marine Divisions in I Corps area.

Combined air effort

Tactical air power was thus employed across a wide variety of combat situations in South Vietnam, and fighter-bombers, B-52s, armed helicopters and gunships were engaged together in what amounted to a war of attrition fought in numerous small engagements.

Major operations such as those in 1967 at Dak To, Con Thien and Loc Ninh called for a more concentrated tactical air effort, as did major search-and-destroy operations such as that codenamed Junction City, the largest single operation of the war in Vietnam, fought from February to May 1967. This was an operation in which three infantry divisions, three brigades[19] and several South Vietnamese units were engaged in efforts to destroy an enemy force consisting of most of the 9th Viet Cong Division in War Zone C, thirty miles north-west of Saigon and the most impenetrable enemy base area in the whole country.

The operation was designed to force the enemy into pockets where air power and artillery could be brought to bear to destroy him, after which the ground forces would withdraw again. Before the start of the operation, B-52s bombed the suspected location of the Viet Cong headquarters, and 200 close air support sorties a day were made available for the operation itself. Since over 300 sorties a day were already being flown over South Vietnam, it became necessary to use aircraft stationed in Thailand as well as US Navy Air from Task Force 77 off the coast.

On the first day of the operation more than 180 sorties were flown by the 7th Air Force alone, but the enemy proved to be very elusive and the air effort was soon cut back. Air transport proved to be a more urgent necessity, however, and for instance forty C-130s, nearly half the C-130 force in Vietnam, were committed for the parachute assault and for resupply missions on the first day. By the end of the operation, in the middle of May, more than 5,000 sorties had been flown in support of the operation, with F-100s and F-4Cs providing most of the attack missions, and AC-47s illuminating the area at night and controlling the tactical air effort.

In the operation, US and South Vietnamese forces lost 289 killed and 1,576 wounded. The Viet Cong were reported to have lost more than 2,700 killed, and 500 weapons were captured. The real gain, however, was that the Viet Cong 9th Division had been badly mauled by a well co-ordinated land/air action and had been forced across the border to sanctuary in Cambodia.

Khe San

Offensive sweeps like at Junction City, though on a smaller scale than that operation, were commonplace by this stage of the war as were Viet

Cong hit-and-run attacks on US fire-bases. Far less common were Viet Cong attempts to besiege and capture US bases, although one notable effort took place at Khe San in January 1968 as part of a general increase in Viet Cong activity that had begun across the country in September 1967.

Elements of three Viet Cong divisions arrived in the area just south of the DMZ and began to move into the area around the US base at Khe San, a few miles to the south, probably as a flanking movement to support a frontal attack on Dong Ha and perhaps Hue.[20]

As the scope of the threat to the fire-bases and Khe San became clear, preparations were made to open an intensified air campaign so as to disrupt the enemy artillery fire coming from the north of the DMZ, which by now was directing more than 1,000 rounds each day into the allied area.

Khe San actually had little military significance for the Americans; its principal value was as an intelligence-gathering centre and as a jumping-off base for long-range patrols in the area. Determined to hold the base in what was thought to be a direct challenge along the lines of Dien Bien Phu, fourteen years before, the Americans increased the garrison to four battalions of Marines and one of ARVN (Vietnamese) Rangers, a total of about 6,000 infantry together with forty-six artillery pieces and other support. The strength of the Viet Cong is more difficult to judge, but the elements of 320th, 325C and 304 NVA Regular Division seem to have totalled six brigades with an artillery regiment and an AA artillery unit equipped with 37 mm radar-guided guns. The total force was perhaps 20,000 men massed in an area of about five square miles.[21]

One very early problem to emerge was that of air congestion.[22] The US Marines at first maintained that Khe San was a Marine air – ground operation, but as air traffic in the area grew it became essential to centralise all fixed-wing air effort, and for the first time in the Vietnam war the regulation of all fixed-wing aircraft in the theatre was placed under single control. The lessons of the Second World War and of Korea were being learned again.

It was just as well that this precaution was taken at an early stage of the operation. Eventually, the Airborne Battlefield Command and Control Centre (ABCCC) established in C-130s to co-ordinate all air and artillery activity, was controlling approximately 850 aircraft movements each day.[23] Another important air contribution to the successful defence of Khe San was made by the B-52 bombers, which not only attacked suspected Viet Cong staging areas around the camp, but were also employed to lay down carpets of bombs up to within 3,000 feet of the defence positions. On the average, 60 B-52 sorties were being flown over Vietnam each day at this time, 48 of them over Khe San. By the end of the siege, these bombers had flown 2,548 sorties in its defence and delivered 53,162 tons of bombs.[24]

The battle began on 21 January 1968 with an assault on a Marine outpost followed by an artillery and mortar bombardment of the camp. Sporadic but heavy fighting then continued until 7 February when the Viet Cong attacked the Special Forces camp at Lang Vei, three miles West of Khe San on Route 9, eventually overrunning it, and on 8 February the attack shifted back to Khe San itself. Despite the air and artillery effort that had been directed into the area in support of the defence, the Viet Cong had by now moved their AA guns forward. On 11 February a Marine KC130 was destroyed as it landed, and this and other incidents led to the expensive C-130s being replaced by the smaller and less costly C-123K Provider in support of the garrison. When a Provider was lost on 6 March more emphasis was given to the use of helicopters, but the helicopters and C-123K Providers together did not have the capacity to sustain Khe San, especially in bad weather, and after parachute drops had proved to be a very inaccurate form of delivery through cloud, the USAF reverted to C-130s and cargo extraction, a technique employing a cable strung across the runway to pull palleted cargoes out of the hold.

The extent of enemy activity varied a great deal through February, although the base was only rarely free from artillery fire. Then on the night of 29 February, the Viet Cong launched what proved to be their final attack. The defenders called for artillery and mortar support as well as for the massive firepower of tactical aircraft and B-52s with the result that the threatened attack was halted by a barrier of high explosive at the eastern end of the main perimeter, and the Viet Cong assault died away before it could reach the forward positions.

The 1972 invasion

On 30 March 1972 the war in Vietnam took on a new quality with the invasion of the South by North Vietnam, whose forces launched major offensives in three of the four military regions. The principal attack was made across the DMZ by about 40,000 troops in three Divisions using weapons such as Soviet-made T34, T54 and PT76 tanks, 400 armoured vehicles all told, as well as SA-2 and SA-7 missiles and 130 mm artillery pieces. Outnumbered, the South Vietnamese forces fell back in disorder and for the first few days of the offensive low cloud prevented any useful intervention by air power to stem the advance. As the retreat of the South Vietnamese continued, the US began to deploy air units back to Thailand,[25] the strength of the 7th Air Force was raised to 1,000 aircraft and the number of aircraft carriers on station Yankee was increased to five, the highest level of the war.

Despite the enemy use of SAMs, and despite the fact that US aircraft were unable to operate safely below 10,000 feet without counter-measures, the invading armour in particular was successfully engaged and 267 tanks were destroyed in the course of the offensive. Meanwhile, by the end of July the attack in Military Region II had been defeated at Kontum and the one in the south had stalled at An Loc, so that all available air power was able to concentrate on the invasion in Military Region I.

The 7th Air Force was soon flying an average of 207 sorties a day against this particular enemy thrust, and B-52s were in action day and night. When Quang Tri fell to the North Vietnamese, President Johnson on 8th May announced an increased bombing offensive against North Vietnam and the mining of Haiphong harbour.

Up until the invasion, US air power was being employed almost exclusively against interdiction targets on the Ho Chi-Minh Trail, and 90 per cent of the missions in South Vietnam were being flown by the VNAF. Within a few days, 55–60 per cent of a greatly increased air effort in the South was being undertaken by US air power, and interdiction attacks were switched from the Ho Chi-Minh Trail to the road and rail network of North Vietnam as part of the Linebacker I interdiction campaign.

THE INTERDICTION CAMPAIGNS

Interdiction, whether on the Ho Chi-Minh Trail or in North Vietnam itself, was a principal feature of the American air effort in Indo-China. But it was interdiction with a wider aim than that covered by the usual definition, which is to attack enemy resources moving towards the ground battle and to disrupt or destroy those resources before they can arrive.

In Indo-China the aims of the air attacks on the North, as given by Secretary of Defence McNamara in testimony before Congress, were: first, to reduce the flow and/or increase the cost of the infiltration of men and supplies from North Vietnam to South Vietnam; second, to make it clear to the North Vietnamese leadership that as long as they continued their aggression against the South, they would have to pay a price in the North; and third, to raise the morale of the South Vietnamese people. Only the first of these aims could be described as interdiction, or even as a purely military aim. The other two were much closer to the objectives associated with a strategic air offensive.

Many of the targets attacked were, however, part of the Communist logistics system, the heart of which lay in North Vietnam, where bulk supplies arrived in the ports and over the border from China, mainly along the two rail routes that cross it. From there the system transported weapons and supplies to redistribution points at Hanoi, Haiphong, Kep, Nam Dinh and Than Hoa for onward movement by truck and barge to smaller depots ready for the final leg by porterage to the combat areas. The vital segment of the northern rail system was the stretch from southern China to Hanoi, a sector eighty-two nautical miles long and with a daily capacity of some 27,000 short tons. There were two principal bottlenecks on the line; one at the Canal des Rapides, and the other the 5,500 foot long Paul Doumer bridge at Hanoi.

In 1964 the road system in North Vietnam had about 5,800 miles of motorable way, 1,070 miles or so of which were all-weather, but by 1972 all the main roads had been made all-weather. At the hub of the system leading to the South was the town of Vinh, 150 miles north of the DMZ, from where supplies were routed down Highway 1 to the DMZ or over three, and later four, mountain passes to Laos where they fed into the main North–South artery in that country, the Ho Chi-Minh Trail.

It was thus in North Vietnam that the most vulnerable bottlenecks were to be found and it was there that the supplies, the repair and the support facilities for the whole logistic network were based. Further south the transportation system became more diffuse and it offered fewer vulnerabilities to air attack. Most supplies arrived at the DMZ by truck, although bicycles and porter-borne A-frames were often used, and the open terrain in the area made it possible for blocked supplies to be re-routed or for it to by-pass damaged roads and tracks.

In South Vietnam itself, most of the supplies were moved by porters together with a limited number of vehicles; but unlike the other parts of the system no major roads were in use, and by the time the traffic had reached the various base areas within South Vietnam interdiction was generally recognised to be an unproductive technique.[26]

Weather had a marked effect both on the pattern of logistics and on the ability of the USAF to attack them. Between May and September the heavy rain and thunderstorms of the south-west monsoon flooded the main roads to Laos and at the same time reduced visibility, making air operations more difficult. During the north-east monsoon, from September to May, the weather over North Vietnam made visual attacks on the upper route areas very difficult, but in general this cycle meant that when the weather was bad over North Vietnam, it was good over South Vietnam and Laos and vice versa, thus playing an important part in target selection.

Mention was made earlier of the split control of air power between the USAF and the Marines before Khe San, but there was another and more intractable division between the USAF and the US Navy. As in Korea, US air power was exercised both by the USAF and the US Navy; but in Korea, Far East Command had been given full responsibility for air and other operations. In Vietnam there was the added complication that Military Advisory Command Vietnam acted as a theatre Commander under the Pacific Command, which was also a theatre command. Not only that, but the 8th Air Force operating B-52s of SAC, aircraft which had a nuclear mission in general war, was responsible directly to the Joint Chiefs of Staff.[27]

Little had, it seemed, been learned from Korea about the need for centralised command and control of the air, but this untidy arrangement was made worse by allocating what were called Route Packages in North Vietnam to the USAF and USN Task Force 77. Route Package I was assigned to the 2nd Air Division but directed by MACV rather than by CINCPACAF. Packages II, III and IV were assigned to Task Force 77. Route Package V went to the Air Force while the most important Route Package of all, No VI, was divided between the Air Force and the Navy along the line of the north-east rail line to China; VIB in the East went to the Navy and VIA in the West to the Air Force.

This compromise solution to a difficult command and control problem was a serious hindrance to the flexibility and power of concentration on which air power relies for so much of its effectiveness. Task Force 77 did not, for example, have the resources with which to maintain a round-the-clock effort against all its assigned areas, while the 7th Air Force often diverted excess effort into Route Package I when weather closed access to Route Packages V or VI.[28]

Two main interdiction campaigns against the North Vietnamese lines of communication can be distinguished; one from 1965 to 1968, and the other in 1972. Each included attacks on the railway system, particularly on the segment between China and Hanoi. This whole stretch was covered by SAM and AA artillery defences, particularly along the last thirty miles outside Hanoi. Near the Chinese border the defences were thinner because the North Vietnamese knew of the 125-mile buffer zone

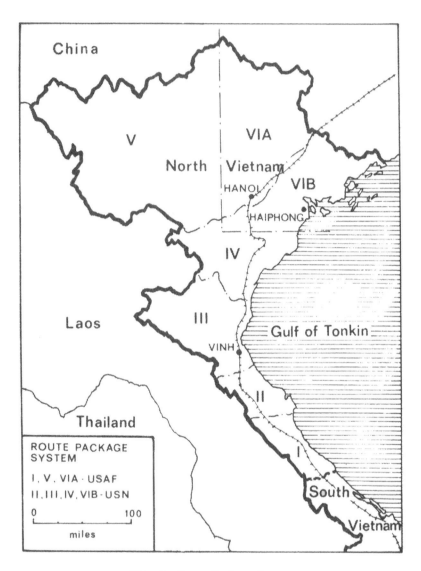

MAP 7 *Route Package System*

that the US had imposed on its aircraft so as to avoid accidental violations of Chinese airspace. Penetrations into this zone by US aircraft could be authorised only for specific targets, and the Vietnamese were able to exploit the situation by marshalling trains in the sanctuary area by day, ready to make night runs along the remaining stretch to Hanoi.

The heaviest AA defences along the line, and indeed the heaviest of the whole war, were deployed around the two bottlenecks already mentioned, the Canal des Rapides and the Paul Doumer bridge.

Political restrictions in interdiction bombing meant that the former bridge was not released for air attack until April 1967, and the Doumer bridge could not be raided until August 1967. When it was finally targeted on 11 August, a force of twenty-six F-105D Thunderchiefs attacked the bridge in three waves, each wave covered by four F-4s as top cover, four to suppress the AA artillery batteries and another four 'Wild-Weasels' for SAM suppression. The bridge was out of action for seven weeks with one railway and two roadspans destroyed.

Attacks on smaller bridges along the line had caused little hindrance to the flow of logistics because they were so easily repaired or by-passed; but once these main bridges were dropped the enemy faced a difficult problem. The Paul Doumer bridge, for example, was 5,532 feet long, and although the ruse that had been so effective in Korea – that of building a new span but floating it away to concealment during daylight hours – was employed, reconnaissance and follow-up attacks on the spans and on the cranes needed to move them usually kept the bridge out of operation. The bridge was put out again in late October, repaired again by the end of November and attacked twice more in December, after which the enemy resorted to a pontoon replacement some distance along the river.

The forty-mile rail segment between Haiphong and Hanoi was also vital to North Vietnamese logistics since it was along this line that bulk goods including food and fuel travelled from the harbour at Haiphong. A third important segment was that south for 165 miles from Hanoi to Vinh. From Thanh Hoa southwards the line was vulnerable not only to air attack but to bombardment from the sea, and the line was usually interdicted to such an extent that the Vietnamese resorted to the kind of shuttle operation between cuts that had been seen during the railway interdiction campaign in Korea.

South of Vinh the line was made altogether unusable by air attack. This sector included the road–rail bridge at Thanh Hoa, on the Ma River eighty miles south of Hanoi. It was a key target during Rolling Thunder attacks as early as April 1965, and all told 700 sorties were flown against this bridge, some of them employing USN Walleye glide-bombs, but although hits were scored the bridge was not brought down. It was not until 1972 that the Thanh Hoa bridge was dropped by a 3000 lb laser-guided bomb.

These so-called 'smart' bombs were standard weapons fitted with a guidance kit, a development dating from 1968 but one that surprisingly seems to have met with a certain amount of scepticism in the USAF.[29] Successes like that at Thanh Hoa and the enthusiasm of the aircrew eventually led first to the adoption of these weapons and later to the acceptance by the USAF of the value of the whole developing field of precision guidance.

One serious drawback to the interdiction campaign was the constraints placed on US air power to avoid civilian casualties, and the facility with which the North Vietnamese took advantage of this by storing their supplies alongside rail and road routes but in residential areas. Because they could stockpile supplies in these sanctuary areas, the North Vietnamese logicians were on the one hand often able to compensate for delays inflicted by air attacks at choke points, and on the other hand they were able to shuttle supplies down the route from one sanctuary to another during the hours of darkness.

Laos – the Ho Chi-Minh Trail

The interdiction efforts in the North were a powerful, but by no means an absolute, answer to the enemy's logistic system, and the flow of supplies down to Vinh continued. From Vinh, supplies for northern Laos went along Route 7 while those for southern Laos and South Vietnam went along Route 1A to the DMZ or up Route 15 to the Mu Gai Pass, or along Route 137 to the Ban Karai Pass. Later, and despite prolonged attack by the 7th Air Force, a new route, 1036, was built by the North Vietnamese across the mountains through the Ban Raving Pass and so into Laos.

In Laos itself lay the so-called Ho Chi-Minh Trail, which was not a trail at all but a comprehensive system of well-developed roads feeding large supply camps in Military Regions I and II and linked with other road and river systems throughout Cambodia to support activities in Military Regions II and IV. The whole network formed a resilient, complex, diffuse and very difficult target for air attack.

Until 1967, the air defences established along the Ho Chi-Minh routes in Laos by the North Vietnamese were slight, and the USAF were able to use daylight armed-reconnaissance missions to locate specific targets as well as to build up an intelligence picture of developing choke points.

Attacks were only lightly escorted by F-4 flak-suppression aircraft, Wild Weasels and ECM EM-66s, and the intensity of the effort that could be applied was increased during the dry season in Laos because aircraft diverted by bad weather from attacks in Route Package VI were often directed into the Tiger Hound, Steel Tiger, or Barrel Roll areas, or into Route Package I.

About 200 sorties a day were flown on average against the Laos routes, most of them in darkness,[30] but during the 1968 halt to bombing in North Vietnam it was possible to put an even heavier air effort against the Laos routes, and more than 400 sorties a day were usually flown. These attacks continued even when, at various stages of the war, diplomatic efforts were being made to start negotiations. This apparent contradiction arose because the North Vietnamese would not admit that they had forces in Laos although by February 1971 it was estimated that they had 35,000 maintaining the routes and another 30,000 actually fighting in northern Laos, and because the US would admit only to armed reconnaissance being carried out at the request of the Laotian government.

At first the air tactics employed were based on those used in Korea using a hunter–killer team of two A-26 aircraft, one illuminating the target for attack by the other. This was effective during 1965–66, as was the use of C-123s equipped with starlight-scopes, an adaptation of a sniper's sight, through which roads could be searched from C-123s flying at about 3,500 feet and 140 knots to direct an accompanying B-26 on to likely targets. Once the enemy began to move more AA weapons into Laos, however, the vulnerability of the team was too high and the B-26s were withdrawn from the war. The C-123s were then replaced by airborne FACs whose higher manoeuvrability gave them a better ability to avoid enemy AA fire. Once a target along a road was located, a pair of F-4s or a B-57 would be called in. As the attack aircraft approached, the FAC would mark the head and the tail of the enemy column with ground-burning flares and bring the attack in.

In 1967 the picture was changing again as the enemy moved more weapons and more advanced systems into South Vietnam and Laos, and by mid-year it was necessary to cover attacking aircraft with Wild Weasel F-105s and EB-66 ECM aircraft. The growing SAM threat meant that by now the provision of support aircraft had become an important factor in resource allocation, but since the SAM threat over Laos was still not as severe as that over Route Packages I, V and VI, those areas were given priority – especially for the use of ECM pods, which were in short supply.

Particularly successful in these night interdiction attacks were B-57s armed with Mk 35 incendiary bombs, especially in 1966 and 1967 when the Viet Cong convoys often carried fuel. Later, as the North Vietnamese logistic system grew more sophisticated and included the use of fuel pipelines, the value of incendiary raids fell off.

AC-130 gunships were also introduced in 1967, and these aircraft became the most potent truck-killers of the whole war. They were particularly successful in lightly defended areas such as Tiger Hound. Most AC-130s were equipped with two 7.62 mm as well as four 20 mm guns and they carried low-light television, infra-red and radar. Later models carried 40 mm guns, and one version (Pave Aegis) had a 105 mm weapon, while other versions used designators for the laser-guided bombs of accompanying F-4s.

The routes in Laos were always at their busiest in the relatively dry winter months, and US air activity was correspondingly stepped up in a series of campaigns codenamed 'Commando Hunt', the first being fought in the Winter of 1968–69. By 1970 the North Vietnamese had so extended the Trail that about 2,500 trucks were in use in Laos and a POL pipeline had been built, and despite continuing US efforts the flow of supplies continued.

During Commando Hunt 3 in the winter of 1969–70, it was estimated that about one-third of the 54,000 tons of supplies that entered the Ho Chi-Minh Trail were getting through, the rest being consumed or destroyed en route, while in Commando Hunt 7 during the winter of 1971–72, the Americans estimated that only one-sixth of the supplies were getting through. But later and more careful analyses of the estimates suggested that on the one hand the figures were grossly optimistic, ignoring for example the fact that damaged enemy vehicles were often salvaged and repaired; and on the other hand even the official US figures for the Communist throughput of about 35 tons a day was enough to account for the enemy build-up before the 1972 offensive across the DMZ.

Interdiction in Laos certainly had some effect in making it difficult and expensive for the Communists to move reinforcements and supplies to the South; but it was not as successful as was claimed at the time, and it did not neutralise the enemy potential to launch large-scale offensives.

AIR BOMBARDMENT OF THE NORTH

Targets in the Hanoi area had first been attacked on 29 June 1966 when raids were made on a POL complex only four miles outside the city, and by 1967 the air offensive had been extended to include other targets such as airfields, the electric power infrastructure and certain factories in efforts to apply strategic air pressure on the Hanoi government.

Until January 1967 attacks were made at 4,500 feet, an altitude that offered a compromise in efforts to avoid AA artillery fire at low level and SAM defence at higher altitudes. Four strikes were normally launched each day, each consisting of the strike aircraft themselves, fighter escorts, 'Iron Hand' escorts carrying Wild Weasel air-to-ground missiles that homed on to SAM radar beams, ECM aircraft, air-to-air refuelling tankers, intelligence collectors and command and control aircraft. When ECM pods became available for all strike aircraft in January 1967, formations began to penetrate North Vietnamese airspace at 15,000 feet, a height that gave better target acquisition, made the control of the formations easier and avoided most of the AA artillery fire.[31]

As to fighter defences, as early as August 1964 the first 30 Migs had arrived at Phuc Yen from China, and those Communist intérceptors posed a potential threat to US strike forces that could never be altogether ignored. By July 1966 there were 10 or 15 Mig-21s and about fifty Mig-17s, and by mid-1967 over 100 aircraft roughly split between the two types. Mig-19s appeared in the North Vietnamese inventory in 1968, but the main threat throughout the war was considered by 7th Air Force crews to be the Mig-21s with Atoll missiles. At first the Americans dealt with the Mig threat by instructing inward-bound F-4s in strike formations to jettison their bombs and act as escorts for the rest of the force, but eventually dedicated F-4 escorts were used. The air engagements that resulted were nothing like the scale of air combat that had been seen, for example, over Korea, and even in the heaviest engagement of the whole war – a carefully planned fighter sweep, Operation Bolo, on 2 January 1967, only seven Migs were destroyed. Meanwhile the same kind of escort tactics that had been proved over Europe in 1944 and over Korea were found to be effective over North Vietnam, and the Migs never became a really serious threat to the attacking strike forces.[32]

SAMs, on the other hand, remained a threat from 24 July 1965 when an F-4 was lost to their fire. After that date the enemy SAM defences expanded rapidly, and in 1965 alone 180 SAMs were fired and 11 US aircraft destroyed. Most of the missiles were deployed on a 40-mile circle around Hanoi, but they were also sited along the railway lines to the north-east and north-west of the city. The missiles near Hanoi were operated by some twenty to thirty SAM battalions each with four to six launchers, giving them a total of perhaps 180 launchers in 1967 and probably as many as 200 during the 1972 offensive. Few if any of the

SAMs were mobile, but they were all transportable and they were regularly moved about so as to avoid pre-planned air attack. It was estimated that the North Vietnamese kept about 100 of their stock of 400–500 missiles at readiness on the launchers, with another 200 at the launch sites and the rest in the supply system.[33]

One particular difficulty in the Hanoi area was that many SAM sites were quite deliberately located in zones which the US had chosen to regard as protected areas, yet the SAMs could of course fire at targets well beyond the perimeters of those zones. This led to some curious rules of engagement. For example, no SAMs within a 10-mile radius of Hanoi could be attacked; outside that 10-mile zone but within a 30-mile radius SAM sites could be attacked only if they were preparing to fire and only then if they were in an unpopulated area. If they were in a populated area they could be attacked only if they were actually firing. Thus was air power prevented from exercising its full impact.[34]

Several American countermeasures to the SAMs were developed during the war. One of the first was a cockpit warning device to indicate to the crew not only that SAM radar was operating and that a SAM launch could be expected, but giving an approximate indication of range and direction. The aircraft could then manoeuvre to avoid the upcoming SAM, usually by making a diving turn towards it followed by a break into a rolling pull-up which the missile could not follow.

Towards the end of the war, chaff was very often used and single clouds rather than corridors of chaff were found to be particularly successful against acquisition and tracking radars. The effectiveness of the various weapons employed by the US air power is shown by the falling loss rates. In 1967 there was an aircraft loss for every fifty-five missile firings; later this fell to one every 100 missiles, and during the 1972 offensive the number of firings needed to bring down an aircraft was more than 150. Where the SAM umbrella did, however, have an effect was in forcing most missions to go in below the most efficient SAM altitude of about 20,000 feet, which meant that the attacking aircraft often became targets for other elements of the comprehensive air defence system.[35]

By the time that the penultimate bombing campaign against North Vietnam, Linebacker I, was launched in May 1972, the 7th Air Force had settled on the use of a single attack force each day instead of the two that had been used earlier in the war. There were two reasons for this. One was that the ratio of support to attack elements had risen to 4:1; the other was that the high precision of laser-guided weapons reduced the size of the attack force that was needed, especially against targets such as bridges. As more targets were released for attack, carpet-bombing tactics were sometimes appropriate – for example against railway yards and logistic depots – and the size of the strike attack elements was then usually 12 aircraft carrying conventional bomb-loads rather than precision weapons.

On 9 May 1972 serious weaknesses in the whole attempt at air interdiction in the North were remedied by the mining of Haiphong harbour, the reduction of the ten-mile wide protected zone around Haiphong to only five miles, and the reduction of the zone around Hanoi from 30 miles to 10. This increased pressure on the North seemed to result in progress at the Paris peace talks, and on 23 October all bombing above the 20th Parallel was suspended. When it became clear, however, that the negotiations were beginning to drag out once again, preparations were made to resume the air offensive, this time in the form of a maximum effort using the whole range of available air power.

The eleven-day campaign, known as Linebacker II, was duly launched on 18 December 1972 against the Hanoi and Haiphong areas. In a series of carefully co-ordinated raids, low-flying F-111s were sent in against North Vietnamese airfields, while F-111s and Wild Weasels dealt with SAM sites. At the same time EB-66s provided ECM cover, F-4s dispersed chaff, and fighter escorts flew ready to deal with any Mig interceptors.

On the first night, the main force of B-52s flew 121 sorties in three waves several hours apart, all attacking at about 30,000 feet from the north-west. More than 200 SAMs were launched against them, destroying three B-52s and damaging two others. A similar raid on the second night suffered no losses although an estimated 180 SAMs were fired. Another three-wave attack was made on the third night, 20 December, but although the first wave met little opposition, a barrage of SAMs was fired at the aircraft of the second wave. Two B-52s were shot down and another damaged – to crash later in Thailand – as they made their turns away from the target and into the prevailing 100 knot north-westerly head winds. These winds not only slowed down the outward flight of the bombers but dispersed most of the chaff that had been laid and thus gave the North Vietnamese SAM controllers good opportunities to exploit gaps in the electronic jamming barrage. In the final wave of the night, two more B-52s were brought down over Hanoi and another so badly damaged that it crashed in Laos, making a total loss of six B-52s for the night – the heaviest in the whole Linebacker II operation.

On the fourth and succeeding nights the number of SAMs fired fell off, and this together with improved tactics brought the loss rate down to two aircraft and held the level of loss and damage down to an acceptable level for the rest of the offensive. After a 36 hour pause in the bombings over Christmas, the attacks were resumed on 26 December after carefully co-ordinated and massive preparation by 120 attack and 100 support aircraft divided into seven waves attacking ten different targets. That night, the B-52s concentrated mainly on Haiphong and Thai Nguyen, and 113 of these aircraft struck their target within fifteen minutes, an unprecedented concentration of firepower in Vietnam and perhaps in the whole history of air warfare. The SAM defences were saturated by this weight of attack, and again only two B-52s were lost – one over the target area and one that crashed on landing in Thailand as a result of heavy battle damage.

On the ninth day, sixty B-52s again attacked. One more aircraft was lost in the target area and one during the return flight. Two more were damaged on 27 December, but these were the last, and on the tenth and eleventh days of the offensive the SAM defences were markedly weaker. At midnight on 29 December 1972 the offensive ended.

A total of 389 B-52 sorties had been flown from Guam and 340 from U-Tapao. Sixteen B-52s had been lost, eleven of them brought down over Hanoi, and all of them victims of the 1,200 or more SAMs that had been fired. Nine other B-52s had been damaged; 13,395 tons of bombs had been dropped on 34 targets including airfields, railway yards, POL and munition storage areas, docks and power plants.[36]

Linebacker II had been a highly accurate and a very concentrated attack on areas that had hitherto been sanctuaries for North Vietnamese military effort and political will, and there was little doubt that the offensive played a key part in bringing about the North Vietnamese decision to accept the remaining terms of the ceasefire and to sign the peace agreement on 15 January 1973.

The North Vietnamese would not admit that the bombing had tipped the balance in what was probably a narrow decision, and in any case it was a decision that was welcomed by both sides. The US could disengage at a time when many observers such as Sir Robert Thompson believed they 'had the war won'[37] and the ceasefire left the North Vietnamese free to rebuild their strength ready for a later offensive against the South – which came in 1975. Meanwhile, after Linebacker II all USAF units left South Vietnam and most of those in Thailand were also withdrawn.

Although the US called the Linebacker campaigns interdiction, they were interdiction only in the global sense that the ultimate strength of the North Vietnamese was perceived to lie elsewhere, either in China or in the Soviet Union, or both. To the North Vietnamese, however, the offensives had all the characteristics of a strategic air offensive, and a successful one at that. US air power had won a clear military victory. It may have been only a local victory, it may have been a victory that was not consolidated either militarily or politically; but air power had, for the first time in the Vietnam war, exerted the kind of leverage of which it had been capable throughout the war had it been applied with determination.

CONCLUSION

An assessment of the impact of air power in Vietnam must distinguish between the quite different air campaigns that were fought. Very broadly these can be seen as: air support of all kinds in the ground fighting, interdiction, air superiority, and the use of air power against strategic targets.

Direct air support could only very rarely be the massive or decisive factor that it had occasionally been in other and earlier campaigns. Khe San was a notable exception, but on the whole the relatively small scale of combat engagement on the ground restricted air power to the function of mobile artillery. Even then, because the techniques were more often based on air strikes on enemy locations rather than on direct opponents in contact, the use of the air weapon was not always efficient, and in a campaign that ultimately depended upon the support of the local population it was often indiscriminate and counterproductive.

Strategic air transport played a vital and an uncontroversial role in supporting the whole US effort in South-East Asia, while tactical air transport and helicopters made possible one of the most crucial contributions of air power in the ground fighting, that of rapidly redeploying combat elements so as to match and often to exceed the mobility and the flexibility of the Communists, based on their knowledge of the country and on the fact that they so often held the initiative.

The interdiction campaigns were far less satisfactory, and the lessons of the European campaigns of 1944, and of the interdiction campaigns in Korea, emerged once again. If the enemy holds the initiative on the ground, then he can either reduce his ground activity so that the level of consumption of supplies is below that which is evading the air interdiction campaign, or he can cease operations until his reserves have increased to the level for a new offensive. Successful interdiction therefore implies a grasp of the initiative in the ground fighting as well as in the air, so that the enemy is compelled to consume supplies faster than they can arrive. In South Vietnam it was not possible to maintain enough of a grasp of the initiative to put the Communists in this position, particularly since the enemy could live off the land, and the quantities of supplies from the North that were essential to the style of warfare being undertaken were very small indeed. Despite the massive resources available, and despite the remarkable ingenuity as well as the determination shown by the USAF, no answer to the problem of interdiction against Marxist-style guerrillas therefore emerged through out the war.

Far more crucial to the overall US strategy for the war, however, was the air campaign to apply strategic pressure against the North Vietnamese. In a pattern of events that bore a remarkable similarity to Korea twenty years earlier, the US adopted a policy of carefully graduated air attacks in the hope of compelling the enemy to negotiate for fear of later and even worse air bombardment. In fact, the slow escalation meant in Vietnam, as it had meant in Korea, that the enemy was given time on the one hand to prepare his population physically and psychologically against the steps in the process of escalation as they occurred, and on the other hand he was given ample time to generate protests of inhumanity on a world scale, and not least in the US itself, where a sometimes less than responsible Press gave an often distorted view of the war.[38] As Admiral Sharp asked in 1978:

> How could our leadership have been aware all along of our negotiating mistakes in Korea and still proceeded along the task we took in negotiating an . . . end to the Vietnam affair? How could we have called time and time again for negotiations with an enemy whose military position was still unquestionably favourable to him . . . and not, at the very least, have played the one quick-response ace we had in the hole, our coercive air power?[39]

General Westmoreland took the same view:

> the kind of bombing that should have been started as soon as a strong military and political base had been established in South Vietnam did in fact induce the Communists to make concessions that were considerably less attractive than those they had striven for at enormous cost for seventeen years . . .[40]

Strategically the war was a defeat for the US, and it was an expensive one. According to US Department of Defence statistics, the US alone[41] lost 44,527 men killed in action from 1966 to 1973; less than in the Korean War, but given the nature of the fighting, a very high figure indeed. The air effort involved in the war was, by any standards, vast. Between 1966 and 1973, US air power flew 1,248,105 fixed-wing combat sorties and well over 37 million helicopter sorties. Over the same period 1,324 fixed-wing aircraft were lost to enemy action, and 2,112 helicopters.[42] The total losses were much higher; 3,221 fixed-wing aircraft were lost altogether in connection with the war, and 4,587 helicopters were destroyed.

As Lord Tedder once said, the important thing is not to look back to the past but to look at the future from the past. The question for the future from the Vietnam experience was put in these words by one commentator in 1980:

Have we learned the expensive lesson to the degree that it will influence allocation of aviation resources? Is the lesson reflected in the preparation of service program objective memorandums and the annual budget? If not, then one must anticipate that future civilian leadership will again trigger the misuse of our air forces.[43]

5 Air Power in the Middle East

While the USAF was focusing primarily on the war in South-East Asia, grappling with problems of jungle topography, monsoon weather and an enemy whose tactics and logistic support made successful interdiction very difficult, a very different war broke out in the Middle East. There, the topography was almost entirely barren rock or desert; the skies were almost entirely cloudless and the tactics of both sides were the product of European habit and weaponry.

THE CRISIS

By the summer of 1967 the ring of enemies round the fledgling state of Israel appeared at last to be achieving greater unity in their efforts to redress Sinai defeat of 1956. During May there was evidence of co-ordinated Egyptian–Syrian staff planning in Damascus; on the 17th the United Nations forces on the Egyptian–Israeli border were forced to withdraw by Egypt; on the 18th the key fortress at Sharm El Sheikh overlooking the Straits of Tiran was occupied by Egyptian troops. Four days later the Gulf of Aqaba was closed to Israeli shipping. Western reaction was lukewarm and when, on 30 May, King Hussein of Jordan flew to Cairo to sign a defence pact with President Nasser, the Israelis believed that the ring was about to be drawn tight and that their fate would lie in their own hands.

The strategy they would choose was influenced by several clear-cut factors. Their country was some 400 miles in length from Galilee to the Gulf of Aqaba but only 9 miles wide near Tel Aviv and 70 across to the Dead Sea with a total population of $2\frac{1}{2}$ million. Consequently, the state would be defended on the territory of the hostile neighbours and, because there were neither the manpower nor resources to fight a protracted war, the strategy would be designed to reach a decision as

MAP 8   *The Arab–Israeli Theatre, 1967–73*

swiftly as possible. Egypt, the most powerful Arab country, with aspirations to Arab leadership, was clearly the major threat and in Clausewitzian terms, the centre of gravity of the hostile coalition.

Israeli strategy therefore postulated an attack against the opponents one at a time: first against Egypt, with a holding operation to the north. The first task would be to attain air superiority, then to concentrate armour to achieve deep penetration until the limited objectives were achieved. There was, for example, no plan to capture all of Sinai.[1] Tactical surprise would be sought, which implicitly meant a pre-emptive attack. Ironically, the strategy and subsequent tactics owed much to the example of Hitler's Germany, even though considerable lip-service was subsequently paid by Israeli generals to the ideas of Liddell-Hart. There was, however, an important change in emphasis.

The Israeli Defence Forces (IDF) believed that air superiority was not just an element in blitzkrieg, but for blitzkrieg in desert warfare it was the key to victory. Reliable reports suggest that General Mordecai Hod, Chief of Staff to the Israeli Air Force (IAF) assured the Israeli Cabinet during the night of 4/5 June that his aircraft could destroy the Egyptian Air Force (EAF) before it was able to bomb Tel Aviv and that thereafter they would swing the land balance of forces in Israel's favour. That assurance is believed to have been a major influence on the Cabinet's decision to go to war.

THE AIR STRIKE

Certainly General Hod had grounds for confidence. By any yardstick except numbers his Air Force was superior to that of the enemy. He had the pick of Israeli young men to fly his aircraft and a pool of technically competent civilians from whom to draw his groundcrews which far exceeded that available to the Arabs. His equipment: the French-supplied Vautours, Mirages, Mystères and Super Mystères was likely to be more effective than the Mig-15s, 17s, 19s and 21s which opposed him.[2] His command, control and communication structure was taut and well co-ordinated. His staffs were efficient, his commanders dynamic and his aircrews trained to far higher standards than the Egyptians and their allies. The whole was supported by an extremely efficient military intelligence system.

At 0845 hours Cairo time on 5 June the first attacks, maintaining complete radio silence, were made on nineteen Egyptian airfields in Sinai and across the Suez Canal. Tactical surprise was complete. The early morning EAF combat air patrols were being turned round, the mists were beginning to evaporate over the Nile delta, staff officers were driving to their offices in Cairo, the largely reservist AA gun crews were preparing for another uneventful day and despite President Nasser's bellicose attitude, the EAF was ill-prepared for war. It had intended to launch its own offensive against Israeli airfields, radars and control centres in support of the Arab plan to cut across the South Negev towards Jordan; but those plans evaporated in the impact of the repeated Israeli air strikes during that Monday morning.

By noon, 75 per cent of Egyptian combat aircraft and 66 per cent of the total strength had been destroyed almost entirely on the ground. An ill-timed Jordani attempt to relieve the pressure on her ally was punished by the total destruction of King Hussein's single Hawker Hunter squadron. Then, in the afternoon, similar treatment was meted out to the Syrian Air Force and to those Iraqi aircraft still within reach. By the end of the day, 500 Arab aircraft had been destroyed for the loss of 20 Israeli machines.

The IAF victory was so utterly comprehensive that there is little dispute about either its numerical extent or the manner in which it was achieved. Israeli aircraft ignored early warning radars, flew below the 138 missiles of the high-level SAM-2 batteries and attacked the airfield runways with French-built 1,200 lb rocket-assisted bombs. Then they strafed the neatly aligned, unprotected Egyptian aircraft with guns, cannons and rockets. They flew about 1,000 sorties achieving turn-round times of as little as 7 minutes: an achievement which prompted the Egyptians to assume that the UK and the USA were contributing to the attacks.

THE LAND – AIR WAR

Thereafter, the Arab ground forces had no protection against a completely free-ranging IAF. Close air support and interdiction was provided in all three theatres: on the Golan Heights, the Jordan Valley and Sinai. Armour and supporting artillery were attacked with rockets, napalm and bombs while AA batteries were neutralised by bombs equipped with variably timed fuses designed to burst in the air above the positions. Any movement was rapidly visible to the unmolested IAF which exacted very heavy losses on the Arab ground forces by both interdiction of reinforcements and disruption of retreats. In Jordan the retreat was turned into a rout while the reinforcing Iraqi brigade never reached the battlefield. In Sinai the Mitla Pass was strewn with burnt-out Egyptian vehicles. In addition, air superiority permitted daylight unopposed helicopter assaults either to support conventional operations as at Abu Agheila, to secure longer-range objectives such as Sharm El Sheikh, or to achieve short-range vertical surprise as at Boutmiye on the Golan.

After six days the war ended, with Israel in control of Sinai, the West bank and the Golan Heights. Air power had made its most spectacular contribution to warfare since August 1945. It had formed the basis of Israeli strategy and prepared the way for victory in battle. In fact it had been so spectacular, and the lessons were so unambiguous, that it was highly unlikely that the opportunities of June 1967 would ever reoccur. At any rate, that was clearly the determination of the Arab Air Forces. Conversely, the Israelis had demonstrated their superior skills, training, equipment, leadership and strategy. They had secured valuable additional territory as a bulwark against further Arab aggressors and they did not have the same stimulus to re-examine their own strategy and the postulates on which it had rested. Had they done so, events six years later might have taken a different direction.

THE YEARS BETWEEN

Until his death in September 1970 President Nasser sought to extirpate the shame of the Six-Day War. Procedures for selection and promotion in the officer corps were revised. Training in the air and on the ground was sharpened and extended.[3] Hardened shelters were constructed on airfields, and aircraft outside them were dispersed in random patterns. IAF electronic countermeasure techniques were studied and copied; security was tightened and, in particular, attention to detail in staff work was considerably increased. President Nasser began the series of local military engagements, collectively labelled 'The War of Attrition' designed to sap the resources of Israel over a lengthy period. Israeli response was again based on superior airpower. Indeed, by the end of 1969, the SAM-2 batteries had been decimated, Israeli aircraft were bombing targets throughout Egypt and President Nasser's own prestige was in jeopardy. As a result, the Soviet Union responded to his call for greatly extended air defence assistance. From February 1970 to July 1972 she constructed an extensive, closely co-ordinated network of SAMs and AA artillery along the West bank of the Canal and across the Egyptian heartland. It is idle, but interesting, to speculate that without the successful Israeli 'strategic' bombing, Soviet assistance in the construction of such a network might not have been so comprehensive.

Nevertheless, the Israelis do not appear to have been unduly alarmed. Visitors to the IAF in 1972 reliably observed that Israeli training had also improved since 1967, that traditional quality of leadership and initiative was being maintained, and that new equipment such as the F-4 Phantom and associated systems was actually extending the technological superiority of the IAF. They also noted that the IAF was fully aware of the increased Egyptian airfield protection and of the new SAM/AA defence net, but that it remained convinced of its ability to overcome them and to take advantage of continued Arab inferiority. The visitors, however, believed that it was most unlikely that the IAF could repeat such a rapid counter-air strike, that they could no longer guarantee such a favourable air situation over the battlefield, and that air support could accordingly be reduced. In retrospect, one can also see that the Israelis attached disproportionate emphasis to their supremacy in air-to-air combat which had produced victims in the ratio of 30:1 during the War of Attrition.

In 1973, however, Israel remained convinced that she could repeat the victory of 1967 should it become necessary: secure behind her extended boundaries, confident in the superiority of her air power and armour and disparaging of Arab preparations for war. The destruction of thirteen Syrian Migs off Latakia for the loss of one Israeli Phantom on 13 September seemed to confirm that superiority. Nevertheless, reprisals were feared along the Golan Heights, an area which was also known to be covered by Syrian SAMs. Consequently, as a precaution, by the end of the month the IAF had been brought to a much greater readiness state. In the light of events in October, this was proved to be a very shrewd precaution.

THE OCTOBER WAR

The contribution of air power in the conflict between Israel and her Arab neighbours in October 1973, known variously as Yom Kippur, The War of Atonement or The War of Ramadhan, has been examined from many points of view. Although considerable attention has been focused on the impact and implication of surface-to-air weapon systems, air power had a considerable, if not decisive, influence on the pre-war planning of both sides, on the way the war was fought, and on the final outcome. It was present in most of its traditional forms: strategic bombing, air defence, interdiction, counter-air, close air support and tactical and strategic transport. Moreover, in some instances, its absence was as significant as its presence.

However, unlike the Six-Day War, comprehensive analysis is on this occasion bedevilled by incomplete and frequently conflicting historical evidence. There is no shortage in the open press of extracts from 'official' records, personal interviews, eye-witness accounts and informed opinion, but problems of factual substantiation, always present in conflict analysis, are unusually extensive in this case. In addition to an acute manifestation of traditional causes of ambiguity, others are symptomatic of the nature of this particular conflict.

For example, assessment of aircraft and other equipment losses should start with the orders of battle on 6 October, subtract the losses over the next seventeen days or thereabouts, add replacement figures and come to an aggregate. Sub-totals require an analysis by aircraft or equipment type, identification of cause, location and timing of losses. Yet Arab, Israeli and neutral sources tend to conflict with, rather than corroborate, each other in many categories. Nomenclature varies: in some cases training aircraft pressed into combat action are included in combat lists and elsewhere they are not. Whatever the hopes and intentions of both sides, neither can discount the possibility of further conflict. Therefore, in the interests of national security alone, both must maximise potential advantage and minimise perceived weakness, as reflected in attrition rates and weapon effectiveness. Among the actual combatants, Israeli fighter pilots might consider it more honourable to acknowledge destruction by SAM-6 than by locally modified Mig-21s, while Egyptian air defence missile commanders might claim the tactical virtue of surprise after a period without firing rather than acknowledge dependence on tardy Soviet resupply. The superpower patrons have their own military and political reasons for being less than candid about the nature and significance of their contributions. Not surprisingly, where evidence is fragmentary and conflicting, many 'lessons' can be confidently drawn; as long as the desired lesson is fully understood before the supporting evidence is elicited, It is, therefore, possible to argue convincingly on the one hand that Yom Kippur marked the end of close air support, counter-air operations and interdiction in the face of well-co-ordinated SAM systems. On the other, it can equally trenchantly be argued that the vulnerability of SAMs to ground attack, ECM, precision munitions, specialised tactics, not to mention their economic demands on highly skilled manpower, place them securely and dangerously in the Maginot tradition. Did the war revolutionise the application of modern air power with considerable implications for future conflict in Europe? Or was it, in fact, fought in such political, geographical and climatic circumstances that most 'lessons' are misleading if translated to a different environment? Perhaps further reflection, even bearing in mind all the contradictions, may suggest different conclusions about the continued impact of air power.

EGYPTIAN STRATEGY

It seems likely that President Sadat's political objective was to break the political stalemate existing since the uneasy truce after the War of Attrition, rather than to secure the whole or a specific part of Sinai. Moreover, such a limited political objective could be supported by Egyptian resources at the time: a harmony preached by Clausewitz but seldom achieved in practice.

The Egyptian Armed Forces seem to have made a very objective and accurate assessment of their strengths and weaknesses *vis-à-vis* their potential opponents. Their armour was generally inferior but their infantry was certainly numerically superior and possibly now as well trained and led as the Israeli infantry, which had been eclipsed since 1967 by the prestige of the tank. In the air, there was no doubt. The ground attack Mig-17 was obsolescent while the Mig-21, although an excellent clear-weather air superiority airframe, was outranged and outpaced by the Israeli Phantoms. The Soviet-supplied short-range air-to-air Atoll missile, whether with infra-red or semi-active radar homing guidance system, was limited to 2G manoeuvres, had only a 25 lb warhead and was in every respect inferior to the US Sidewinder or Israeli developed Shafrir II. Nor did the EAF have any weapon to match the longer-range, radar-guided Sparrow, and the Soviet Union had not supplied Egypt with third-generation Mig-23s. One squadron of SU-20s, the export version of the SU-17 Fitter 'C', had been supplied but was still undergoing conversion training and was not used during the war.

A deliberate decision, therefore, seems to have been made to accept the consequences of technical inferiority and to avoid air-to-air combat except under the most favourable circumstances. The implications of that situation were that no air cover against the IAF could be guaranteed for Egyptian ground forces. On the other hand, since 1969 Egypt and, to a certain extent, Syria, had come to depend increasingly on SAMs for national air defences against Israeli incursion. The early static high-altitude SAM-2s were supplemented first by the relatively mobile and lower-level SAM-3s and then, in 1973, by fully mobile SAM-6s. All were laced into a complex which in Egypt, according to Israeli Intelligence[4] included 146 SAM batteries and several different calibres of AA guns. Of these, some sixty batteries were deployed in an area 140 km by 25 km down the entire length of the Suez Canal. SAMs and guns were carefully co-ordinated under the central control of the Air Defence Service which was responsible for some fifty control centres and 400 radars on 180 sites. Together, the system provided a defensive umbrella extending from 100 feet to above 60,000, not only above the Egyptian heartland, but extending several kilometres east of the Canal above Sinai. Similarly, the thirty or so Syrian batteries and accompanying guns provided dense, but geographically limited, cover over the Golan area. Therefore, if Egyptian strategic planning had included the well-tried Staff College 'Appreciation' it is highly probable that potential Israeli aircraft superiority and Egyptian surface-to-air protective cover would have been classed as 'pervasive' factors.

Thus it is possible to agree with Chaim Herzog[5] that the EAF might have been inhibited by their long exposure to Soviet doctrine while the IAF were 'naturally' more adventurous. But whatever the influences before 1973, it is difficult to see how else President Sadat could have prepared for war when the technical balance in the air was so clearly defined.

THE ISRAELI ASSESSMENT

Consideration of air power by the Israelis, however, does not seem to have been quite so objective. They were aware of the capabilities of the SAM-2 and, to a certain extent, the SAM-3. They had observed the Russians dismantle and withdraw SAM-6s from Egypt, together with a great deal of other equipment, in July 1972. They had seen a number returned later that year and early in 1973, together with large numbers of mobile ZSU-23/4 AA weapons. But according to General Elazar[6] they did not expect them to produce a qualitative change in force balance because of assumed Arab dependence on Soviet advisers and, by implication, because their combined technological and tactical impact was seriously underestimated. IAF victory in 1967 and individual successes during the War of Attrition suggested that the IAF could continue to win air supremacy and then, in close support of Israeli armour, take the customary toll of exposed enemy ground forces.

OPERATIONS

So, even before a shot was fired, the opposing strategies were either dominated, or heavily influenced by, perceptions of the likely contribution of air power to the conflict.

The major actions in the war have been thoroughly documented. The co-ordinated Syrian and Egyptian attacks took place at several places along the Suez Canal and on the Golan Heights at 1400 hours, Saturday 6 October: the Jewish Feast Day of The Atonement. By the end of Sunday, the 7th, the Syrians had pushed across the 1967 cease-fire lines and the Egyptians had established positions along the entire East bank of the Canal except at the north end of the Bitter Lakes. By 10 October the positions had been consolidated to a depth of some ten miles. In the North, however, Syrian advance had been held and slowly pushed back until by 13 October there seemed to be an Israeli threat to Damascus itself.

On 14 October the Egyptians struck out over Sinai with the tactical objectives of extending the bridgeheads and seizing the Sinai Passes but also apparently with a broader objective of drawing away Israeli pressure from their Syrian allies. The offensive was held, and countered by an Israeli attack across the Canal in the Bitter Lake area on 15 October. During the next seven days heavy fighting took place on the West bank of the Canal, a section of the Egyptian air defence belt was overrun and by the first cease-fire of 22 October the Egyptian 3rd Army on the East bank was threatened with encirclement. The truce broke down, the encirclement of the 3rd Army was completed and, with the Israeli Army only fifty miles from Cairo, a superpower crisis arose. From 10 and 13 October respectively, the Soviet Union and the USA had been resupplying their clients. On 24 October the USA believed that the Soviet Union was about to intervene unilaterally in the conflict, and President Nixon brought US nuclear forces to a Defence Condition 3 Alert in the early hours of 25 October. Thereafter, both sides agreed to a UN resolution to accept a UN Emergency Force in the Middle East. The fighting died away in the North on the 24th and in the Suez area on the 28th. It was swiftly followed by analysis and the search for lessons.

THE ISRAELI DILEMMA

By 6 October the Israeli military staffs were convinced that war would break out on two fronts later that day. In a meeting summoned for 0800 hours Prime Minister Meir authorised the Chief of Staff of the IDF, General Elazar, to begin partial mobilisation but rejected his request for a pre-emptive air strike against the Syrian missile system and airfields. After the Latakia engagement on 13 September the IAF had been at a higher degree of readiness than the other forces and General Peled had advised General Elazar in the early hours that he could be prepared to launch such a pre-emptive attack at 1100 hours.

The precedent of June 1967 was tempting but was in fact of doubtful relevance. Arguments will continue over the likely military achievements of a pre-emptive air strike. Presumably, just three hours before the Arab attack was due to begin, the Syrian air defences would have been fully manned, alert and, possibly, even expecting some IAF attention. Consequently, a large-scale pre-emptive attack by IAF squadrons could have produced a large-scale disaster for the aircraft themselves in the face of unexpected, undistracted and well-coordinated SAMs and guns. On the other hand, the impact of an 'unscheduled' attack on the would-be attackers could have thrown them off balance, unhinged the co-ordination between Damascus and Cairo and seriously impaired Arab confidence. So much is speculation. The fact was that on the advice of Defence Minister Dayan the Prime Minister refused the request for pre-empt on the grounds that the international political disadvantages would outweigh the immediate military gains. Israel was no longer universally perceived as the David among Goliaths as in 1967, and Mrs Meir did not wish to jeopardise international sympathy and support. So the proposed strategy was not in harmony with political considerations, and air power, like any other form of military power in such circumstances, was impotent.

THE ARAB AIR OFFENSIVE

Thus the initiative, as they had planned, remained with the Arab allies at 1400. Details of their initial use of close air support or deeper attacks are still a little vague but an overall impression can be reasonably accurately made. The Syrians began the war with a nominal orbat of some eighty Mig-17 and thirty SU-7 ground attack aircraft,[7] and perhaps 150 Mig-21 fighters. Assuming a maximum serviceability effort there were probably eighty to ninety aircraft employed in attack on Israeli defensive positions and armour, with perhaps the same number of Mig-21s providing top cover for them. All the air attacks seem to have been restricted to targets near the 1967 cease-fire line or in northern Israel behind it, that is either within or very close to the protective umbrella of the ground-to-air defensive systems. Israeli accounts of the ensuing chaos on their northern flank do not distinguish between the results of artillery and of air attack but clearly the subsequent air-to-air combats were extensive and bitter.

Meanwhile, the EAF had also contributed to the opening offensive but over longer ranges than those flown by their Syrian allies. Assuming a 75–80 per cent serviceability at the outset of hostilities they probably had seventy Mig-17s, sixty SU-7s and twenty twin-jet medium-range TU-16 bombers with which to launch their attacks and, in theory at least, almost 200 Mig-21s to provide top cover. Over 200 pre-planned sorties were flown against Israeli airfields in Sinai, command posts, Hawk SAM batteries, logistic centres and radar installations. The difference between the range of air attacks in the north and south is probably explained by Egyptian possession of the TU-16 and a deeper area of purely military significance in Sinai than in the Golan. Both Arab Air Forces appeared to be flying to the same co-ordinated strategy: to force a diversion of IAF activity over two fronts, to support ground operations directly within the limits of friendly SAM cover and indirectly by attacking command and control centres and reinforcement targets and to rely on tightly co-ordinated SAMs and AA to deny Israeli air superiority.

However, even if all the Arab claims for their air offensive are accepted, its impact on the overall campaign was of little more than nuisance value. If, however, the Egyptians and Syrians could have extended their activity, what would the implications have been for Israeli strategy?

A factor in the Israeli pre-war Intelligence assessment was a belief that large-scale Arab attack was unlikely until their Air Forces had the equipment to mount an offensive against strategic targets throughout Israel. Indeed, hints at the development of an Israeli nuclear weapon were regarded as a deterrent to such an offensive. In the event, neither Arab country had any real option because the handful of Egyptian TU-16s did not permit a large-scale strategic bombardment and the Soviet Union had consistently refused to provide them with other aircraft suitable for that role. Consequently, on the Feast Day of Atonement, Israeli mobilisation and reinforcement was able to take place throughout the country without any disruption from the air. Bearing in mind the Israeli planning assumption that she would be able to rely on such mobilisation, it may well be that Arab offensive air power, however limited, should wherever possible have placed greater emphasis on deeper interdiction.[8]

ISRAELI RESPONSE

A further consequence of the relatively light threat to Israeli airspace was the opportunity for the IAF immediately to take the air war to the enemy. In 1967 the attacks of 6 June had annihilated the Egyptian, Syrian and Jordanian Air Forces. Thereafter, IAF aircraft had roamed at will across Sinai and the Golan, creating havoc among the un-protected Arab land forces. But on this occasion the opposition had the initiative and threatened both north and south. Israeli land forces in position were, for the most part, overwhelmed. In little more than twenty-four hours Syrian forces were within sight of Galilee and fifty miles away from Haifa. In Sinai the Egyptians had established bridgeheads across the Canal along its entire length. Israeli commanders could not know that Egyptian military objectives were limited or that the Syrian divisions would come close to exhaustion after twenty-four hours hard fighting across country far from congenial to armour. There was no time in either theatre for the IAF to seek traditional air superiority before contributing to the land battle, to prevent what could well have been the most serious threat since 1949 to the Israeli state's existence.

The IAF had a nominal front-line combat strength of 100 multi-role Phantom F-4Es, 160 ground attack A4 Skyhawks, sixty multi-role Mirages and eighteen Super Mystère interceptors. Although Egyptian forebodings were quickly substantiated by the loss of several of their longer-range intruders into Sinai to Israel fighter response, in the first forty-eight hours there was little else for the IAF to celebrate.

A relatively small proportion of IAF sorties were flown against Egyptian airfields but with little impact. Hardened shelters had been constructed since 1967, rapid runway repair facilities introduced and practised and ground–air defences strengthened. The Israelis them-selves only claimed to have destroyed twenty-two aircraft on the ground throughout the entire war and no airfield appears to have been closed for more than a few hours.[9]

The great majority of IAF sorties were flown in direct or indirect support of ground forces. But whereas in 1967 they had been supporting rapidly advancing ground forces, now they had to support those desperately defending. Instead of free-ranging armed reconnaissance the need was for precise and timely succour, given for the most part within the range of Arab SAMs. The missile controllers, the reload teams, the radar technicians and the rest of the 50,000 or so highly qualified men who manned the systems were fit, fresh and confident of early success. Their weapons were well-prepared, carefully sited and closely co-ordinated. In the first forty-eight hours they exacted a heavy toll of Israeli aircraft on both fronts, but the proportion of losses to each element in the defences, and the overall loss as an attrition percentage of Israeli sorties in the war as a whole, are difficult to establish.

For example, in pre-war planning, the Egyptians prepared to allocate three SAMs to each aircraft carrying ECM and one source suggested[10] that in the event, slightly fewer missiles were actually fired. Yet, a later Egyptian statement admitted that eleven SAM-2s were fired for each confirmed kill. Several thousand SAM-7 missiles were launched, yet the Israelis reliably admit to only a handful of losses to this particular heat-seeking weapon. On the other hand, the very low-level, highly mobile SAM-6 speedily acquired an awesome reputation. The Israelis had no effective ECM to its frequency agility and the combination of very high-speed flight, continuous wave target illuminator, pulsed radar tracker and optional optical guidance made it a very difficult weapon to detect at or after launch. Moreover, because it was highly mobile it was equally difficult to locate and attack. The Egyptians further capitalised on its presence by using spoof techniques against IAF airborne missile release warning radars and claimed to have prompted several unnecessary ejections. Undoubtedly, also, the four-barrel 23 mm ZSU-23 Shilka, on its tracked chassis, exacted a heavy toll. In the wide horizons and relatively uncluttered countryside of the Suez and Golan areas the radar-laid guns would not need to reach the theoretical rate of 1,000 rounds per minute (rpm) to erect an unpleasant barrier to low-flying Skyhawks and Phantoms.

The combined impact of this defensive array seems to have been to destroy about forty Israeli aircraft in the first forty-eight hours of the war, which may be represented either as approximately 3 per cent of attack sorties flown, or 2 per cent of all sorties flown or, rather more meaningfully, 40 per cent of all losses throughout the war or 14 per cent of the front-line combat strength of the IAF. It has been reliably assessed that these losses fell almost equally to SAMs and AA artillery, but attempts to allocate each kill to an individual weapon are no more likely to be accurate than the well-intentioned, sincerely believed but wildly extravagant claims of pilots and gunners in the Second World War. Clearly, the impact of each weapon was enhanced by its co-operation with others, both of the same kind with a complementary field of fire, and of a different kind with a complementary altitude or acquisition system. For example, an aircraft seeking to intervene in the land battle had to fly below the SAM-2s, which automatically increased its vulnerability to SAM-3s and SAM-6s. The Israeli pilots were tactically and electronically prepared for the SAM-2s and SAM-3s but had to improvise against the SAM-6. They sought to attack it by steep dives designed to take advantage of the relatively shallow launch angle of the SAM but general evidence suggests that it remained their most serious threat. If they approached their targets at very low altitude they increased their vulnerability to Shilka. Moreover, if they sought to reduce that vulnerability by high-speed manoeuvre their unguided weapon delivery accuracy was obviously impaired. Perhaps partly because of this difficulty, an increasing proportion of attacks seem to have been made using bombs rather than rockets, on the grounds that even a near miss with the former could inflict damage on armour or other targets. In any event, the cumulative impact of the air defences severely curtailed the contribution of the IAF to the land battle in Sinai, and to a certain extent on the Golan. Repeated attacks were made on the temporary bridges across the Canal but – partly because the Egyptians were able to repair them promptly, partly because of their ability to maintain activity at night, and partly because Israeli attacks had to be pressed home in the face of highly concentrated fire – the Egyptian crossings were neither greatly disrupted nor very much delayed. The bridgeheads themselves were so well protected by the air defence net that there may well be truth in an Egyptian claim that on 7 October General Peled ordered his aircraft away from the immediate vicinity of the battlefield.

On the other hand, the reduction of IAF presence could have been caused by a decision to give priority to the Golan front. There, the cost-effectiveness of offensive air power was not measured by attrition rates but by how much effort was needed to stop Syrian armour descending into Galilee when there was little or no opposition remaining on the ground. There seems little doubt that air attack was a major contributory cause of the Syrian loss of impetus. By flying close to ground contours, on very high-speed single-pass attacks, the aircraft reduced the effectiveness of radar-assisted missiles and guns while the speed alone was usually too much for the rear hemisphere approach and angle of attack limitation of the SAM-7 infra-red Strella. Moreover, the Syrian SAM/AA artillery net was not as dense nor as extensive as the Egyptian, and the IAF was able to attack both deeper interdiction targets such as communication or logistic parks and more traditionally strategic targets such as oil refineries and, indeed, Damascus itself.

TRADITIONAL LESSONS

After the first two days of combat, significant new factors were to influence the air war and IAF losses were to dwindle rapidly, but one or two age-old lessons of military conflict had already been heavily reinforced.

Although the Israelis had been aware of their presence, the performance of the SAM-6 and ZSU-23 came as a complete technical surprise and was probably the most important factor in the achievement by the Egyptians of their first limited objective of the bridgeheads. On the other hand, their inability to disrupt Israeli mobilisation and counterattack was to have very serious longer-term implications for the war. For the Israelis, a military strategy divorced from political considerations had been proved unacceptable. Tactically, the resurgence of air defence would force a reconsideration of offensive profiles and equipment, but strategically, air power's defensive capability had been confirmed. No other kind of military force could have responded so swiftly on two fronts; only aircraft possessed the reach and speed to be switched in a matter of minutes from one theatre to another.

ASSISTANCE FROM THE SUPERPOWERS

In retrospect, one can see that the Arabs began to lose the initiative from 9 October. In Sinai, General Ismail continued to consolidate and reinforce his position on the East bank within the confines of his air defence umbrella. In the Golan, Syrian efforts became exhausted and Israeli counterattacks were mounted. Consequently, the IAF was able to direct more of its attention to counter air, defence suppression, and deeper interdiction operations on both fronts. This marked the beginning of a second phase, from 10 to 14 October, which saw the entrance of the superpowers into the arena: the Soviet Union on 10 October and the US on 14 October.

The rationale for Soviet assistance to Egypt and Syria awaits clarification from scrutiny of documents in Moscow. But whether it was pre-planned, whether in reaction to the killing of Russians in Damascus, or because the Soviet Union wished to join a winning bandwagon in Sinai or because of unease at the intelligence returned by Cosmos 596 on 9 October which probably disclosed the extent of Syrian disarray; whatever the reason, the Soviet airlift introduced a new dimension of air power into the conflict.

Two years previously, the SAM defences in the Hanoi area had been saturated by the Linebacker II operation to the extent that missile stocks had been used up in a very few days. Now, the London *Economist* of 3 November 1973 reported President Sadat as stating that Syria and Egypt had planned for a ninety-day war, but it seems that the extremely high expenditure of missiles and other ammunition took all combatants by surprise and both sides turned to their patrons for assistance.

Soviet response was swift and comprehensive. From 10 October until the Cease Fire some 750 sorties were flown from Russia to the two major Allies. Of these, the great majority were by the four turboprop Antonov-12s with a payload of 20,000 kg, but heavier cargoes were flown into Cairo by the Antonov-22 with its payload of 45,000 kg. Examination of the actual number of aircraft involved suggests that the Soviet Union devoted at least one-third of its medium-range transport fleet and well over half its heavy-lift aircraft to assist its clients. Altogether some 12,500 metric tons of equipment were airlifted to Damascus and Cairo. President Boumedienne alleged[11] that early sorties carried 'medicines and merchandise' but it is a safe assumption that higher priority was given to replacement missiles, SAM components, radars, trucks and ammunition of all kinds. The Soviet Union also mounted a sea-lift, primarily to Latakia in Syria, which was to move far more equipment than could be supplied by air: for example, tanks and other armoured vehicles. But comparatively little could arrive in time to influence the conduct of the war whose duration was already being measured in days.

It may be that the wider implications of the Soviet airlift are more significant than its impact on this particular war. Had the resupply of air defence components been available at the outset, so that both Syrian and Egyptian ground forces could have been accompanied by a truly mobile, rolling air defence umbrella, the Israeli problems of close air support would have continued to be very serious indeed. As it was, the resupply restricted the limits of Israeli counterattack rather than enhanced initial Arab advantages on the ground.

For the West, however, it was an ominous display of greatly improved Soviet military transport efficiency and a correspondingly significant increase in Soviet political influence based on military reach. VTA (Military Transport Aviation) demonstrated a capability to turn round and recycle aircraft at rates well beyond those seen in Prague five years previously. The convenience of being able to represent military aircraft as units of Aeroflot facilitated over-flights of Yugoslavia, Turkey and Iran from airfields in Hungary and The Crimea. Moreover, such over-flights were conveniently invisible to the population below, if not to Allies and potential opponents.

The Israelis had also been quick to request support from the US. El Al and charter aircraft had begun an airlift on 9 October after President Nixon had authorised limited sales of equipment. A detailed report in the magazine *Electronic Warfare* of January/February 1974 alleged that the first aircraft carried ECM AN/ALQ-119 and AN/ALQ-101-V(B) underwing pods for use against the radars of the SAM-2 and 3, whose acquisition and tracking frequencies were well known. They were followed by chaff dispensers and pods for Skyhawks and Phantoms. On 13 October President Nixon authorised a large-scale airlift by USAF Military Airlift Command which – according to its Commander-in-Chief, General P. K. Carlton, in a briefing on 27 June 1974 – flew 45 C-5 sorties and 421 by the C-141 in 33 days, lifting 22,395 tons which included M-60 and M-48 tanks, replacement tails for Skyhawks, CH-53 helicopters, missiles and ammunition at a total cost to the Israeli government of 42 million dollars. The replacement tails indicated that more realistic attrition figures should have included those aircraft grounded by battle damage.

In addition to the ECM equipment, two other items of considerable importance were received by the IAF from the US. The initial serious aircraft losses were made good during the war's duration by flights of Phantoms and Skyhawks from Europe and the US. The fact that some arrived in Israel still with USAF markings gave rise to accusations, later quietly dropped, of USAF direct participation in the conflict. Altogether, just under 100 F-4s, A-4s and C-130s were flown into the war zone. Subsequently, the *Armed Forces Journal* of January 1974 carried Israeli reflections on the need for many more reserve aircraft and aircrew. This particular resupply illustrated the ability of aircraft designed for short-range tactical operations to be moved swiftly over long distances to contribute in a very different arena: an increasingly important attribute of modern air power.

But once in the theatre, the aircraft had to be able to make that contribution and the other very important item of equipment in the US airlift was a number of guided air-to-surface weapons of different kinds. The Shrike anti-radiation missile was used against surveillance and SAM radars, but operating passively against E-Band only it had limited opportunities in the Egyptian and Syrian air defence systems. On the other hand, three other air-to-surface weapons proved extremely effective. The Walleye unpowered bomb, delivering a 2,000 lb warhead, was guided from the launch aircraft by television in the missile. Hobo was also an unpowered television or infra-red-guided weapon which could also be adopted to work with a laser designator. Maverick, with a completely autonomous optical tracker, could deliver a 1,300 lb warhead from a launch point outside the range of low-level air defences. Reliable evidence suggests that all three had an extremely high kill percentage despite the fact that Israel crews had not trained with the weapons in peacetime. Maverick, in particular, combining high destructive accuracy with reduced aircraft vulnerability, was a weapon with considerable potential.

Nor was Soviet or US assistance restricted to the provision of equipment. A House of Representatives Armed Services Subcommittee Report[12] stated that a number of Foxbat B sorties were flown over Sinai in the closing days of the war. This would not be surprising because the Mig-25's speed and height made it invulnerable to Israeli air defences and clearly there had been hitherto a lamentable gap in Egyptian reconnaissance provision, as the failure to spot General Sharon's attack across the Canal on 15 October dramatically demonstrated. Indeed, tactical air reconnaissance seems to have left something to be desired on both sides. General Peled commented later[13] that in previous campaigns the IAF had operated under benign conditions which gave complete freedom for reconnaissance. Not any more; but the need remained because information from ground sources tended to concentrate on fine topographical points whereas the need was more often for accurate information beyond the ground visibility horizon. And so it would remain, in conflict elsewhere.[14]

The Soviet Union also made use of information from at least four satellites: Cosmos 596, 597, 598 and 600, which returned to the Soviet Union between 9 and 23 October. How much was passed to the combatants is not known, but there is strong evidence to suggest that the Soviet Union's own activity on 24 October might have been prompted by information from Cosmos 600 about the extent of Israeli disregard of the Cease Fire and the gravity of the threat both to the Egyptian 3rd Army and to the client state herself.

SUPERPOWER CRISIS

That activity introduced a further element of air power into the arena: not by actually appearing but because of a recognised ability to appear. Proposals for joint action by the superpowers to intervene to stop the conflict had broken down when, on 23 October, flights of AN-12 'Cubs' were drastically reduced. On 24 October Mr Brezhnev informed Washington that he was considering taking 'appropriate unilateral action'. It was believed by the US that VTA could move up to seven airborne divisions and that possibly the 'Cubs' were being diverted to that task. At the same time, flights of the larger AN-22 'Cock' to Cairo had also decreased and there was, in theory at least, additional airlift capacity available. It was these factors which prompted Mr Nixon to proclaim a Defence Condition 3 Alert which, in turn, was swiftly followed by a diplomatic defusing of the crisis. The threat by Mr Brezhnev had to be taken seriously, whether it was bluff or not, because his transport aircraft gave him the capability to take such action, while the US could not respond in kind.

EGYPTIAN DILEMMAS

The flurry had no impact on the war itself, but the airlifts had allowed the combatants to fight on until the first Cease Fire of 22 October. On 13 October General Ismail did finally launch an attack towards the Sinai Passes. He was subsequently criticised for failing to take advantage of Israeli disruption on 7 and 8 October and for not continuing his offensive at that time. He later explained why he had not done so.[15]

> We had begun the operations under the protection of our famous missile network. If I had to advance beyond that I would have to wait – whether there was an opportunity someone else could see or I saw it myself – until I made sure that my forces had adequate protection. Our Air Force has performed heroic feats but if I had thrown in my Army in the footsteps of an available opportunity without any air defence cover against the enemy's air superiority, it would have meant that I was throwing the entire burden on the Air Force and assigning it to its tasks which were more than it could stand. . . . [Therefore] I abided by our plan. . . . I mean our original plan . . . which envisaged a build-up pause after completing the crossing operation. . . . A pause during which I could make a re-valuation of the situation in the light of the enemy's reaction.

The General had moved some air defence units across the Canal but clearly such an operation carried a very high degree of risk. As has been noted, the air defence system depended for its effectiveness on close co-ordination and complementary operations. Moreover, both ZSU-23 and SAM-6 were untried in mobile combat operations, as opposed to using their mobility to change from one static position to another. The availability of reserve missile crews is uncertain and until after 10 October the General did not have any Soviet weaponry supply. Bearing in mind the absolute reliance of Egyptian land forces on their surface-to-air defences, and that Egyptian Intelligence could not accurately assess the remaining combat capability of the IAF, it would have been extremely foolhardy for an Egyptian commander to risk sacrificing all his current advantages by dismantling and diluting his air defence system to redeploy the mobile units in what had to be an inferior mode. Under such circumstances accusations of 'rigidity of thought' or 'over-caution' against the Egyptian leadership are a little harsh. In the event, the advancing Egyptian armies, under diluted air cover, did become vulnerable to the IAF with its newly US-supplied precision-guided munitions.

ISRAELI AIR SUPERIORITY

Then, on 15 October, General Sharon's controversial attack across the junction of the Egyptian armies at Deversoir had the additional bonus of neutralising four SAM sites, thereby opening a gap in the original Suez air defence lines.[16] As the effectiveness of the air defence system declined, so IAF air superiority was regained. Egyptian interceptors, hitherto largely held back behind the Canal, flew as bravely and skilfully as their Allies on Golan had already done. But the pre-war assessments of both sides were proved to be accurate. The comparative air-to-air shortcomings of the Mig-21 and its weapons, already known over Sinai and Damascus before 1973, were sternly re-examined. Of almost 500 Arab aircraft destroyed during the war, over half fell to the IAF.[17] Significantly, there is sufficiently reliable evidence to suggest that a further 15–20 per cent of Arab losses were to their own air defence systems.[18] The problem of airspace management was observed in its most acute form to date. Egyptian aircraft did carry 'identification friend or foe' (IFF) equipment but not only was it susceptible to spoofing or jamming, its reception by SAM recognition challenge might have been impaired by high-speed low-level flight which was the EAF's preferred method of returning from operations. IFF problems could also be magnified by simple navigational errors, faulty operation of procedures[19] and straightforward inaccurate recognition by tense and fatigued operators of manual and optically laid weapon systems: all producing a modern manifestation of Clausewitz's fog of war. Nor did the Arab Air Forces have much more success against Israeli ground–air defences. They flew some 1,500 offensive sorties, unsupported by ECM, but lost 75 aircraft to Hawk batteries and AA artillery: a 5 per cent sortie attrition rate and a total loss approximately equal to that of the Israelis against Arab surface-to-air defences. They achieved a minor technical surprise by launching anti-radar versions of the Soviet supplied AS-5K 'Kelt', destroying two Israeli radars. But the subsonic missile, of the size and speed of an early Mig fighter, was vulnerable to air interception and

AA artillery fire during its thirty- to forty-mile flight and had little impact on the Israeli air defence system as a whole.

Nor were offensive operations by helicopters much more successful. Israeli sources[20] reliably stated that the Egyptians lost 42 helicopters, or about 25 per cent of their orbat, and the Syrians 13, about the same proportions. Members of the US House of Representatives Armed Services Subcommittee found the Israelis very disparaging about the value of helicopters in opposed operations. Certainly, Egyptian daylight sorties in Sinai placing paratroopers across Israeli reinforcement routes and close to installations at the foot of the Gulf of Suez were badly ravaged by the IAF. But the groups placing troops across the routes were only destroyed after discharging their mission, and although a further 7 were destroyed *en route* to Sharm El Sheikh, an undisclosed number also reached their objective. Moreover, in the northern theatre the Mount Hermon position was taken by both sides by heli-borne troops. The Syrian offensive achieved complete tactical surprise while the recapture at night by the Israelis was an operation which still awaits detailed description and analysis. On the other hand, the crews who sought to disrupt the Israeli counterattacks across the Canal were swiftly knocked down by Israeli groundfire. This, and the Sinai experience, supports the deduction that helicopters flying in clear weather, without surprise and over open hostile terrain are extremely vulnerable to both ground and air-to-air fire. But helicopters able to fly at night or in marginal weather, armoured against lower-calibre groundfire and with heat sources shielded or deflected against IR-seeking weapons, clearly offer a potential for short-range surprise attack and tactical battlefield mobility which any commander would be very pleased to have at his disposal. However, their major limitations compared to fixed-wing aircraft, of speed and range, make them much more fitted to an offensive which possesses the initiative of location and timing, rather than to a defensive which cannot be sure that its firepower will be in the right place at the right time. The subsequent large-scale production and deployment of the Mig-24 by the Soviet Union may well be in accord both with October war 'lessons' and with her own strategic inclinations. The impact of tactical surprise with its potential to paralyse or throw off-balance a local riposte may be thought worth the costs of high attrition.

WHICH LESSONS?

The major problem in seeking to identify any 'lessons' from the October war lies not in conflicting details of evidence, but in the fact that no one knows who the next examiner will be, or where the examination will take place. For example, both Maginot and Guderian had learned their lessons from the First World War, but the examination set in the Second World War found one to be very short of revision. There are similar dangers in projecting forwards from October 1973. For example, the Suez and Golan air defence nets did severely restrict the close air support contribution of the IAF, but only when they remained unscathed, closely co-ordinated systems and only as long as the ground forces fought below them. When the IAF was able to direct more effect against them, and in particular when they became vulnerable to groundfire, they began to display some of the less desirable Maginot characteristics of inflexibility and immobility. Even the much vaunted SA-6 depended on far less mobile surveillance radars at divisional level for its early warning, while when deployed in truly mobile mode it competed with several other equipments for positions most favourable for its ac- quisition and tracking radars. Indeed, its mobility in this conflict may have been a more valuable defensive asset. So, assessment of the interaction between SAM-6 and close air support should distinguish most carefully between static and mobile air defence.

In the analysis of the electronic warfare (EW), generalisations and confident assertions are even more dangerous. In most other aspects of modern war it is, access permitting, possible to see some of the hardware, count some of the items and examine some of the damage. Not so in EW. Both sides in the October war, and both patrons, had much to lose and little to gain by giving access to highly classified data about electronic intelligence (ELINT), electronic support measures (ESM), electronic counter-measures (ESM), and electronic counter- countermeasures (ECCM). Moreover, some of the early commentators, otherwise highly qualified, seemed to have little knowledge of the state of the art even in the skies over Germany in 1944 and 1945, when General Kammhuber's night fighters grappled with the Allied bomber offensive, and therefore they saw in the 1973 EW a major transform- ation of war, rather than a further stage in a well rooted evolution.

A highly regarded Israeli ELINT capability failed to give adequate warning of Egyptian preparations. Had there been any doubt about it before, it became clear that good signals discipline and exercise 'cover', together with awareness of an opponent's ELINT efficiency, could beguile him into a certain complacency. Moreover, just as ELINT did not preclude strategic surprise, it did not give warning of the SA-6 impact either. SA-2 and SA-3 were old, well-known missiles whose target acquisition radar frequencies could be easily jammed by IAF airborne ECM equipment. The frequency of the Straight Flush radar associated with SA-6 was not known, nor apparently was its heavy dependence on acquisition information from other radars at regimental level. It is beyond reasonable doubt that IAF ECM pods were quickly modified with the assistance of technicians from the United States, but what is in doubt is the proportional effectiveness of the modified pod when compared with modified anti-SA-6 tactics, reduced SA-6 missile availability, SA-6 mobility and SA battery vulnerability to ground forces.

There was, on the other hand, an unambiguous lesson in the destruction of the two IAF radars in Sinai by stand-off missiles equipped with anti-radiation warheads. But routine jamming by both sides was much more common even though an old lesson was reinforced rather than new ones discovered. The Commander's dilemma: whether to jam or to listen-in, was aggravated by the complexity and capability of the equipment. There is no evidence to suggest, for example, that Israeli jamming contributed to the vital unhingeing of the Egyptian position, or lack of it, at Deversoir, nor that Egyptian interference unbalanced IAF command and control.

Most evidence seems to justify aircrews' traditional mistrust of identification friend or foe (IFF) equipment. There is little doubt that self-inflicted losses on both sides were increased by spoofing and jamming of IFF. Safe lane, height and time procedures were preferred, avowedly by the EAF and probably by the IAF, despite the problems of misunderstandings, damaged aircraft and information security inherent in such attempts to cut the Gordian knot of airspace management.

Overall, electronic advantage assumed an importance which is unlikely to diminish in the foreseeable future. Here, the Israelis were able to call for superpower assistance to reset their ECM pods, but in a conflict between the superpowers themselves there would be no patron to redress an initial disadvantage. High technology ELINT could induce complacency and is unlikely ever to be a foolproof guarantee against either strategic or tactical surprise. Once combat has been joined EW adds a further, complex dimension to the traditional fog of war. Any strategy which fails to take such factors into account is likely to pay a heavy penalty.

Precision-guided air-to-surface munitions will certainly influence the outcome of electronic combat. In 1973, the anti-radar weapon typified by AS-5 'Kelt' was slow and vulnerable to countermeasures. Its high-speed successors, with passive guidance reinforced by computer memory, presents such a serious threat to early warning radars that the weapon carrier must be destroyed before it reaches its stand-off launch point. In air-to-surface operations generally, successors to the 1973 editions of Walleye, Hobo and Maverick are already affecting the defensive—offensive balance as they increasingly combine destructive accuracy with stand-off distance.

Overall, however, in addition to providing equivocal lessons, the air wars in the Middle East confirmed underlying principles of air power. For example, like any other kind of military power, it must be in harmony with contemporary political factors: it was in 1967 for the Israelis, but in 1973 it was not. In the first case a strategy was well-founded and successful, in the second it was invalidated before the war had begun.

The inherent flexibility of air power – the ability to switch military force between theatres of operations and from one target array to another – proved invaluable to Israel in both wars. It underpinned her offensive successes in 1967 and her two-front defence in 1973. Moreover, it also conveyed an ability to withdraw rapidly beyond the reach of technological surprise over Suez: a negative asset perhaps, but not one possessed by infantry or armour. Indeed, the intrinsic relationship between air power and technology was again clearly demonstrated, whether it was in the re-emergence of surface-to-air defences or in the air-to-air superiority of Israeli aircraft which neither numbers nor bravery were sufficient to offset.

Concentration on technology could, however, obscure the fundamental importance of people power. Not only did Israel misjudge the technical competence of her enemies; she overlooked the significance in the EAF of improved leadership and the acquisition of motivation. Rapidly advancing technology had demanded that imagination and forward thinking should keep pace with it, to allow intellectual mastery of both weapons and environment. Defeat was clearly a much greater spur to such activity than the complacency of easy victory. It is difficult to avoid a conclusion that the IAF had, by 1973, come to concentrate on the kind of war it would like to fight, rather than the kind of war it would likely be called upon to fight.

But perhaps of greatest significance of all was the long-range impact not only of air power, but of its shadow: the perceived ability to project political influence with the speed and as far as the reach of the weapon system; the ability of air power to create more favourable circumstances which the statesman might then seek to consolidate. Whereas in 1967 the outcome of the war was determined by the IAF in the first few hours, in 1973 it was influenced by the ability of both the US and the Soviet Union to come rapidly to the assistance of their friends.

REVISION: SYRIAN ANNIHILATION 1982

In June 1982, however, the IAF showed that it had revised its lessons and comprehensively removed any doubts about its supremacy when it annihilated the Syrian Air Force in a short sharp campaign which, because it coincided with more widely publicized events in the South Atlantic was quickly overshadowed by the drawn-out and bloody battle with the PLO in Beirut.

In an interview on 15 June, Premier Begin announced the destruction of 80 Syrian aircraft for the loss of one Israeli fighter in a massive encounter over the South Lebanese and Syrian borders. Reliable independent reports suggest that this time these almost incredible figures could be accurate. There may have been several reasons for the IAF success: the greater agility of the F-15s and F-16s over the Russian-built Mig-21s and 23s; piecemeal and comparatively inflexible tactics by the Syrians; the extensive use by the IAF of flare infra-red decoys and various electronic countermeasures and almost inevitably the individual superiority of IAF pilots. In a melee of that scale it is highly unlikely that the IAF used longer range air-to-air missiles but rather old-fashioned guns and short range infra-red missiles to which their opponents were fearfully vulnerable. Helicopter losses, on the other hand, seemed to have been less uneven. Again, while they considerably enhanced the mobility of ground forces they proved particularly vulnerable to SA and AAA fire.

Presumably, the IAF fully employed its handful of electronic warfare EC-707s and E2Cs both for stand-off jamming of Syrian radars and communications and for providing a measure of airborne control. Drones or mini RPVs were probably used to supplement reconnaissance. But according to an IAF spokesman the well-publicized destruction of 18 SA-6 batteries on the Syrian border was achieved by ground-launched anti-radiation missiles after the SA radars had reacted to IAF overflights. Assuming a range of about 30 kilometres this action had considerable significance for operations in Central Europe where similar treatment could probably be meted out to SA-6s and SA-11s advancing with a Warsaw Pact offensive, provided that NATO land and air forces could co-ordinate their target plans.

The net result of the Israeli combined operation was to give the IAF complete freedom to provide whatever air support the offensive into South Lebanon required. All in all, if the Soviet Union had been tolerably satisfied with the performance of her equipment in the Middle East in 1973, she had grounds for grave concern after the events of 1982.

6 Soviet Air Power 1945–80

In 1980 the Soviet Air Forces (SAF) were equipped with some 10,000 modern fixed-wing aircraft and 4,000 helicopters.[1] The Soviet aviation industry was producing a further 1,800 planes each year. The result was that Soviet air power was a vitally important element in any assessment of the military balance between East and West and, moreover, was increasingly permitting the Soviet Union to demonstrate a potential for military influence far from its own national boundaries. Indeed, the comparative growth in Soviet air power since 1945 far exceeded that of any other country. Its progress, generally shrouded in secrecy but occasionally exposed for dramatic international effect, has often been both underestimated and overemphasised. Problems of contemporary analysis remain, but its evolution from the aftermath of the Second World War, through the debates of the Khrushchev period to the current expansion under Mr Brezhnev is now much more clearly discernible.

THE SECOND WORLD WAR EXPERIENCE

After a traumatic start, Soviet military aviation ultimately made an important contribution to the 'Great Patriotic War'. In October 1941 the Soviet Union admitted to the loss of 5,316 aircraft,[2] which suggests that German claims to have destroyed 4,000 in the first seven days of the war in June were not quite so wildly exaggerated as was first thought. Thereafter, the Soviet ground forces were ravaged by free-ranging hostile air power. In 1941/2 '60–87 per cent' of all fighters and '60–80 per cent' of AA artillery were required for defence against attacks against 'rear area targets'[3] and only subsequently, as a result first of Allied assistance and then increases in Soviet production, could the war slowly be taken back to the enemy over his troops and rear areas. Soviet authors tend to use examples from the Second World War to illustrate points of contemporary doctrine or operations and, therefore, can occasionally be a little selective in their statistics and illustrations. There seems, however, little reason to doubt that the great majority of all Soviet Air Force activity in the Second World War was directed towards the support of the ground forces.

'The Air Force was destined primarily to support the ground forces in actions taking place directly over the battlefield.'[4] Forty-six per cent of sorties were flown in close air support, 35 per cent to achieve air superiority but only 0.2 per cent on 'independent' air operations against economic and political targets. Seventy-six per cent of all SAF sorties were carried out by tactical aviation.[5] By 1944, for example, the SAF were able to concentrate 6,000 aircraft from four Air Armies in Belorussia to support offensive ground operations. Indeed, by 1945 the SAF were thoroughly imbued with the spirit of the offensive 'throughout the depth of the whole offensive zone' concentrating on the lines of the main land force thrusts.[6] While the main strength of the SAF continued to be concentrated on the battlefields and close enemy rear, the depths of the operations steadily increased to hinder enemy reinforcements, interdict supplies and disrupt communications. Principles of air supremacy, massed force and offensive operations were well established.

Consequently, if folk memories passed on to the post-war SAF, they would have been the danger of inadequate air defences and the value of tactical offensive operations.

THE LEGACY OF THE WAR

In June 1945 the first line strength of the SAF was approximately 20,000 aircraft[7] and the aircraft industry had finally been able to produce 42,000 aircraft in a year. But the majority had single engines and timber airframes. There was limited experience of metal airframe construction and multi-engine design, and virtually none of electronics or gas-turbine production. The Western allies, on the other hand, had jet fighters in squadron service, a war's experience of multi-engine long-range bomber operations, a wide range of electronic equipment on the ground and in the air, and above all the atomic weapon. The disparity was, in Soviet eyes, extremely serious.

The origins of the Cold War and subsequent antipathy between East and West have been widely analysed. Whether they lay in Soviet ambition or fears, or in Western misunderstanding and fears, the fact was that by June 1945 there was on both sides an assumption of hostility.

Therefore, perception of Western capability and intention was, and was to remain, a strong influence on the evolution of Soviet military policy and hence on the development of her air power.

Soviet armies controlled Eastern Europe and the rear was consolidated in Manchuria. While the decisive arena for a power struggle would continue to be Europe, the only threat to Soviet security came from the US in the form of the manned bomber carrying the atomic weapon. We do not yet know whether Stalin was aware of the limits of the US atomic stockpile but even if he had been, his decisions would perhaps have remained the same. Soviet resources had been ravaged and his options were restricted; therefore his priorities had to be very clearly defined. They seem to have been first to construct an air defence system for the Motherland and, second, to prepare weapons which could take a war across the North Pole to the US itself.

But after 1942, little air defence had been required and the country lacked early warning radars, all-weather fighters and a co-ordinated command and control system. Indeed, in 1945, ground-to-air defences were still the responsibility of the Commander-in-Chief of Red Army Artillery. In offence, the expertise of tactical aviation was no longer sufficient, but there was little experience or equipment from which to build a long-range bomber force.

However, the SAF received an immediate windfall, indirectly by courtesy of the Western Allies' strategic bombing offensive. A very large proportion of the German aviation and associated industries had been moved, or reinforced, as far East as possible during the war to reduce the impact of British and American air raids. Consequently, some four-fifths of all German aircraft production fell into Soviet hands in 1945.[8] Large numbers of airframe designers, project engineers, chemists and fuel specialists were quickly swept back to the Soviet Union. Subsequently, by 1947, some 300,000 highly skilled members of the aviation and missile industries were believed to have been rounded up and put to work for new masters.[9] Complete aircraft which were taken included the twin-jet ME-262 fighter, the Arado 234 twin-jet bomber and the rocket-driven short-range ME-163 fighter while the experimental I-270 rocket fighter was based heavily on German inspiration. Among the engines were the HWK-109-509 rocket, the S.011 jet and the BMW-003 co-axial jet. In addition were large quantities of electronic and optical equipment, together with their research staff. Nor was the legacy restricted to airframes and engines. Also captured were production models of the Junkers Schmetterling radar-guided surface-to-air missile, with a range of twenty miles up to

50,000 feet and the larger but experimental Wasserfall as well as air-to-air missiles and air-to-ground radio-guided bombs. Finally, of course, from Peenemunde and elsewhere, the Soviet Union retrieved production model V2 weapons and details of the A9/10 two-stage transatlantic rocket project which were to accelerate considerably Soviet surface-to-surface missile development, just as the other acquisitions were to benefit airframes and engines.

THEORY AND PRACTICE

The first priority, air defence, was urgently pursued. By 1950 partial early warning radar coverage had been extended from the Baltic across the Continent to the Pacific coast and there seems to have been little controversy over its extension. German early warning Freya and Wurzburg apparatus, trained Luftwaffe operators and radar engineers from Siemens and Telefunken had been included in the 'reparations' package.[10] The practice, however, was not facilitated by the theory.

Stalin had good domestic and international reasons for publicly denigrating the impact of nuclear weapons on warfare: 'atomic bombs cannot decide the outcome of a war',[11] and for suggesting that 'surprise' had been only a temporary factor in strategy. In the face of US atomic superiority, but possessing a large land force, he advised his generals that the 'permanently operating factors' in warfare were stability of the rear, morale of the Army, quantity and quality of divisions, armaments, organising ability of commanders and adequate reserves.[12] He was subsequently criticised for stultifying debate on strategic issues but, nevertheless, he took a personal interest in ensuring that practice would be rather different.

Active air defence of the country would for several years depend heavily on the manned interceptor. At first, Stalin ordered concentration on the proven piston-driven LA-11 rather than the complicated, jet-powered Mig-9[13] and indeed the unreliability and relatively low power of available jet engines justified his decision at that time. Moreover, he supported Yakovlev's argument not to produce the ME-262 but rather to develop new Russian aircraft.[14] Not only was the 262 a complex aircraft which presented handling problems, but production would have absorbed too many resources to the detriment of future indigenous development. Yakovlev's arguments may have had more than a tinge of self-interest but they do, nevertheless, offer a sharp insight to the limitations of the Soviet aviation industry in 1946. In the event, two jet

fighters were built: the Yak-15 and the Mig-9; both used engines of
German origin and both flew for the first time on 24 April 1946, which
was an astonishingly short time after the acquisition of the engines.
Stalin summoned both designers to the Kremlin the following day and
instructed them to build fifteen of each in time to fly over Red Square on
7 November.[15] The aircraft were produced on time, and only bad
weather caused their public appearance to be postponed until the
following May Day parade. This was the first occasion when Soviet air
power was deliberately revealed to the world; not of course as a total of
thirty aircraft, the product of desperately stretched resources, but as a
symbol of the might of the air defence forces of the Soviet Union.

Later that year, Soviet air power did in fact take a major step forward,
thanks to British industry. Twenty-five Rolls Royce Nene and thirty
Derwent V engines were supplied to the Soviet Union. The Nene became
the RD-45 and was fitted to the new swept-wing product of the
Mikoyan/Gurevich design bureau: the Mig-15, which first flew on 30
December 1947 and which appeared publicly at Tushino airfield
Moscow on Soviet Aviation Day the following July. The original 5,000 lb
thrust of the Nene was later developed by Soviet engine designer,
Klimov to 6,615 lb and as the Mig-15 *bis*, it surprised United Nations
pilots in Korea in November 1950. After the radars and the interceptors
the third element in the air defence system was established when in 1948
the PVO: Soviet Air Defence[16] was established as a separate force co-
equal with ground, air and naval forces. It had responsibility for all
aspects of air defence: radar, surface-to-air and air-to-air. Until 1981
it remained separate from other air arms with its own academies,
training programmes, promotion patterns, aircraft and organisation.

Although improvements to PVO would steadily continue, its equipment was superior to that produced to achieve the second priority: the
long-range bombardment capability. Long-range Soviet military aviation (LRA)[17] had had a chequered history. The four-engined Il'ya
Murometz of the First World War and the TB-3 bomber of the 1930s
had been superior to their foreign contemporaries, but the proponents
of LRA received a severe setback with the execution of Tukhachevsky,
Khripin, Lapchinsky and others in the purges. Thereafter, as has been
noted, LRA played little independent part in the Second World War and
indeed 'the possibilities of bombers were underestimated and insufficient attention devoted to their construction'.[18] This was, in fact, a
considerable understatement. Between 1941 and 1945 bombing operations were carried out almost entirely by twin-engined medium-range
aircraft and numbers of the four-engined Petlyakov PE-8 never

exceeded seventy-nine. Indeed, they had all been built before the war, were rapidly obsolete, and even when modified with uprated engines in 1943 only reached a maximum speed of 280 mph. Although ultimately possessing a nominal range of 3,600 miles with an 8,000 lb bombload, their operational radius in practice seldom seems to have exceeded 700 miles.[19] Consequently, there was virtually no heavy bomber operational and industrial experience on which to build a post-war long-range force which could compare with the aircraft already in service with Bomber Command and USAAC.

Again, however, foreign expertise became available. Two USAAC B-29s which had force-landed in the Soviet Far East, in August and November 1944, were dismantled and swiftly copied by the Tupolev Bureau at Kazan. The most modern US engines, navigation aids, weapon control systems and other associated avionic and airframe components thus became instantly available. Entering squadron service in 1947 over 1,000 'TU-4s' were subsequently built and although their American cousins were proved vulnerable and obsolescent in the Korean war, their contribution to the development of Soviet long-range aviation is difficult to overemphasise. Moreover, in April 1946, the Soviet Union removed Dal'nyaya aviatsiya from its subservience to Army control, re-establishing its 'independent' status within the SAF, one year before the USAAC was similarly emancipated from the US Army.

Even so, as in fighter production, Soviet jet bomber development was at first impeded by lack of powerful jet engines. A prototype Ilyushin four-engined jet bomber flew in 1947 but could achieve only a range of 1,200 miles at 450 mph and never went into production. The medium range IL-28, on the other hand, powered by engines developed from the Nene, was successful and became the standard medium-range bomber of the Soviet Union, her allies and favoured customers for the next twenty years.

Nevertheless, Stalin's second priority had not been met and in 1949 he ordered the establishment of a new design bureau at Fili under VM Myasischev, to produce a bomber with a range of 9,940 miles to reach and return from the US. The four-jet Mya-4, 'Molot', flew in 1953 and entered squadron service the following year, but it lacked the power to produce the required range, achieving less than 6,000 miles. It was subsequently severely criticised by Mr Khrushchev[20] for its inadequacies and the fact that it killed several test pilots. Although not scrapped as he claimed, the M-4B Bison[21] was never produced in the numbers expected by the West.

Also built to the 1949 long-range bomber specification was a further product from Tupolev at Kazan: the TU-20(TU-95). This aircraft, which made its first public appearance at Tushino in 1955, was powered by four turbo-prop engines and did possess the necessary range to reach the US and return but only with a maximum speed of about 500 mph with a 25,000 lb bombload. It, too, was criticised by Khrushchev on the grounds that its speed and altitude made it too vulnerable to USAF defences and, therefore, it 'could not be used as strategic bomber'.[22]

That, however, was not the perception in the US at the time. The Soviet Union had exploded the atomic bomb in 1949 and the thermonuclear one, well ahead of the date expected by Western scientists, in 1953. Soviet publicity given to the M-4 and TU-20 assiduously emphasised their range and naturally enough omitted to mention handling, operational and industrial limitations. Meanwhile, new air bases were constructed in Soviet Arctic territories. Consequently, while a strong body of opinion in the US continued to stress the importance of a nuclear retaliatory capability, it was considered prudent to invest in an extensive air defence system of early warning radars, interceptors and command and control.[23]

THE KHRUSHCHEV INHERITANCE

Thus, in 1955, Khrushchev inherited Air Forces which were respected in the West far more than could have been envisaged ten years previously. The skill and ultimate potential of Soviet designers and engineers had been considerably enhanced as a result of British private enterprise and US military misfortune, which gave Soviet fighter and bomber development an unexpected acceleration. In particular, the Mig-15 fighter and the successors, the Mig-17 and 19, seemed comparable with their Western contemporaries, despite limitations of range, avionics and all-weather performance.

But elsewhere there were serious deficiencies. The only specialist ground support aircraft, for example, remained the Second World War IL-10 derivative from the IL-2 Shturmovik. It was supplemented by the IL-28 medium bomber and the fighter/ground attack Mig-19 but a post-war specialist replacement was still several years away. Transport aviation depended on modified bombers or on medium-range twin-engined aircraft such as the IL-14 or Yak-16. Naval aviation was being expanded and re-equipped but still lacked modern maritime attack and reconnaissance aircraft. Even the bombers had not met their specification: 'the range requirements set by our military planners for a strategic bomber were beyond the reach of our technological capability', was the blunt assessment by Mr Khrushchev.[24]

Khrushchev, however, was not necessarily an objective commentator on the merits of a manned bomber when compared to other methods of waging war. In 1955 there was no Soviet doubt about the significance of the long-range bomber with a large operational radius and an ability to destroy 'important strategic targets in the deep rear'.[25] Only six years previously reference to a strategic role for aviation had still to be expressed in traditional terms of support of the surface forces:

> One of the most important tasks of aviation is active assistance to the ground and naval forces in all forms of their combat activity [but it is] not contradicted by the need to employ part of its forces to strike the deep rear of the enemy on his military industrial targets . . . but such blows are not an end in themselves, only a helpful means of creating favourable conditions . . . for combat operations of ground and naval forces.[26]

But at the 20th Party Congress in February 1956 Marshal Zhukov asserted that 'in the composition of our Armed Forces, the relative weight of the Air Forces and Air Defence Forces have significantly grown', and 'the task of defence of the rear of the country has never loomed so large as under contemporary conditions'.[27] Indeed, in general, the mid-1950s was a period of SAF self-assertion; but other factors were already at work to challenge it.

DEBATE AND DISSENSION

For several reasons, long-range bombardment did not become the major issue in the SAF that it has frequently been in the US. First, as has been noted, there was not the organisational or operational experience on which to build a pressure group: long-range bombardment had simply never achieved a comparable status. Second, even if it had done so, there was clearly not the scope for public pressure that was projected by groups such as the Air Force Association in the US. But, most importantly, arguments in the later 1950s about the roles of military aviation were subsumed in the Soviet Union in the broader debate about the impact of nuclear weapons on traditional Marxist–Leninist theories of warfare and, by implication, their impact on the roles and organisation of traditional forces. Of those, LRA was but one, and despite the rhetoric, by no means the most influential.

Nevertheless, despite the absence of a public forum, there is no reason to doubt that various branches of the Soviet military sought to influence the debate. There is no need to look for personal ulterior motives, even though they might not always have been absent. A soldier who believes in the contribution of his arm to the nation's defence will argue it vehemently enough without necessarily thinking of career implications. As Khrushchev himself observed:

> In our country, of course, . . . we have no militaristic class as such. But our military puts similar pressure on our government . . . Soldiers will be soldiers. They always want a bigger and stronger army. They always insist on having the very latest weapons and on attaining quantitative as well as qualitative superiority over the enemy.[28]

Nor were weapon designers less persistent, according to Khrushchev's honourable exemption of Tupolev from such an attitude.[29] Moreover, if as it seems likely, Khrushchev owed his position to some extent to military support at a time when strategic debate was emerging from the stultifying effects of Stalinist dogma, it would be surprising had his defence policy deliberations not been made under strong military pressure.

Broadly, the debate divided those who believed nuclear missiles would dominate future warfare and those who argued that balanced forces would still be necessary. There was consensus that a war could be fought with nuclear weapons and that the nature of warfare would be changed by them; the question was, how far? The extreme case was presented by Khrushchev himself in a speech to the Supreme Soviet in January 1960. He reminded his audience of previous reductions in the size of the Soviet Armed Forces, proposed a further reduction of 1.2 million men out of a total Armed Forces complement of 4.5 million and observed:

> Given the present development of military technology, military aviation and the Navy have lost their former importance. This type of armament is not being reduced but replaced. Military aviation is being almost entirely replaced by rockets. We have now sharply reduced and probably will further reduce and even halt production of bombers and other obsolete equipment.[30]

Several factors had influenced that conclusion. First, there was the obvious evolution of Soviet missile capability, from tests of the V2 in the eastern Baltic in the late 1940s through the launching of Sputnik in 1957 to the construction of the first generation of medium- and long-range liquid-fuelled ballistic missiles, 'rattled' by Khrushchev during the Suez, Quemoy and Berlin crises of the late 1950s. This sequence had culminated in 1959 in the creation of a new arm, the Soviet Rocket Forces, which became independent in May 1960 and was quickly elevated to the position of senior Armed Service. Second, the reduced birthrate of the Second World War years was making itself felt by 1958. Shortage of industrial manpower has frequently been a Soviet problem and with Khrushchev's ambition to overtake capitalism in consumer production and standards of living, the appeal of a defence policy which freed more manpower for civilian employment obviously had an attraction. It may also have seemed no bad idea politically to reduce the Armed Forces' potential for domestic pressure. Militarily there was the precedent of the decision in 1954 by NATO to rely to a much greater extent on tactical nuclear weapons to counter Soviet conventional numerical superiority, thereby reducing the military value of those numbers.

Indeed, some Soviet officers did not believe the emphasis was strong enough. In 1958 or 1959, Khrushchev appears to have instigated a series of highly classified studies on the employment of nuclear weapons and missiles in future war. They included the assessments that long wars were more profitable to capitalists, that 'the new world must strive to keep war losses to a minimum . . . to keep war short (by swift use of nuclear weapons)' and that it was insufficient simply to modernise old arms: 'obviously we must go faster and further both in the theory of using nuclear missile weapons and in their production'.[31] Such debate apparently took place in secret sessions of the Central Committee of the Communist Party in 1959 and the emphasis was so strongly on nuclear missile attack that it prompted Penkovsky, at least, to believe that Khrushchev was preparing for a pre-emptive strike against the West.[32]

But however strong the influences in favour of missile predominance, the case for maintained conventional strength could not be overlooked. We now know that Soviet missile development did not proceed anything like so quickly as was feared in the West at the time. For example, not only were costs considerable, but there was a shortage of raw (fissionable) material which restricted simultaneous development of tactical and intercontinental missiles.[33] And whatever the speed of deployment, there were obvious limitations on missiles as instruments of day-to-day Soviet foreign policy. Whereas Stalin had been heavily preoccupied with events in Europe, and while succeeding Soviet governments have probably continued to believe that Eastern Europe is the most important security region, Khrushchev increasingly sought to extend Soviet power further across the world. He was ideologically committed to the support of revolution and spurred by the contemptuous rivalry of China, but inhibited by fears of nuclear escalation and particularly by his lack of conventional means. He could extend military assistance and arms sales to favoured clients, but it is also possible that he, and his military advisers, drew a common lesson from the Western military activities in Suez 1956, Lebanon and Jordan in 1958 and in Kuwait in 1961. Despite Khrushchev's bluster, the Soviet Union was impotent in each case although Western military operations were taking place less than 1,000 miles from Soviet territory and against the interests of countries he was seeking to befriend.

Within Russia itself, he faced opposition from within the Armed Forces. Cuts before 1960 seem to have been accepted, perhaps inevitably in the circumstances of a falling birth-rate which would naturally reduce conscription and its associated infrastructure. But the dangers and implications of missile emphasis caused extensive professional concern.[34] There was a strong attachment to conventional forces; for example in the artillery:

> we were carried away by missiles . . . we have ignored conventional artillery, which still exists in all our regiments and divisions and, therefore, because of these missiles, we are suffering shortages in the classic artillery arm. And, in general, because of these missiles, we are also short of other types of armament.[35]

And although the missiles were being brandished, the aircraft of LRA were still on regular airborne alert. From bases near Zhitomir and Lvov in the Ukraine, for example, they flew with atomic weapons 'in a westerly direction all the way to the border of the USSR'[36] and 'across Rumania and Bulgaria'.[37] Such activity symbolises the difference at this time between Soviet military theory and its practice. Moreover, one area of military activity which was not cut back was research and development.[38] The roots of conventional military expansion which took place in the mid and later 1960s lay not in the reaction to the Cuban debacle of October 1962, but in the five years preceding it. While the equipment was being prepared, its doctrinal environment was being constructed. Far from being eclipsed, air power was to be given wide-ranging responsibilities.

NUCLEAR PRE-EMINENCE

A landmark in the modification of Soviet military thought appeared in 1962 with the publication of Sokolovsky's *Military Strategy*.[39] The book was given great prominence in the Soviet Union and in the West, where commentators observed that the views were a reliable indication of Soviet thought if not necessarily of all Soviet thought.[40] It was the work of fifteen senior officers and reflected a compromise between the emphasis of Khrushchev on the missile and its deterrent effect and those more traditionally minded officers who insisted that nuclear war simply demanded new concepts and modified organisation.

Sokolovsky therefore emphasised the prime importance of nuclear weapons, but not to the exclusion of the other arms. There were two reasons for this. First, that a war fought with nuclear weapons would also require conventional forces; and second, that not every war would necessarily be nuclear.

Military strategy under conditions of modern warfare becomes a strategy of deep nuclear missile strikes in conjunction with operations of all branches of the Armed Forces in order to inflict a simultaneous defeat and destruction of the enemy's economic potential and Armed Forces throughout the whole depth of his territory, for the accomplishment of the war aims within a short timespan.[41]

In other words, 'the annihilation of the enemy's Armed Forces, the destruction of objectives in the rear and disorganisation of the rear will be a single continuous process of the war'.[42] But, 'at the same time, the Armed Forces of the Socialist Camp must be prepared for small scale wars that could be unleashed by the Imperialists',[43] which could require different ways and means from world wars and which would need to be prevented from developing into world war. This view may be contrasted with the fear expressed by Penkovsky that Khrushchev regarded 'local wars as a prelude to a future "big" war, for which intensive preparations are being made'.[44]

The continuity of the argument that combined arms would be required in a nuclear environment goes back to the position taken by Marshal Zhukov five years previously when he had said that nuclear weapons and air power could not, by themselves, determine the outcome of an armed conflict. 'We are proceeding from the fact that victory in future war will be achieved only by the combined efforts of all arms of the Armed Forces and on the basis of their co-ordinated employment in war.'[45]

THE CONTRIBUTION OF AIR POWER

Thus, in 1962, it was envisaged that military aviation would be required to operate primarily in a nuclear environment: 'The basic weapons that will be used to solve the main problems of war on land, in the air, and at sea are nuclear weapons; therefore, they will primarily determine the development and construction of Armed Forces'.[46] Although ritual references were made to the likelihood of the US initiating nuclear warfare, as in the statement by General Power, Commander-in-Chief of SAC in May 1959 quoted by Sokolovsky, 'We must never find ourselves in a position where we are not free to start a war . . . we must have the ability to deliver the first blow . . .',[47] the question of first use is generally academic in Soviet writings.

   Against this background, Soviet ideas about the contribution of military aviation are quite explicit, covering all the traditional roles: air superiority, air defence, offensive support, reconnaissance, long-range bombardment, tactical mobility and naval aviation.

AIR DEFENCE

The concept of air supremacy was well rooted in Soviet Second World War experience, tending to be expressed in terms of 'local air superiority'. It had been a major task of the tactical air armies and had usually been sought by air-to-air combat, even though counter-air missions against airfields may have been more statistically successful: thirty sorties for each German aircraft destroyed in the air against five for each one on the ground.[48] Even during the period of the strategic bombardment debates in the mid-1950s the concept was not lost. Air supremacy was sought, 'not only to resolve the tasks of the Air Force, but above all to create favourable conditions for the operations of the ground forces and on the coastal sectors for the navy'.[49] Slowly, greater emphasis began to be placed on the counter-air element also. Partly because modern jet aircraft were becoming more dependent on long runways and complex support facilities, but primarily because of the increasing nuclear role of NATO European-based aircraft after 1954. Also because, at the end of the decade, new Soviet aircraft would be better equipped to attempt attacks on airfields.

As in the Second World War, air supremacy blended into the overall provision of air defence, through and beyond the armies' rear areas back into the heartland. Provision of defence by AA artillery had previously been very costly and not very effective: requiring 'between 400 and 600 shells to destroy each German plane'.[50] Now, however, 'modern air defence has become almost impenetrable to modern bombers', which 'can be shot down with a first or at most second missile'.[51]

Indeed, throughout the 1950s development of Soviet interceptors had continued. In 1955, the first of the 'second generation'[52] had appeared at Tushino: the Yak-25 twin-engine, two-seat, all-weather interceptor whose design and development between 1949 and 1951 had been personally hastened by Stalin.[53] In the following year three other supersonic types were revealed: the Mig-21 Fishbed, the SU-7 Fitter and the SU-9 Fishpot. Fishbed, a single-engined, high-altitude, single-seat day fighter was to be widely exported and subsequently modified many times over the next twenty years. The Sukhoi 7 Fitter, although of limited range, light weapon load and lacking all-weather capability, succeeded the Mig-19 in the dual fighter/ground attack role and could deliver either conventional or nuclear ordnance. Sukhoi 9 Fishpot had a similar role to that of the Yak-25 but with superior engines, airframe and radar. Appearance at Tushino, however, was an unreliable indicator of design progress because whereas Yak-25 had entered squadron service in 1954, Fishbed and Fitter did not do so until 1959 and Fishpot in 1961. In addition, a much longer-range interceptor, the Tupolev 28 Fiddler, first flew in 1957 and entered squadron service in 1962. It operated largely from north Russian airfields and, with an endurance in excess of three hours, seems to have been designed as a specific response to the threat from the B-52 carrying stand-off nuclear weapons. Indeed, it is reasonable to assume that the major impetus behind the development of the entire Soviet air defences, and in interceptors in particular, lay in the actual or expected development of Western offensive aircraft. In 1961, for example, the Soviet Union seems to have expected that both the USAF B-70 and the RAF TSR-2 would enter squadron service.[54]

The second element in the air defence system, the SAM, had progressed more slowly, reflecting perhaps the need of the Soviet Union in 1945 to build a guided missile industry from virtually nothing. By 1954, rudimentary SAMs, descendants of Schmetterling and Wasserfall, were deployed but it was not until May 1960 that their full potential was revealed to the West. On 1 May, Gary Powers' U-2 high-altitude reconnaissance aircraft, on a regular flight from Peshawar in Pakistan to Bodö in northern Norway, was shot down by a SA-2 near Sverdlovsk in the Ukraine. Not surprisingly, the dramatic event was well publicised from Moscow and certainly seemed to foreshadow the demise of the manned bomber. But, in fact, the Soviet Union was far from making her airspace 'impenetrable' as Sokolovsky claimed, and certainly not automatically to the 'first or second' missile launch.

Deployment of a second SAM system had been reported in the West in 1957. We now know that it was the SA-2 'Guideline' with a radar-guided high-altitude reach in excess of 70,000 feet. We also know that at the time it was far from the efficient weapon implied by Sokolovsky. On 1 May Colonel Oleg Penkovsky was duty officer at the Chief Directorate of Intelligence of the Soviet General Staff (GRU) in Moscow and quickly received the details of the interception. 'They wanted to fire when the aircraft from Turkey flew over Kiev, but there was nothing to fire with and the aircraft escaped. Powers would have escaped if he had flown a mile or so to the right of his flight path.'[55] The implications of very restricted resources and indeed of the limits of a static SAM system are quite clear but, in addition, in this very first confrontation between SAM and aircraft, two other difficulties immediately emerged. It was not the first or second missile which brought down the U-2, but one of fourteen. Moreover, another hit and destroyed a Mig-19 attempting to intercept. Problems of aerospace management had received a sudden complication, while provision of adequate missile stocks in the right defensive area would be much more difficult in practice than in theory. Nevertheless, air power generally received a nasty jolt on May Day 1960 and the air defences of the Soviet Union in particular seemed to have been considerably enhanced. Continued heavy Soviet investment in SAM systems would not only improve the air defences still further, but would have a significant impact on her offensive capability also.

OFFENSIVE SUPPORT

Tactical offensive aviation had been relegated in priority to air defence and LRA since 1945. Despite its considerable contribution in the Second World War it had remained completely subordinate to the ground forces. The phraseology used in its description illustrates very sharply its different status from the tactical air forces of the West. For example, 'In land theatres, the mission of armed combat will be accomplished primarily by offence. But this will be done by the ground forces, including tactical aviation . . .',[56] or 'The Socialist countries have at their disposal ground troops equipped with nuclear weapons, tanks, front line aviation and other new military equipment and arms.'[57] Moreover, Western analysts agreed that by the early 1960s the strength of Soviet tactical aviation had been reduced by over 50 per cent[58] or even more from some 10,000 to 4,000 aircraft.[59] This was perhaps partly due to the withdrawal of the IL-10 and later, the IL-28 and to Khrushchev's increasing reliance on short and medium long-range missiles for nuclear weapon delivery.

Nevertheless, the theoretical roles of offensive support did not change much in the same period. The emphasis was on conventional capabilities within an overall nuclear posture: to support troops in the field of battle and to employ 'sweep tactics against the enemy's means of nuclear attack', to disorganise it and reduce the effectiveness, if not 'frustrate' it altogether.[60] Tactical air power was considered particularly effective for attacking mobile targets: tanks and troops on the march, mobile nuclear weapons, mobile command and control units and various kinds of troop and logistic concentrations.

Theory tended to reflect the limited capability of the existing equipment, for example the short-range SU-7, but also looked forward to a greater contribution from more advanced aircraft including those able to take off vertically.[61] The Royal Air Force VTOL Kestrel had flown in 1960 and the three Soviet VTOL aircraft which were to appear at Domodedovo in 1967 would almost certainly have been in the design stage and probably known to Sokolovsky. Soviet concepts of battle during the period stress high-speed offensive operations with nuclear attack either present or imminent. There would, therefore, tend to be 'a broken front, porous war, uneven development of the front, or simply the absence of a well defined forward edge of the battlefield'.[62] Almost in Second World War style, 'aviation escort of ground troops' meant rapid response to requests from advancing forces and particularly from those which might be outrunning the main ground force support of artillery and reserves.

RECONNAISSANCE

Such a fluid environment, threatened or already engulfed by nuclear weapons, required extensive and timely knowledge of events on 'the other side of the hill'. Aerial reconnaissance was essential for several specific reasons. First, ground force commanders needed to know the location of lightly defended or lightly occupied areas which could be swiftly penetrated in depth. Second, the position of every nuclear weapon needed to be accurately fixed and a new customer for the information, the Rocket Troops, had appeared. Third, traditional information was required on troop movements, concentrations and associated equipment. Finally, post-attack details would be required: the extent of damage, levels of radioactivity, and direction of tank retreats and pursuit. As with other air forces, tactical reconnaissance aircraft tended to be variants of interceptor models, eg, the Mig-21 and Yak-28 which entered service in 1962. Indeed, further development of the Yak-28 might have been foreshadowed by observations about the increasing importance of electronic warfare, not just in reconnaissance, but throughout the entire tactical aviation environment. Indeed, by 1960, the Soviet Union considered the development of electronic warfare equipment to be as important as the development of nuclear missiles.[63]

BOMBER DEVELOPMENT

While the need for reconnaissance was indubitable at the turn of the decade, the function of the long-range bomber was rather more ambivalent. On the one hand, it was clearly becoming more vulnerable to air defences and was 'quickly giving way to ICBMs and IRBMs. Tactical bombers are gradually being replaced by missiles'.[64] But the same author also wrote that 'Missile carrying aircraft are being used more and more; they are able to inflict upon an aggressor widely spaced missile attacks over long ranges without entering the air defence zone',[65] and because rockets and bombers would be used simultaneously, 'it is all the more likely that aviation has not lost its combat potential'.[66] Indeed, it was argued that the manned bomber was particularly well suited for specific missions such as following up missile attacks and destroying mobile or insufficiently reconnoitred targets. Even Mr Khrushchev, despite his advocacy of missiles, authorised Tupolev to carry out research into an atomic-powered bomber.[67] Perhaps such decisions were additional insurance against lack of development potential of contemporary ICBMs which were very expensive, complex, liquid-fuelled and relatively vulnerable. Their relative costs, however, perhaps depended on the political and military interests of the assessors. For example, Marshal Zhigarev, Khrushchev's Commander-in-Chief of the

SAF is alleged to have said in 1955 that missiles were cheaper, easier to build, smaller, required less logistic support, were easier concealed and were less vulnerable to air attack.[68] But 10 years later, after Khrushchev's disgrace, another eminent soldier could write that 'The production of nuclear missile weapons requires greater budgetary appropriations for the solution of complex laboratory design problems',[69] with a detrimental effect on conventional weapons development which receives a 'considerably lesser amount of materials and fuel as a whole'.[70]

However, development of the manned bomber did continue. In 1961 the Tupolev-22 'Blinder' appeared at Tushino. The twin-jet bomber had a range of some 1,400 miles, maximum speed of 1.5 Mach and, significantly, one of the ten aircraft in the fly-past carried an air-to-surface stand-off missile. This combination of bomber and missile corresponded exactly to the theory of the time.

TACTICAL MOBILITY

Through the bomber, Soviet air power could be applied directly; but it could also be distributed indirectly by providing additional mobility and speed to ground forces. Until the purges of 1937 and 1938 the Soviet Union had steadily increased its allocation of resources to airborne forces. Large-scale exercises were held, for example in 1935 when a fully equipped rifle division of 14,000 men was transported from Moscow to Vladivostok. In the same period parachute troops were trained for reconnaissance and sabotage operations behind enemy lines. Although the execution of Tukhachevsky and his colleagues, including K. A. Kalin the leading transport aircraft designer, checked the development of airborne forces they were used against the Finns in 1939 and later in 1942 and 1943 against the Germans. They also contributed consistently to the Soviet partisan campaigns behind German lines. However, they fought more often as ground troops, primarily because there was neither the quantity nor size of transport aircraft available for them but also because the Soviet High Command could not afford to have large numbers of elite troops inactive for long periods between airborne operations.

Air transport of men and supplies was also handicapped by lack of suitable aircraft as well as by the absence of any centralised organisation. Consequently, despite massive operations such as the reinforcement and resupply of the Stalingrad garrison the role of military air transport was not regarded with the same satisfaction as some of the others; for example 'a weak aspect of the Soviet Air Forces [which had] a negative effect on the use of airborne troops as well as on the organisation of the air supply of rapidly advancing forces'.[71]

After the Second World War air transport was low on the list of military aviation priorities, even after the formation of the Soviet Transport Command, known as Voenno-transportnaya-aviatsiya (VTA). Until 1956 it relied heavily on twin-engined medium-range piston aircraft such as the LI-2 adaptation of the US C-47, the IL-12 and the IL-14. But as more resources became available, so production of larger aircraft could expand. In 1956 the twin turbo-prop Antonov 8 'Camp' entered service and was followed in 1959 by the four-engined AN-12 'Cub' which, with a range of 2,200 miles carrying 45,000 lb of payload, may be compared to the Lockheed C-130 Hercules. Several hundred Cubs entered service with VTA and were to confer upon the SAF a much longer reach.

Meanwhile, helicopter production facilitated the distribution of small numbers of troops to or behind enemy positions. The Mil-4 'Hound' produced in 1952 could carry twelve soldiers for 370 miles at 130 knots. Its descendant, the MI-8 'Hip', first shown at Tushino in 1961, had a similar maximum speed but could carry four tons of freight or combinations of troops and air-to-surface weapons. Tactical heavy-lift mobility was provided by the Mil-6 'Hook' which entered service in 1957 and could lift up to ten tons of equipment.

Not everyone, however, was happy about their airworthiness and Mr Khrushchev himself was warned against flying in Soviet-built machines in 1959.[72] Nevertheless, the equipment was to hand and the ideas to go with it. The combination of long-range fixed-wing transports and tactical helicopters made possible airborne operations whose tasks 'include the independent capture, retention or destruction of missile, air and naval bases and other important objectives in the rear of combat theatres',[73] rather than defeating enemy ground forces; while the result of massed nuclear strikes could best be exploited by helicopters landing tactical airborne troops.[74]

Moreover, although not strictly part of military aviation, the Soviet civilian fleet was also expanded during the period of the strategic debate. Aeroflot had, since 1945, been commanded by senior SAF officers and its aircraft provided an immediate reserve to those of VTA. Consequently, the introduction into civilian service of the four-engined IL-18, TU-114, TU-104 and IL-62 even further enhanced the potential of Soviet military airlift.

NAVAL AVIATION

There was not the same continuity in naval aviation theory and practice during the debate which marked the other roles of air power. Just as the naval surface units had tended to be of 'white water' character so Naval Air Force operations had been essentially coastal. It had begun to receive more modern aircraft as early as 1951, first with the twin-jet TU-14 and, subsequently, with the Mig-15 and IL-28. The TU-14 flew only with Naval Air Forces but that might have been a result of its inferior performance rather than a deliberate policy of producing an aircraft specifically for the Navy. In any event, the roles of coastal air defence, anti-surface shipping, mining and reconnaissance differed little from those of the Second World War. But then, in the later 1950s, two factors brought about a major change in role.

First was the threat posed to the Soviet heartland by the US Navy's strike carriers with their nuclear-capable aircraft, and by the US Navy submarine-launched ballistic missile force. It was considered essential that the majority of long-range aviation assets, both naval and LRA, should be used against these targets at a range beyond aircraft or missile launch point.[75] Second was the expansion of, and increased emphasis on, the Soviet's own submarine force from 1953 onwards which demanded longer-range reconnaissance and communication co-operation. Consequently, although destruction of enemy transportation and coastal targets remained a requirement[76] the NAF began to range much further away from Soviet coasts. The TU-16 'Badger', the M-4 'Bison', TU-20 'Bear'[77] and the TU-22 'Blinder' all appeared with NAF to fill one or other of these requirements. Meanwhile, the Beriev Bureau unveiled at the 1961 Tushino display a twin turbo-prop amphibian, the BE-12 'Gull' (NATO 'Mail') with a combat radius of some 1,000 miles in the anti-submarine and anti-surface shipping roles. At that same display at least three different types of long range air-to-surface missiles were observed, all of which would be developed for use against surface shipping.

THE KHRUSHCHEV DENOUEMENT

From the year of the Tushino air display to the downfall of Khrushchev in October 1964 the arguments of the 'all arms' proponents steadily gained in strength against those who, like Khruschev himself, wished to place greater emphasis on the deterrent effect of the combination of missile and nuclear weapon.

There was perceptibly a credibility gap between Khrushchev's declaratory policy and the ability of the Soviet Union to sustain it. A more realistic appraisal of Soviet missile development had been made by the J. F. Kennedy government, and in the Kuwait and Berlin crises of 1961 the Soviet military options were extremely limited. The humiliation in Cuba the following year was dramatic and seems to have contributed to Khrushchev's personal downfall, but to the Soviet marshals it must have been also the latest in a series of incidents which confirmed their belief in the need for strong conventional forces in all arms.

There seems also to have been reaction to the adoption by the US of the strategy of flexible response in 1961. A clue to such an attitude may lie in Sokolovsky's long analysis of the US shift.[78] After the standard reference to the inability of bourgeois military thought to cope with major strategic problems, and before concluding with an appreciation of all those who condemn the American aggressors and support the Soviet government's proposals for the attainment of peace on earth, he grudgingly acknowledged that 'The vast scientific and technical progress taking place in the main capitalist countries to a certain extent facilitates the development of military strategy in accordance with the changing conditions of war.'[79] Such an observation would not be lost on his audience, who would thereby be encouraged to draw their own conclusions 'in accordance with the changing conditions of war'.

Nor were conditions changing only in warfare. The international political map was rapidly changing colour as the European empires either disintegrated or were dismantled at the beginning of the decade. Opportunities for making and assisting new friends increased. Soviet arms sales reached 3 billion dollars by 1964[80] including Mig-21s, TU-16s and SAM-2s to Egypt. Military aid programmes began to give military personnel wider overseas experience. With influence came the opportunity to secure facilities and other favourable agreements which, in turn, encouraged the practice of longer-range airlift and ultimately the spread of further influence. The fact that Soviet diplomacy and political objectives were occasionally self-defeating, as in Guinea, should not be allowed to obscure this first flexing of long-distance Soviet military muscle. The assumption of position as protector of Cuba and the desire to counter Chinese rivalry provided good specific reasons for expansion of conventional reach in both directions. But despite the pressure from the marshals, despite the strength of the research and development programme, there were extensive and palpable deficiencies beneath the pretensions of the superpower.

THE BREZHNEV INHERITANCE

As usual, however, the Soviet leadership took care to ensure that only the strength was visible. The Soviet space programme, the extensive ground force re-equipment of the Warsaw Pact forces, the overseas activities in Egypt, Iraq, Indonesia and, apparently, in India, the steadily expanding national economic base and the greatly improved air defences all contributed to the image. Nor was the strength by any means simply illusory. Of particular importance for air power was the continued deployment of surface-to-air missiles and AA air defences both in the forward Warsaw Pact area and in the Soviet Union itself. Quite apart from strengthening the defence, the deployment began to free Soviet fighter aircraft for other roles.

But if, as seems likely, there is in the Soviet government a continuing consensus that the country must rely entirely on its own resources for its security; that it cannot depend on bilateral agreements with the capitalists nor on international treaties, no matter what its declaratory policy, then much remained to be done in 1965.[81]

There was certainly unanimity over the view that 'Strategic defence and defensive strategy should be decisively rejected as being extremely dangerous to the country',[82] but air power, for example, still lacked offensive reach and impact. Tactically, aircraft like the SU-7 Fitter or Mig-21 Fishbed could present little threat to NATO rear areas in conventional warfare. They were limited in range, in payload, in all-weather navigation and target-finding equipment. While tactical mobility had been considerably enhanced by the production of the AN-12 it was still only a medium-range transport, it lacked a pressurised freight or passenger compartment and its long-range deployment depended on facilities at foreign airfields. The value of long-range bombardment had been emphasised in theory, but by 1965 no Soviet heavy bomber had been put into large-scale production in the role for which it was designed.

Moreover, there had been major omissions in the construction of the theory itself. It had concentrated on war between the central powers in either an actual or imminent nuclear environment. While acknowledging the likelihood of 'local wars' it had assumed that they also would involve a central power confrontation. But nowhere did Sokolovsky, for example, refer to the traditional use of the threat of force as an instrument of policy, except implicitly in reference to the deterrent element of Soviet nuclear weapons. Doctrine was preoccupied with the war-fighting aspects of military force. The ability of conventional arms to deter by their own presence or imminence was neglected. Consequently, when nuclear deterrence only deterred nuclear activity, there was insufficient equipment and doctrine to cope with other conventional pressures.

Moreover, whether military force was to be applied in an intensive nuclear environment or over longer conventional periods and distances, command and control would obviously be as important as ever, but much more difficult to maintain. The importance of centralised command of air power had been realised in 1942 when command of tactical aviation was elevated from Army level to Front with the STAVKA (Supreme High Command) exercising overall control. Far from inhibiting flexibility, such control enhanced concentrated support for ground forces at decisive points and times. In 1965 problems of command and control had begun to be identified and remedial action begun, but the necessary equipment was not yet in service. To a country whose basic military security rested on an ability to fight and win a nuclear war, such a deficiency was extremely serious.

THE RESURGENCE OF OFFENSIVE AIR

Since the mid-1960s the military strength of the Soviet Union has increased dramatically in all arms, from ICBMs to conventional tactical weaponry.[83] When the outcome of the doctrinal debates, the provision for research development and the international challenges and opportunities of the later Khrushchev period are summarised, there is little need to look for new factors after his demise except for a naturally increasing confidence among his doctrinal critics.

Less than three years later a new 'third generation' of Soviet aircraft began to appear. But the production of several different types did not take place in weeks or months, as in 1945. Aircraft which flew publicly at the Soviet air display at Domodedovo in 1967 were not the product of a 'new look' in 1965, nor even necessarily the manifestation of a response to the Cuban debacle at the end of 1962. The development of this 'third generation' of Soviet aircraft may have been expedited by Brezhnev's regime, but bearing in mind lead time, production schedules, bureaucratic control and still not unlimited industrial facilities, not a great deal of acceleration could have taken place between 1964 and 1967. Subsequently, however, there has been a dramatic shift in Soviet budgetary provision for defence of which air power has been the main beneficiary. 'Between 1967 and 1977, "spending for the Air Force

increased more rapidly than spending for any other military Service",
and grew at over 3 times the rate for defence spending as a whole from
1969 to 1973.'[84] Whereas the previous priorities in air power had been
first for air defence and then to long-range aviation, now the major
recipients were the tactical air armies of Frontal Aviation (FA). 'Of the
total spending for the Air Force between 1967 and 1977, the largest
increase by far was for Frontal Aviation, which increased by about 50 %
its inventory of tactical aircraft over this period.'[85] Moreover, whereas
the primary contribution to FA of earlier post-war aircraft had been
largely defensive, with only limited offensive capability, the new aircraft
were to contribute to a much more effective offensive posture.

It must be remembered, however, that this was not a new departure
for the aircraft of FA. It did not mark a radical change in the traditional
attitudes of the SAF. But it did mark the opportunity for the first time in
over twenty years, to return to the traditions of the Second World War;
traditions which had been kept alive throughout the lean years of the
Soviet aviation industry and throughout the Khrushchev debates.

Details of the 'third generation' aircraft have been well documented in
the Western press.[86] They include the Sukhoi SU-17, Fitter 'C' which
was basically the SU-7 modified by a variable-geometry outboard wing
section, a much more powerful engine and greatly improved avionics
which together approximately doubled its range and payload. SU-17
was later further modified to the mark of Fitter 'D' with enhanced
navigational and weapon accuracy. In the similar period the original
Mig-21 Fishbed clear-weather short-range fighter was given a ground
attack role with improved engines, avionics and weapon systems. But
perhaps the most significant introduction was the family of the
Mig-23/27: also first shown publicly in 1967.[87] From the aircraft first
observed at Domodovodo four similar, but operationally distinctive,
models have been developed. Floggers 'B', 'G' and the export version 'E'
are all-weather fighters with a variable-geometry wing which permits
them to operate with greater effectiveness either as a high-level
interceptor or in the air superiority role at lower altitudes. The 'High
Lark' radar fitted in Flogger 'B' is believed to give it a limited ability to
engage targets below it and, unlike any of its predecessors, it can also
attack from a beam as well as head-on or from the rear. Its radar is
supplemented by infra-red target acquisition equipment which will aid
low-level detection in good weather. It normally carries four air-to-air
missiles: two long-range Apex with either infra-red or radar guidance,
and two short-range Aphids with infra-red warheads. Both these
missiles have greater manoeuvrability and are better suited to low-level

operations than their predecessors. In addition, Flogger carries a fuselage-mounted double-barrelled 23 mm cannon. In common with its contemporaries it is fitted with a receiver to give warning of hostile radar emissions. Flogger 'C' is a two-seat model for conversion and operational training at home and as an export model and, therefore, although resembling the Flogger 'B', its radar and other avionics equipment is probably inferior to the primary interceptor.

Flogger 'D', also labelled Mig-27, is in many respects a very different aeroplane. It is the first Soviet aircraft since the piston-driven IL-10 to be designed and enter production for the specialist ground attack role. It is equipped with laser rangefinder and computerised navigation/attack system. It has a rapid-fire six-barrelled 23 mm Gatling gun and can carry a large variety of conventional and nuclear ordnance. Its cockpit has additional armour-plate protection and the undercarriage is fitted with large low-pressure tyres to facilitate operations away from conventional runways.

The fourth model, Flogger 'F', is rather more of a hybrid. It carries the engine and greater part of the Flogger 'B' airframe but from the cockpit forward it resembles the Flogger 'D' and is also equipped with laser rangefinder and marked target-seeker, terrain-avoidance radar and a cockpit shape designed to improve the pilot's downward vision. It seems, therefore, to be a genuinely multi-role aircraft designed to fly and fight in a ground support environment.

It is significant that despite the considerable increase in Soviet SAM defences over both the Warsaw Pact armies and the homelands, there was still considered to be a demand for a manned interceptor and air superiority fighter. Part of the explanation was given at the time that Flogger 'B' was still being developed:

> A special role belongs to aviation, which will be the main long-range means in these (conventional) conditions. Aircraft are capable of destroying operational–tactical type missiles, as well as aircraft on the airfields and in the air. However, in order to carry out those missions the aircraft must overcome very strong air defences on the opposing side. To suppress it in conditions where nuclear weapons are not used, the aircraft must allocate a large portion of their forces.[88]

This was a concept of air superiority over the enemy's territory which could not be guaranteed by the SAMs protecting one's own forces and rear areas. Moreover, the effectiveness of SAM defences in Sinai and in Golan in 1973 must have been closely analysed and the differences noted between the impact of the carefully integrated static system and that of the much less co-ordinated mobile units, especially in Sinai.

Nevertheless, the presence of the multiple SAM and AA artillery umbrella over the Warsaw Pact forces and rear areas did mean that more Mig-21s could be adapted for the ground attack role and more multi-role Floggers could be similarly employed. Together, this marked a decisive shift in the contribution of FA from local air superiority to much more offensive activities. Indeed, as greater emphasis continued to be placed on conventional warfare, so greater emphasis was placed on the contribution of tactical aviation to it. For example, in a conventional phase tactical aviation could be given targets such as airfields or known reserve concentrations which would otherwise have been targets for the rocket forces. Attacks on nuclear targets would be especially important when the ground forces launched a main conventional attack against a weakly defended area or position, because NATO doctrine was interpreted to mean that at such times the Western alliance was likely to resort to a nuclear response. Such philosophy continued the change in emphasis which had occurred during the Khrushchev debate of a move away from the very close air support of the Second World War to the wider and deeper operations required in both nuclear and conventional environments. The two were regarded as complementary; there was no suggestion that conventional warfare had now replaced the nuclear environment. Offensive tactical air power would best be used against land-based mobile targets, and nuclear weapons were held to be particularly appropriate for use against tanks both on the line of march and in concentration, 'This guarantees effective and efficient use of nuclear weapons and affords the opportunity to strike at the most appropriate spot at the proper time.'[89] Thus, demands on tactical aviation would be considerable in either nuclear or conventional scenarios: air superiority, indirect support by deeper attacks and when the rapidly advancing armour outran its indigenous ground fire support, air-delivered firepower.

The potential offensive reach of FA was extended still further by the advent of the Sukhoi 24 Fencer. Entering squadron service in 1974, the twin-engined two-seat light bomber resembles the USAF F-111 in shape and size, and also carries a specialist weapons system operator whose presence suggests a complex avionics fit in the aeroplane which could confer all-weather navigational and attack accuracy greater than hitherto possessed by other aircraft in FA. Operating from bases in western Russia it could discharge the offensive responsibilities of tactical aviation in and beyond a land battle in central Europe. If it were to be deployed forward to bases in Poland or East Germany it could obviously extend its combat radius proportionately to attack deeper NATO reinforcement lines and bases throughout western Europe. By August 1980 it looked as if Fencer would become the mainstay of the light bomber force of FA.

There was in addition a further important newcomer to FA's offensive strength. The Mil-8 'Hip' helicopter which had appeared at Tushino in 1961 in Aeroflot colours reappeared at Domodedovo in 1967 in military aviation camouflage. That year Hips participated in Exercise Dnepr, not just to provide tactical mobility but close offensive support with guns and rockets. Since then, some 4,000 helicopters have been deployed with the SAF, largely with FA. The Mil-8 has been supplemented by the Mil-24 'Hind', now developed from its original form as an assault helicopter to a heavily armed and armoured gunship capable of discharging several offensive tasks.

The earlier assault responsibility continues to be very important. Helicopters would be expected to exploit and develop a successful nuclear attack by crossing contaminated ground and by penetrating swiftly into weakened rear areas. In conventional scenarios they would mount independent missions against anti-air defences, command and control points, nuclear weapons, important road junctions and river crossings. In more covert operations they would place 'diversionary forces' in political and military administrative centres, scatter agents for sabotage and place troops on air bases to seize them for subsequent use by regular airborne forces.

'Hip' and 'Hind' were always expected to be able to fight their way to their assault objectives, but Hind 'D' is now also regarded as a close air support anti-tank and even anti-helicopter weapon system. One Soviet report claimed that it was

> superior to other anti-tank weapons in terms of field of vision, manoeuvrability and firepower; and capable of hitting armoured enemy targets while remaining out of reach of anti-aircraft weapons. The correlation between tank and helicopter losses is 12–1 or even 19–1 in the helicopter's favour.[90]

It seems likely that Hind 'D' was developed after a close examination of helicopter operations in South-East Asia. Whereas the West has tended to be concerned about vulnerability, the SAF wished to exploit its meteorological flexibility and relatively low sortie attrition rate. It tends to be used in the short take-off rather than the vertical mode and, with an all-weather capability, infra-red sensors, infra-red emission control, heavy armour, four-barrelled Gatling gun and laser-guided anti-tank missiles it is a very formidable weapon system, provided that its tactical environment is appropriate for helicopter operations. For example, pre-positioned in the right place its relatively restricted range and top speed of 200 mph would not inhibit a major contribution to an offensive. If, on the other hand, it had to respond rapidly over a long distance to contribute to an urgent defensive, its utility would clearly be reduced. However, within the assumptions of Soviet offensive doctrine it considerably enhances the mobility and firepower of Warsaw Pact land forces.

Nor is its contribution restricted to the European environment. In 1981 it was widely reported and photographed in action in Afghanistan providing both mobility and firepower in terrain unsuited to traditional land operations. Yet, even there, its degree of vulnerability remained in doubt because while some press reports referred to its relative invulner-ability to groundfire, others stated that anti-aircraft weapons had been withdrawn by the Russians from their Afghanistan 'allies'.[91] There was a clear implication that the allies were not quite so fraternal as the Russians would have liked and that consequently the SAMs did present a threat to their own helicopters. Nevertheless, 'Hind' and 'Hip' were most valuable instruments of power well away from a central confron-tation and confirmed the views of those who had long maintained that 'local wars are fought as a rule with conventional arms'.[92]

The combination of helicopters, SU-17, Mig-23/27, SU-24 and uprated Mig-21 ensured that not only could the Soviet Union con-fidently consider conventional options in such local wars but that her capacity to attack was considerably greater than that enjoyed by Khrushchev. In the decade between 1967 and 1977 the numerical strength of FA grew by almost 50 per cent[93] and of the 4,000 or more front-line combat aircraft, 70 per cent had entered service after 1970.

Meanwhile, the striking power of long-range aviation and the NAF was also being increased by the entry into service of TU-26 (or as designated by the SAF, the TU-22M) a twin-engined variable-geometry medium-range bomber whose actual combat radius was still in dispute in 1980 but believed to be in the region of 2,500 miles. 'Backfire' was first observed at Kazan in 1970[94] and entered squadron service with LRA in 1974. Since then, it entered LRA and NAF squadrons evenly at the rate of approximately thirty-five a year. It was observed both with and without air-to-air refuelling probe and seemed designed to implement the bomber and naval aviation doctrine evolved in the Khrushchev period: to attack rear areas either as a supplement to nuclear missile strikes or, in conventional conflict, to destroy command and control centres, reinforcement concentrations, coastal targets and especially carrier groups beyond missile or aircraft release point. It could carry either conventional or nuclear weapons including the AS-4 Kitchen stand-off missile which could be launched more than 100 miles from its target. In fact, Backfire and her remaining modified older LRA colleagues, Bear, Badger and Bison prompted a nervous US observation in 1979 that

> There is increasing evidence that the Soviet bomber and cruise missile force may be overtaking their submarine force as a threat to our fleet and to our forces necessary for the resupply of Europe. They can concentrate aircraft, co-ordinate attacks with air, surface or submarine-launched missiles and use new technology to find our fleet units, jam our defences and screen their approach.[95]

DEFENSIVE REINFORCEMENT

Although Soviet priority in the decade after 1967 was given to offensive air power, steadily strengthening air defences were not neglected. SA-2 was supplemented by SA-3, 4, 5, 6, 7, 8 and 9 with SA-10 and 11's entry into service imminent. Defensive cover was drawn across Warsaw Pact forces in eastern Europe back into Russia, projecting with the now completed radar net and the manned interceptor force a complex challenge to any intruder. The Sukhoi 15 Flagon also appeared at Domodedovo in 1967. Single-seat, twin-engined and with all-weather capability it could fly higher, faster and further carrying superior weapons to its predecessors and by 1980 was the mainstay of PVO-Strany. Yet, paradoxically, it was a newcomer which had the least significance for Soviet air power which made the greatest initial impact: the Mig-25 Foxbat. Foxbat development would be well known by Sokolovsky and seems to have been designed as a counter to the then expected USAF B-70. It was the third new interceptor to appear at Domodedovo and later claimed a world altitude record of over 120,000 feet and a speed record over a closed circuit of 1,800 mph. It rapidly acquired a formidable reputation, assiduously cultivated for obvious political reasons by its Soviet sponsors. Only in 1976, when defector Lieutenant Belenko flew his aircraft to Hokodate, was the West able to make a thorough evaluation. It was, not surprisingly, a product of

Soviet technology of the early 1960s. It was built almost entirely of steel, with titanium only at high temperature points; it possessed no computerised avionics and depended for its efficiency on two extremely powerful engines which not only allowed it to climb very rapidly to a high altitude, but also generated the power for its Foxfire radar which had a range of some fifty miles and comparatively good anti-jamming qualities. With four long-range missiles it was clearly a high-altitude interceptor of considerable effectiveness but only against high-level intruders who would present no problems of identification. Foxbat, therefore, was a very effective weapon system but with a very restricted role compared, say, to the wide-ranging activities of Flogger 'B'.

On the other hand, a different development of Foxbat did become most important. The value of reconnaissance at all stages of conflict continued to be stressed in Soviet writing and Foxbat variants 'B' and 'D' were designed to carry it out. Capable of Mach 3, equipped with cameras, sideways-looking radar and more advanced navigation equipment, the later marks of Foxbat have considerably strengthened the reconnaissance capability of FA.

IMPACT ON MILITARY BALANCE

The tentative move by the Kennedy government away from dependence on nuclear strategy to more balanced forces was followed in 1967 by the adoption by NATO of the strategic posture known colloquially as 'flexible and appropriate response'.[96] It was an ironic coincidence that the same year saw the beginning of the major Soviet conventional expansion and re-equipment as the products of the research and development of the previous period emerged to match the modified theories of warfare. Marshal Jakubovskii, Commander-in-Chief of Warsaw Pact Forces, commented in 1967 that nuclear weapons should not be treated as absolutes and that it was a very good thing that Party and Government had improved 'the capability of the ground forces to conduct military operations successfully with or without the use of nuclear weapons'.[97]

Consequently, by 1980 the Western alliance not only faced Soviet strategic nuclear parity but superior numerical strength in tanks, armoured personnel carriers, manpower and artillery in all the main NATO regions.[98] Soviet land forces were trained for an offensive doctrine which called for surprise, rapid mobility and manoeuvre and large concentrations of strength with or without nuclear weapons.

Western response required a defence of territory as far east as possible but, because of local numerical inferiority and the almost certain concession of tactical initiative to the enemy, there was clearly a need for rapid reinforcement both from beyond the threatened region and tactically within it. Soviet incursion on land could only be halted by the combined land and air power of the West supported by heavy reinforcements which required precise and complete control. Yet the new Soviet offensive air power threatened the reinforcement routes, concentrations, command and control positions, airfields and air defence upon which NATO strategy depended, while the Alliance's own ability to disrupt and dislocate Soviet offensive action had been complicated by the continued expansion of Soviet air defences. Moreover, Soviet land forces were trained to mount continuous operations in all weathers. Hitherto, not only had their supporting tactical aircraft been limited in range and payload but also to operating in clear weather. SU-7, Mig-17, 19 or 21 had inadequate navigation and target acquisition equipment to allow them to fly and fight 'round the clock'. SU-17, Mig-27, SU-24 and, above all, Hind 'D' on the other hand, were all capable of supporting ground operations at night and in reduced daylight visibility.

Moreover, there is one further aspect of Soviet air power which is likely to complicate NATO's defensive strategy. For many years now the SAF have approached EW through a concept of Radio Electronic Combat Support (RECS) which, as an integral part of war-fighting, includes not only traditional activities such as ELINT or ECM but also active suppression and destruction of the enemy's radio and electronic equipment. To the SAF, therefore, EW is not a separate aspect of war and the air armies are equipped and train accordingly. In view of the implications for strategic and tactical surprise, Western official sources are justifiably tight-lipped about the details of Soviet RECS, but a reasonably reliable overall view can be gleaned from the open press and occasional guarded Congressional Committee reports.

As befits a Service which pays close attention to military history, the SAF has closely studied the activities of Bomber Command in the Second World War and RAF methods adopted and developed against the German night fighter force. Thus Soviet bombers could be expected to use self-screening devices such as CHAFF – the precisely cut threads of tinfoil once known in Bomber Command as 'Window' – to disguise the size of an incoming raid or even to suggest the presence of a raid when none exists. Photographs of Yak-28, Brewer E, available in the open press display aerials which suggest the presence of on-board active jamming equipment which presumably would be used to mask the transit of Flogger, Fitter and Fencer Squadrons and to jam Western air defence radars and communications.

Longer range early warning and surveillance radars are naturally vulnerable to longer range jamming which would almost certainly be provided by SAF aircraft, perhaps by modified AN-12 Cubs, standing back beyond Allied fighter combat radius. It is also reasonable to assume that the most modern SAF aircraft will, like their Western counterparts, carry integral or pod-mounted self-screening or weapon radar jamming equipment for use when directly threatened themselves. In other words, SAF has a capability to threaten active and passive jamming of Western defensive radar and communications over a wide proportion of the electromagnetic spectrum.

Nor is RECS only concerned with offensive operations. In the extensive Soviet military expansion and re-equipment of the 1970s, defensive RECS equipment has not been neglected. ECCM theory is naturally unclassified and, indeed, techniques are widely discussed in Western specialist journals. It is therefore possible to speculate that new Soviet communication systems have been duplicated and 'hardened' against Allied disruption while new radar systems are incorporating new improved methods of frequency diversity, side lobe suppression, moving target indication and height and azimuth location. In addition, active jamming and spoofing methods of interfering with Allied airborne radars and communications can be expected to become more sophisticated. Meanwhile, the assiduous collection of Western signals intelligence will continue in peacetime: by the ever-present 'trawlers' hovering coincidentally off Allied coasts where military bases are located; by the regular probing of Allied airspace by appropriately equipped long-range aircraft; by ground receivers strategically located in Eastern Europe and beyond; by satellite and, inevitably, by the traditional methods of espionage. The combined impact of Soviet RECS must be to make the Western Allies extremely conscious of the threat of radar and communications disruption and to view with caution any strategy or tactics which would depend for their success on detailed, inflexible and unimpeded communications.

The implications for Soviet air power of all these improvements to aircraft, weapons and RECS were clearly considerable. Ironically, there were no new Soviet ideas about airpower underlying the resurgence, simply traditional military thinking of a kind castigated by Khrushchev:

Superiority in numbers and equipment creates favourable real

possibilities for active and decisive action on the enemy for the
purpose of suppressing him and disrupting his combat formations,
and the dis-organisation of all his activity . . . creates conditions for a
variety of combat actions . . . enlarges the range for a combination of
fire and manoeuvre . . .[99]

THE GLOBAL REACH

Khrushchev had managed to castigate the soldiers who always wanted
more at the same time as he had begun to turn Soviet attention beyond
the immediate strategic problems of the European region. Ignominy had
swiftly followed in Cuba but also, five years later in the Middle East,
three Soviet friends, Egypt, Syria and Iraq, were dealt with very severely
by the Israelis without any prospect of Soviet assistance. Two weeks
later the London *Economist* carried a leading article headed 'Bears Can't
Fly'. It reflected on the inability of the USSR to intervene in the Arab–
Israeli conflict because of its lack of strategic mobility: its lack of forces
to employ a 'flexible response' of the kind which lay at the heart of Mr
McNamara's strategic thinking. The West enjoyed advantages in long-
range sea power, air power and distant bases; there was a contradiction
between Russia's claim to global influence, its propagation of an
ideology with universal potential and its power to translate the ideas into
action. 'The combination of an offensive ideology with a defensive
strategy', observed *The Economist*, 'is apt to produce diplomatic
defeats'. The article then concluded with a very ominous reflection:

> To avoid more Cubas and Sinais the Russians will have either to resist
> the temptation to take on commitments in the Third World (which
> includes encouraging 'wars of liberation'), or else to acquire the
> military capacity this sort of policy calls for. This means building
> aircraft carriers and acquiring staging posts for airborne troops. It
> will be a bad omen for East–West relations if there are signs that they
> have chosen this second way out of their dilemma.[100]

We now know that there had always been an offensive strategy as well
as an offensive ideology. By 1967, the Soviet Union had already
identified its need for stronger conventional forces and an extended
global reach. Naval expansion was well under way[101] but the extended
reach of Soviet air power was not yet so obvious. Already, however, a
new Antonov four-engine transport, the AN-22 'Cock' had flown in

1965. This turbo-prop strategic transport could lift close to 100,000 lb of heavy equipment in excess of 4,000 miles. It has been observed to carry armoured vehicles, surface-to-surface missiles and SAMS with their supporting equipment. It entered squadron service with VTA between 1970 and 1974 and contributed to the assistance given to Egypt and Syria in October 1973.[102] Perhaps because of various technical weaknesses production was cut short in 1974; at least two had been lost in 1970 while on long-range relief missions: one off Iceland en route to Peru and one near Calcutta while returning from East Pakistan. It has since been supplemented in the long-range strategic role by the four-jet IL-76 'Candid' which first appeared publicly at the Paris Air Show in 1971 and which began to enter service with both Aeroflot and VTA in 1974. With a payload of 80,000 lb, approximately twice that of the AN-12 'Cub', it has a range of over 3,000 miles or half as much again as 'Cub'. 'Candid' was still in production in 1980 at the rate of about three aircraft a month.[103]

The implications of this increased capability as an instrument of Soviet foreign policy are considerable. As early as 1971 in Exercise Dvina, admittedly in carefully pre-planned conditions, a Soviet airborne division with 160 vehicles was landed in only 22 minutes.[104] Since then, strategic airlift has facilitated, or indeed made possible, Soviet intervention in the Middle East in 1973, in Angola in 1975, in Ethiopia in 1977–78 and in Afghanistan in 1979 and 1980. In each case, strategic air power had a decisive effect on the outcome of the local conflict. Further, one US analyst in 1980 estimated that the Soviet Union could deliver ten airborne motorised rifle division equipments to the Persian Gulf in the same two-week period that the US would need to deliver a single fully equipped mechanised infantry division.

Clearly, the further away from the Soviet Union's own boundary that a crisis area may be located, the more complicated her problems will be. But the more access she is given to distant air bases, and the more reluctant Third World countries become to deny her over-flying rights, the easier those problems will be to resolve. Moreover, Soviet transport aircraft, unlike their Western counterparts, are accustomed to domestic conditions which are frequently of moderate quality. Consequently, they tend to be equipped to operate with a minimum reliance on ground handling equipment, with rugged undercarriages and variable-pressure tyres to permit landing and take-off from semi-prepared strips, and with two or three flight engineers capable of minor servicing with little or no local assistance. Clearly, such aircraft are readily adaptable for long-range operations in Third World countries.

In addition to the land-based aircraft, new arrivals in naval aviation also contribute to the global reach. By August 1980, two aircraft carriers, *Kiev* and *Minsk*, equipped with anti-submarine helicopters and Yakovlev Forger VSTOL fighter-bombers, were operational with a third nearing completion. Their war-fighting capability has been variously assessed and they certainly appear vulnerable both to submarine and to stand-off air attack. But their contribution to Soviet diplomacy is by no means restricted to their war-fighting capability.

In Sokolovsky's work, and in most of the military debates of that period, military strength was considered solely in its war-fighting role. Nothing was said of the importance of its perception or its potential, which are not necessarily the same thing. Yet in practice, as has been noted, the Soviet Union has been adept at producing opportunities for perception which have greatly exaggerated potential. By the beginning of the 1970s, however, Soviet doctrine began to rediscover ideas of force without war:

> The greater the combat might and readiness of the Soviet Armed Forces and the armies of the fraternal Socialist countries, . . . the more secure is peace on earth . . . and the broader are the opportunities for consolidating the successes of the policy of peaceful co-existence.[105]

Similarly, Admiral Gorshkov had on several occasions echoed Mahan's ideas of the use of 'the fleet in being' to bring 'pressure to bear in peacetime on potential opponents. *Kiev* and her sister ships seemed admirably suited to such a role. Indeed, one could reflect on Anglo-French options in 1956 had there been a *Kiev* or a *Minsk* anchored off Suez; or the inhibitions on US activity if they had stood between the Marines and Beirut in 1958.

Indeed, it may be argued that the functions of Soviet maritime air power and land-based long-range air power are complementary. The former has a capability to influence, threaten, hinder and generally to thwart traditional Western methods of exercising influence while her long-range land-based air power offers much more positive options. Already the Soviet Union has demonstrated the potential to intervene swiftly in local instability: perhaps to pre-empt a competitor, to stabilise and reassure a client or in other ways to create by military strength alone more favourable circumstances for the diplomat to exploit. Because there are now few areas of the world which are not of direct or indirect interest to both superpowers, any subsequent attempt to redress a temporary military advantage could be prolonged, expensive and associated with risks of escalation. In such conditions, even a small-scale military intervention in a relatively unsophisticated environment can have a disproportionate political influence. Power begets influence; influence begets anchorages, support facilities and bases. From bases, power can be further projected and the cycle is renewed. For example, from Afghanistan Soviet air power can threaten Western access to the Gulf and freedom of movement in the Indian Ocean. The Straits of Hormuz fall within the combat radius of even medium-range tactical aircraft flying from bases in south-west Afghanistan. The influence of air power, whether in direct attack or as a distributor of airborne forces, is in direct proportion to its radius of action and its speed of transit. Should the Soviet Union succeed in subduing Afghan opposition to its presence and in establishing permanent bases, the direct threat, first to Iran and Pakistan and then beyond them to the Gulf, the Indian Ocean and southern Asia, would become very serious. Such a threat, before the development of long-range Soviet strategic offensive and transport aircraft, would have been unthinkable.

In an era of nuclear parity between the superpowers, the impact of such long-range military aviation could be even greater:

The establishment of a dynamic balance in strategic forces between the USSR and the USA substantially limits the military activities of imperialism in the international arena and forces it to take into account the peaceful policies of the Socialist community of states.[106]

Consequently:

International relations have also been greatly influenced by conventional Armed Forces, used either independently or in combination with nuclear forces. Both forms can be used extensively not only in the process of military preparations in order to establish a military presence, but also for applying pressure during the course of negotiations.[107]

Moreover, there is ample evidence to suggest that while the speed and reach of military aviation have been greatly and dramatically enhanced, the ability to exercise precise control has also improved well beyond the levels inherited by Mr Brezhnev. Frequent Soviet reference is made to the 'revolution in military affairs' brought about by the potential extent of nuclear devastation, the great range of nuclear weapons, and their speed and delivery which expands the spatial boundaries of combat while accelerating the pace of operations.[108] Since 1970 Soviet provision for, and writing about, command, control and communication (C^3) have been a natural outcome of a strategic position which accepted the possibility of fighting with and the need to win a war involving nuclear weapons.[109] The SAF appear to see centralised command and control not as a potential weakness which would induce rigidity or reduce local initiative, but as a means of deriving the greatest possible flexibility to concentrate force over great distances wherever it should be required. This was the reasoning behind the organisation of FA in 1942, and is believed to be valid in potential nuclear circumstances.

The logic of the assumption has been translated into the practice of protecting C^3 by concealment, dispersal, hardening, mobility and redundancy to an extent that reduces considerably the overall system's vulnerability to either nuclear or conventional attack. In addition, Soviet officers are encouraged to become familiar with cybernetics to speed the decision-making process and the passage of information through the levels of command.[110] Consequently, there is little doubt that Soviet commanders can exercise a degree of precise and effective control down to individual units which is a potential source of great strength, provided that if the unexpected should occur, there is a residual initiative at the appropriate level to respond to it. It may not be a coincidence that the most heavily automated arm of the Soviet Services, PVO, was apparently uncertain and dilatory in its response to the incursion of a South Korean airliner in 1976. A complex combat management system which incorporates improved communications, improved commuter processing, graphic tactical displays, effective information-distribution systems and swift application of appropriate algorithms is not necessarily flexible. The question is whether the theoretical flexibility in reaction would be matched in practice by the flexibility of imagination unrestricted by fears of the consequence of error or the stigma of misplaced initiative. It may also be no coincidence that another well-used expression is 'to lead is to foresee'. If, as is generally assumed, a military organisation tends to reflect the society from which it is drawn, the SAF may have a particular problem in developing the imagination and initiative which air power demands for its fullest exploitation. Independence of thought and action have somehow to be blended not only with military discipline and the combined reliability demanded and recognised the world over, but with the peculiarly bureaucratic and stultifying application of Marxism–Leninism. The problem is recognised and publicly treated, as in a recent reference to a FA exercise in which the indecisiveness of a local commander was responsible for the loss of a tactical air battle.

Automated systems help resolve many questions of command and control in a new way that considerably eases the job of a commander who is a flight leader in combat formation. However, in modern combat the most unexpected situations are possible. Therefore, it is necessary for the commander to always be ready to direct his subordinates in the most complex situation, nourishing in them independence, combat aggressiveness, and an inflexible will for victory over the enemy . . . No matter how great the potential of command and control from the ground, the success of a group in an air battle depends in the first place on the Commander/Flight Leader – on his tactical preparedness and his ability to quickly evaluate a developing situation and to make sound decisions in order to effectively complete his assigned task.[111]

Nevertheless, by 1980, Soviet air power had reached formidable proportions and its growth showed no signs of slackening. Indeed, the last major demonstration of potential at Domodedovo was thirteen years before: a longer gap than at any time since 1946 when the annual air displays were again to be used as public manifestations of the power of Soviet military aviation. Not surprisingly, therefore, rumours of new projects were rife: a new all-weather Foxbat able to shoot down low-flying intruders – logical in view of NATO's offensive air capability; a new air superiority fighter – certainly in harmony with Soviet tactical doctrine; a new manned bomber – perhaps another attempt to meet illusory specifications for a manned intercontinental weapons platform; a new airborne early warning and control aircraft to replace the handful of ageing TU-114s still working optimistically with the TU-28s over the northern provinces; a new in-flight refuelling aircraft, like the AWACS, perhaps to be derived from the most recent wide-bodied IL-86 Camber transport. In 1979 the Soviet Union allocated some 12 per cent of its gross national product to defence, and of that approximately one-fifth to research and development. Doctrine had agreed that all arms were required for both nuclear and conventional conflicts. Unless domestic circumstances were to force a reduction in defence allocation and hence a need to redefine weapon and role priorities, there was good reason to assume that the speculations of 1980 about future Soviet aircraft would soon be verifiable in the public domain.

Yet already, Soviet air power threatened the heart of Western strategy in Europe and Western interests well beyond it. NATO countries were being forced to reassess their provision for air defence at a time when financial allocations were no more readily available than hitherto in the democratic alliance. It was indeed a far cry from the time when the SAF had needed to cannibalise B-29s, adapt Rolls Royce engines and naturalise German science and scientists in a desperate attempt to begin to narrow the air power gap with the West just thirty-five years before.

7 Air Power in NATO

Since its formation on 4 April 1949 the North Atlantic Treaty Organisation has achieved its primary and enduring objective: to deter aggression against member states. Consequently, its air forces have not seen combat as Alliance formations although US, UK, Dutch, Belgian and French aircraft have all contributed to national operations outside the NATO area. Yet air power, in one form or another, has dominated strategies designed to provide security to the Atlantic area ever since tension between the wartime allies began to threaten another conflict.

TOWARDS AN ALLIANCE STRATEGY

The origin and pattern of the deteriorating relationship between the Soviet Union and her Western allies from the Second World War have been amply and variously explained but comparable post-war military strengths were readily identifiable. By August 1946 US forces in Europe had dwindled from 3.1 million to 391,000; British from 1,321,000 to 488,000 and Canadian from 299,000 to none. The Soviet Union, on the other hand, was perceived to 'maintain their forces on a war footing and to keep their armament production going at full blast'.[1] In fact, partial Soviet demobilisation did take place but some 3 million men remained under arms. Estimates of Soviet strength varied from 100 to 200 available divisions, but Western defence analysts would have agreed that 'Soviet Russia possesses ground and tactical air forces greatly superior in numbers to those any combination of probable opponents could hope to bring to bear against her in the early stages of a war'.[2]

Indeed, when in August 1946 two unarmed C-47 transports were shot down over Yugoslavia, Major General Lauris Norstad had to advise the US State Department that the Air Force was too weak to risk a war.[3] The response which was made, however, was to foreshadow a major contribution by air power to Western security. On 13 November six B-29 long-range bombers flew the Atlantic to land at Frankfurt in Germany.

From there, for the next twelve days they flew along the borders of Soviet-occupied territory and 'surveyed airfields to determine their suitability for B-29 operations'.[4]

The B-29 had, of course, a particular significance. It was the aircraft which had carried the atomic weapons a little over a year previously to Hiroshima and Nagasaki. At the time, the world in general could not know whether the B-29s of the 43rd Bombardment Group were carrying atomic weapons or not, but the gesture was very clear: a threat of considerable retaliation for the destruction of two aircraft. Although the US might no longer be able to match Soviet conventional and numerical strength they had an obvious advantage in technology. They had the atomic weapon, and in the B-29 the delivery system. Moreover, the US had already shown that she was prepared to use both. Such were the ingredients in 1946 of embryonic nuclear deterrence: the capability, and the precedent, for massive retaliation.

In May 1947, the US Joint Chiefs of Staff (JCS) formally assessed the relative strengths and weaknesses of East and West:

The Allies do not have the capability of mobilising or transporting, in the early stages of a war, ground and tactical air forces of sufficient strength to destroy the Soviet Armed Forces which would have to be encountered in depth along any of the avenues of approach which lead to the heart of Russia. . . .

On the other hand . . . the United States has a capability of undertaking soon after the beginning of the war an offensive strategic air effort against vital Russian industrial complexes and against Russian population centres. If this effort, adequately expanded, did not achieve victory, it would destroy elements of Soviet industrial and military power to such an extent that the application of this and other forms of military force should accomplish the desired end . . .

Approximately 80% of the entire industry is within the radius of B-29s operating from bases in the British Isles or the Cairo-Suez area.[5]

Less than twelve months after that document was written in the growing crisis over development of the four regions of Germany, the Soviet Union began to increase her pressure on the allied garrison in Berlin until on 24 June 1948 all road and rail transport from the West to the city was halted. A Royal Air Force air-lift was mounted the following day and on the 26th the Commander of the USAF in Europe,

Lieutenant General Curtis le May, started the USAF operation with his locally available transport planes. On 15 October a combined Airlift Task Force was established, which by the time the Soviet Union abandoned its restriction on surface transport twelve months later, had flown 277,728 sorties carrying 2,326,205 tons of supplies. Of this tonnage, 76.7 per cent was carried by USAF and US Navy aircraft, 17 per cent by RAF and 6.3 per cent by UK civilian transport. At no time did the Soviet Union seek to interfere with the traffic although several 'buzzing' incidents occurred in the air corridors to Berlin. Immunity may have been granted because of the frequent presence of superior British or American fighters, or because the USAF deployed more than just transport planes to Europe during the summer of 1948. On 2 July two squadrons of 301 Bombardment Group arrived at Furstenfeldbruck airbase in Germany to join the third squadron already there, while the 307th Bombardment Group moved to the UK on 17 July, and the 28th the following day. All the groups were equipped with B-29s.

Thus, even before the formal construction of the Western Alliance, the shadow of the US atomic capability had beeen projected into Europe in response to two separate Soviet, or Soviet-associated, military activities. How far the USAF gesture was supported by the actual presence of atomic weapons is still in doubt.[6] It has been asserted that by 1948 bomb teams could assemble only two bombs per day and that the total inventory may not have exceeded 200 weapons. But unless the Soviet Union could be sure that they were not carried by the three Groups deployed to Europe, she had to consider that if provoked, the US could use them again. Memories of August 1945 were, after all, still only three years old.

Nor was there any lack of understanding by the European Allies about the potential role of air power. Secretary Forrestal had been uneasy that the British Labour Government would be unwilling to accept a forceful diplomacy backed by an atomic threat, but he was reassured in October 1948 by the far from hawkish Stafford Cripps:

> Britain is placing its main reliance on the development of fighter aircraft to ensure the security of Britain. Britain must be regarded as the main base for the development of American airpower and the chief offensive against Russia must be by air.[7]

This acknowledgement of the significance of the UK to US air power reinforced the JCS analysis of the previous year. It also illustrated that the UK was, in 1948, already looking beyond the resources of the recently formed Western Union Defence Organisation created the previous month as the military arm of the Brussels Treaty Organisation comprising Belgium, France, Luxemburg, Netherlands and the UK. The limitations of those resources in 1948 were subsequently recalled by General Beaufré: 'Western ground forces numbered only ten divisions. In-theatre combat aircraft probably numbered no more than four hundred.'[8] At the same time, the Soviet Union probably had 15,000 aircraft in addition to the 3 million men under arms.

From July 1948 US and Canadian representatives had attended Brussels Treaty meetings. Co-operation grew steadily closer, discussions about extending the Alliance were held on both sides of the Atlantic and on 4 April 1949 the North Atlantic Treaty was signed in Washington by the Foreign Ministers of Belgium, Canada, Denmark, France, Ireland, Italy, Luxemburg, Norway, the Netherlands, Portugal, the UK and the US. Nine months later the Alliance was in a position to produce its first strategic concepts paper. Not surprisingly, it reflected the development during the previous two years of USAF ideas about the contribution of strategic bombardment and the relative weaknesses of conventional forces in Europe.

The JCS Short Range Emergency War Plan 1844/13 of July 1948, codenamed 'Half Moon', had 'aimed at the early initiation and sustaining of an air offensive against vital elements of the Soviet war-making capacity'.[9] It had proposed to 'deploy available units of the Strategic Air Command to bases in England (alternatively to Iceland) and to the Khartoum, Cairo–Suez area and conduct operations from these bases and Okinawa utilising available atomic bombs against selected targets'.[10]

Meanwhile, prompted by the pressures arising from the Berlin Airlift, SAC prepared its own simplified emergency war plan, 'I-49' which was accepted by the JCS in December 1948. The highest priority target system for atomic weapons would be 'the major Soviet urban-industrial concentrations'.[11] It was considered that SAC could deliver all the available atomic weapons even if accepting a 25 per cent rate of attrition, because of the weaknesses of Soviet air defences. These were estimated to comprise an obsolescent early warning system susceptible to jamming; anti-aircraft defences limited to 30,000 feet and weaker than those overcome in Germany in the Second World War; no all-weather fighters; no effective fighter control system and ineffective Soviet electronic countermeasures. Soviet attacks on B-29 bases would be restricted by their bomber range and would be insufficient to stop the strategic air offensive. Consequently, it was assumed that a successful all-weather and night offensive by aircraft relying on height, speed and ECMs was well within the capability of SAC despite the competing demands of the Berlin Airlift for transport support.

In the same month that the North Atlantic Treaty was signed, the implications of a strategic air offensive were reviewed in Washington by a Joint Service Committee. It observed that SAC plans envisaged an initial strike of 'attacks primarily with atomic bombs on 70 target areas' and a second phase, after thirty days, carried out 'with both atomic and conventional weapons'.[12] Although the Committee Report reflected that 'from the standpoint of our national security the advantages of its [atomic weaponry] early use would be transcending',[13] it also emphasised the shortcomings of such an offensive. The 30–40 per cent loss in Soviet industrial capacity would not be permanent, nor would it *per se*, bring about capitulation, destroy the roots of Communism or critically weaken the power of Soviet leadership to dominate the people'.[14] Indeed, the offensive would 'validate Soviet propaganda . . . unify the people . . . and increase their will to fight'.[15] Nevertheless, the Committee endorsed the strategic air offensive by unequivocally stating that 'every reasonable effort should be devoted to providing the means to be prepared for prompt and effective delivery of the maximum numbers of atomic bombs to appropriate target systems'.[16]

INITIAL ALLIANCE STRATEGY

Thus, the route was well charted to the construction of the first North Atlantic Strategic Concept of 1 December 1949. Its 'Principles', 'Objectives' and 'Basic (military) undertakings' naturally reflected both the strategic facts of the time and the thinking which had already taken place among the Allies. One of six Principles underlying NATO planning was to be 'that each nation should undertake the task, or tasks, for which it is best suited. Certain nations, because of their geographical location or because of their capabilities, will be prepared to undertake appropriate specific missions'.[17]

Consequently, the 'Basic undertakings' included:

Ensure the ability to carry out strategic bombing promptly by all means possible with all types of weapons, without exception. This is primarily a US responsibility assisted as practical by other nations . . .

and

> Neutralize as soon as practicable enemy air operations against North
> Atlantic Treaty Powers. In this undertaking the European nations
> should initially provide the bulk of the tactical air support and air
> defence, other nations aiding with the least possible delay in
> accordance with overall plans.[18]

Other undertakings allocated the 'hard core of ground forces', initially,
to the European nations while sea power would primarily be the
responsibility of the UK and the US.

Thus, North Atlantic Alliance strategy, right from the start, in the
event of an enemy offensive, was to rest on prompt atomic retaliation
together with conventional air and ground defence which would be
reinforced from the US and Canada as swiftly as possible. Yet even by
the time the concepts were formulated, they had been overtaken by two
events and threatened by an almost permanent set of other circumstances.

INFLUENCES ON THE STRATEGY

The first event was the British decision to proceed with atomic weapon
development independently of the US after Anglo-US atomic co-
operation had broken down in 1946. The political roots of the British
decision have been examined elsewhere,[19] but two observations are of
relevance to NATO strategy. In January 1947, Foreign Secretary Bevin
commented: 'We could not afford to acquiesce in an American
monopoly of this new development [atomic weaponry].'[20] Later that
year, the Chief of the Air Staff, Marshal of the Royal Air Force Lord
Tedder, in response to a suggestion that Britain might rely on the US for
the maintenance of her nuclear striking force, replied:

> This would involve a close military alliance with the United States in
> which Britain would be merely a temporary advance base, would
> involve complete subservience to United States policy and would
> render Britain completely impotent in negotiations with Russia or any
> other nation.[21]

So, despite the apparent division of labour in the Strategic Concept
Paper, the UK had already elected to develop her own atomic capability

and to build aircraft capable of delivering it. Moreover, in the person of Marshal of the Royal Air Force Sir John Slessor she had her own influential and articulate theorist. After his retirement he expressed his views publicly:

> The RAF today, without a long range bomber force, would be like the Royal Navy of Nelson's day without its line of battle. If we were to provide as our contribution to the Pax Atlantica only ground support and maritime aircraft and fighters to defend ourselves – the gunboats and frigates and seaward defences of the modern air fleet – then we should sink to the level of a third-class Power.[22]

The Air Marshal had already expressed similar views officially in 1952, in a paper on global strategy prepared by the British Chiefs of Staff for the Cabinet.[23] It argued for a strategic British bombing force which would complement that of the US by covering targets such as submarine pens and air bases which did not present a direct threat to the US itself. Development of four-engined medium-range jet bombers capable of delivering atomic weapons had begun after the specification had been given to the British aircraft industry in 1947. Although the Socialist Government of Mr Attlee authorised the production of prototypes the decision for the production of 215 planes was not made until 1952. Ultimately, 370 Valiants, Victors and Vulcans, collectively known as 'V-Bombers' entered Royal Air Force service, the first Valiant reaching its squadron in 1955. The last Victor B-2 was produced in 1962. The UK's V-Force would be available for use within NATO, but it could equally well discharge British national responsibilities outside the NATO area, as it was to do at Suez in 1956 and in South-East Asia in 1965. Thus, although strategic bombardment would indeed remain 'primarily a US responsibility' in accordance with the 'Basic undertakings' of the NATO Strategic Concept, the preparation of a British supplement would inevitably blur the original distinction between US nuclear provision and European conventional defence.

The second event which was to modify the basic concept was the explosion of a nuclear device by the Soviet Union in August 1949. Radioactivity detected in the upper atmosphere by the USAF on 3 September was evidence of a Soviet detonation some ten days before. General Bradley, then Chairman of the JCS, observed in October that:

> the making of an atomic bomb is not so difficult as the problem of turning it out in quantity and delivering it. As long as America retains

a tremendous advantage in A-bomb quantity, quality and deliverability, the deterrent effect of the bomb against an aggressor will continue. Sustained research and development can keep us far in the lead with methods for intercepting enemy bomb carriers.[24]

And, indeed, it may be argued that as long as the General's own preconditions were met, his forecast would be correct. But the ability to intercept bomb-carriers had to exist in Europe as well as over the North American mainland and, in the longer term, Soviet possession of nuclear power would invalidate the assumptions underlying the Strategic Concepts of December 1949.

But perhaps the third factor which was to influence NATO strategy and hence NATO air power would be the most consistent and pervasive. Concept 'Defence principles' included the observation that:

In developing their military strength consistent with overall strategic plans, the participating nations should bear in mind that economic recovery and the attainment of economic stability constitute important elements of their security.[25]

Yet there was considerable disparity between the members of the Alliance. There was disparity in wealth, disparity in vulnerability to threat and disparity in national priorities for allocation of resources. There was, in fact, the disparity to be expected from this group of nations which had voluntarily combined to protect their freedom to make their own selection of priorities. The political and economic consequences to individual Alliance members of promoting common security interests would frequently be unacceptable and the provision for air power would be affected accordingly.

AIR POWER AND NUCLEAR WEAPONS

Soviet intransigence, declaratory policy, possession of the atomic bomb and the apparent emergence of China as a major ally had already generated Western unease, but the invasion of South Korea in June 1950 seemed to justify every fear of Soviet military expansion. Within two months, all NATO members had agreed to take urgent measures to increase their military strength. By December, further agreement had been reached on the desirability of including Western German forces in the Alliance and creating an integrated force, designating a Supreme Commander and establishing an international staff.

During 1951, US air bases were established in France, Morocco, Greenland, Iceland and the Portuguese Azores. Canada prepared to send eleven fighter squadrons to Europe. The Royal Air Force increased its squadrons in Second Tactical Air Force Germany (2TAF) from ten to sixteen and a re-equipment of several Allied air forces with US-built F-84 Thunderstreaks began. By December 1951 NATO combat aircraft had increased by 2,500 to almost 3,000[26] and a large-scale airfield and communications infrastructure programme had been started. Meanwhile, the newly formed international staffs were directed to identify shortcomings in overall defence provision and to make proposals for force targets to a Temporary NATO Council Committee. In the same period, Secretary of State Acheson was among those who believed that despite the previous optimistic assessment of General Bradley, the US lead in retaliatory air power would decrease and that, therefore, the best use of it was 'to move ahead under this protective shield to build the balanced collective forces in Western Europe that will continue to deter aggression after our atomic advantage had been diminished'.[27]

Subsequently, on 20 February 1952, the North Atlantic Council met at Lisbon and accepted proposals from the Temporary Council Committee, which included force goals of 4,000 combat aircraft by the end of 1952, 6,500 in 1953 and 9,000 by the end of 1954. The council also prepared the way for a renascent Luftwaffe by re-affirming the urgency of the need for a German contribution to a 'military effective European Defence Force'.[28] Britain took the Force Goals very seriously and planned to increase the number of her 2TAF squadrons progressively to fifty-six by the end of 1954, comprising thirty-nine light bomber, sixteen fighter/ground attack and one communication squadron. In the event, however, neither Britain nor any other Ally was to meet the Force Goals specified at Lisbon.

This was, in part, due to rapid development of atomic weapon technology. In May 1950 the USAF had been advised that an efficient atomic bomb could be produced small enough to be carried by a fighter type aircraft. 'Where nuclear weapons had been previously available only for strategic air warfare employment, they could now be developed for tactical air warfare applications.'[29] Moreover, the Atomic Energy Commission could now build atomic weapons 'on a production line basis'.[30] Britain exploded her own atomic device at Monte Bello in October 1952 and a potential atomic weapon carrier, the English Electric Canberra began to enter service. More seriously, however, in several countries the contrasting demands of rearmament and economic development began to create political pressures. Britain, in particular, found her resources severely strained. Consequently, although by 1954, the Secretary General of NATO could claim that the strategic concept of deterring aggression had never changed,[31] the contribution of air power to the underlying strategy had changed significantly since December 1949.

General Beaufré, on the NATO staff in Paris, was given the task during 1952 to begin studies of the use of small 'tactical' nuclear weapons, probably 10 KT (kilotons) and below, for use against enemy airfields and ground forces.[32] Although heavily outnumbered by their Soviet counterparts, NATO aircraft generally had superior performance and many were now nuclear-capable. Air-launched nuclear power could not only substitute for allied manpower, but could relieve pressure in other ways as well. A strategy which called for the use of nuclear weapons in a relatively short war did not demand extensive joint-Service staffs to produce the meticulous plans essential for protracted joint-Service campaigns nor require as large a logistic tail to support them. In short, tactical nuclear power was a very effective and politically attractive substitute for the Lisbon Force Goals.

For the UK it was not only politically attractive but very timely. The Socialist Government at the time of the Korean crisis in 1950 had adopted a rearmament plan which increased from £100 million to £4,700 million in less than a year.[33] The plan had produced a split within government ranks because of a well-justified fear that the proposed scale of military expenditure would have a detrimental impact on the economy as a whole by increasing the quantity and price of imported raw materials for defence purposes and by diverting engineering industries from peacetime reconstruction. The Socialist Government fell in the midst of a financial crisis in 1951, and the Conservative Government of Mr Churchill had no alternative but to reduce the scale of defence provision which would have been necessary to meet the British share of the Lisbon Force Goals. The Prime Minister now had very good practical reasons for increasing his country's reliance on the combination of atomic and air power, quite apart from his own personal belief in its efficacy.

Consequently, the availability of tactical nuclear weapons, at first built in the US, provided an opportunity to reduce 2TAF expansion from the fifty-six originally envisaged for 1954 to thirty-five squadrons in 1955. In December 1953 the Chairman of the JCS observed: 'Today, atomic weapons have virtually achieved conventional status within our Armed Forces',[34] which was just as well because earlier in the year General Ridgway had assured the NATO Standing Group that despite the efforts of the Alliance, Allied Command Europe 'would be critically weak to accomplish its present mission'.[35]

But even as NATO's reliance on atomic weapons was increasing, a new factor intruded. On 12 and 23 August 1953 the Soviet Union detonated her first thermonuclear explosions. General Beaufré considered, perhaps prematurely, that they made NATO air power plans obsolete. He envisaged such Soviet weapons could produce a thirty-mile explosive diameter with fall-out belts 30–625 miles wide depending on the yield of atomic or thermonuclear weapons. Airfields would be extremely vulnerable both to the initial impact and to the ensuing fall-out. Writing in 1967 he argued that the need for aircraft dispersal and vertical take-off and lift or short take-off and lift qualities were, therefore, already apparent by the end of 1953.[36]

Whereas General Beaufré's assessment, made with the certainty of hindsight, was perhaps premature, other Western responses seem to have taken no account whatever of the Soviet acquisition of thermonuclear power and its longer-term implications. For example, General Gruenther was reported in the *New York Times* as saying that the outcome of future warfare in Europe would be decided by the forces in being; the war would be atomic in nature and that therefore NATO forces would be reorganised by reducing ground troops and by developing air atomic power.[37] Six months later the Council of NATO approved a report by the Military Committee which laid the defence of Europe squarely on nuclear weapons. Indeed, the most succinct but comprehensive exposition of the rationale of tactical nuclear weapons occurred in the annual British Statement on Defence of February 1955. Deterrence would continue to

rest primarily on the strategic airpower of the West, armed with its nuclear weapons . . . But we cannot rely only on strategic airpower . . . The Communist world also maintains, and can continue to maintain, a great preponderance of conventional land forces. These, moreover, operate on internal lines of communication. The Soviet Union and her Eastern European satellites had some six million men under arms backed by enormous reserves. On the German Front the Soviet Army could be increased to well over one hundred divisions within thirty days. Over the whole field of deployment East and West, the Soviet and satellite land forces could be raised to the level of four hundred divisions. Even allowing for the essential German contribution, the free world cannot put into the front line anything comparable to this strength in conventional forces. The use of nuclear weapons is the only means by which this massive preponderance could be countered. But with their aid and with the European contribution we can adopt a forward strategy on the ground in Europe and so defend the Continent, instead of contemplating again the grim process of liberation. If we do not use the full weight of our nuclear power, Europe can hardly be protected from invasion and occupation – with all that this implies both for Europe and the United Kingdom.[38]

Thus, strategic air power would continue to provide strategic deterrence, now about to be shared by the UK as the new family of V-Force aircraft neared entry into service.

Tactical air power was no longer primarily concerned with close air support, interdiction or counter-air operations with conventional weapons. Instead, nuclear weapons would be used for interdiction and counter-air tasks. The exercise 'Carte Blanche' of 1955, for example, used tactical air power for nuclear operations. Conventional weapons would remain, and the training to go with them, but inevitably the incentives to develop, let alone accelerate the development, of conventional tactics and equipment, would be considerably eroded. Reflecting this change of emphasis the number of 2TAF squadrons was further reduced from thirty-five in 1955 to seventeen by 1957.

Production of the Canberra bomber, ideally suited to conventional tactical roles in Europe, was cut back to give greater priority to the medium-range V-Force nuclear bomber programme. The US greatly enhanced its own nuclear capability and at the same time responded to the increasing threat from the Soviet's nuclear bomber force. It gradually withdrew its weapon carriers back to the American mainland. It accelerated the introduction of in-flight refuelling, airborne alert, extended ground alerts, a greatly improved communications net and a new generation of intercontinental B-52 bombers capable of high-speed, high-level penetration.

In short, although the Soviet thermonuclear explosions were observed in 1953, NATO strategy does not appear to have been unduly influenced. Tactical atomic provision continued, while the US and the UK increased both the size and effectiveness of their own strategic nuclear power. The potential of the threat was not sufficient to shake the conviction of those who believed that the European allies could not afford to meet the Lisbon Force Goals and that, in any event, nuclear weaponry made them unnecessary. Thus, existing Western nuclear programmes continued, including the introduction of atomic weapons to European theatre strategy, until conventional forces assumed the explicit role of a tripwire to trigger a nuclear response against both invading military forces and the Soviet heartland.

A further result of the move to a 'tripwire' posture was a reduced incentive to improve conventional air defence. Strategic Concept 6/1 had envisaged this to be a major responsibility of European air power and, indeed, greater co-ordination was sought by General Gruenther in 1954. In 1955, four co-operative geographical regions were created but 'equipment was becoming obsolete and there was little exchange of air defence information throughout NATO Europe'.[39] In that same year, Fighter Command was reduced and was actually threatened with reduction to two 'air policing' squadrons. In the Defence Review of 1957, the number of squadrons was drastically reduced, but of longer-term significance for European air defence was the conclusion that there was no further need for a manned interceptor. The premise was deceptively simple. It would not be possible to intercept all attacking nuclear bombers, and even a small number would inflict unacceptable nuclear devastation. There was, therefore, little or no strategic require-ment for air defence and, most seriously for future Alliance options, there was little commercial incentive for Western aircraft companies to continue development of interceptors or air superiority fighters. Such an influence would be far-reaching. With a gestation period of up to ten years between concept and squadron service for a modern aircraft, any attempt to redefine the strategic requirement would be very difficult. Yet, even before 1960, the need for such a change was becoming apparent.

AIR POWER AND FLEXIBLE RESPONSE

No amount of conceptual exposition could disguise the fact that the NATO strategy of nuclear response to aggression, known familiarly as 'massive retaliation', depended for its efficacy on maintaining NATO nuclear superiority as desired by General Bradley a decade earlier. If the opposition had only very few nuclear weapons deployed, then the basic inflexibility of the strategy was of little import. If the Soviet inter-continental threat was restricted to subsonic massed bombers, then the newly constructed North American Air Defence Organisation, ampli-fied by the Canadian glacis, would not only protect the US heartland but allow the B-52s to get airborne in retaliation. Their different geographical circumstances had enabled the US and the UK to respond in different ways to long-range Soviet atomic air power. The US could envisage a practical defence; the UK, on the other hand, could not.

But by the end of 1957 the premises on which European theatre nuclear strategy and US national air defence strategy both rested, had already been challenged. The Soviet Union began to deploy short-range surface-to-surface nuclear missiles in Europe and, after Sputnik, apparently had the ability to strike in similar manner against the US. Now, the inflexibility of 'tripwire' began to seem a liability, not an asset. The smallest conventional conflict in Europe could precipitate another World War with inevitable nuclear devastation in North America. Pressure for change began to accumulate in Washington in President Eisenhower's later years and a further strategic shift was subsequently formalised and codified by Secretary of Defence McNamara.

The 'unofficial' view from the US was expressed in 1960 by General Maxwell Taylor:

At the outset of this reappraisal, we should recognise and accept the limitations of our atomic retaliatory forces. Under the conditions which we must anticipate in the coming years, it is incredible to ourselves, to our Allies, and to our enemies that we would use such forces for any purpose other than to assure our national survival . . . [which would include] a major attack upon Western Europe, since the loss of that area to Communism would ultimately endanger our national survival . . . Limited war would then be left to cover all other forms of military operations. The question of using atomic weapons in limited wars would be met by accepting the fact that primary dependence must be placed on conventional weapons while retaining the readiness to use tactical atomic weapons in the comparatively rare cases where their use would be to our national interest.[40]

After the Berlin crisis of 1961 Mr McNamara summarised the view of the US government before the Senate Arms Services Committee:

Believing that the Western World would be very reluctant to invoke the use of nuclear weapons in response to anything short of a direct threat to its survival, the Kremlin leaders hope to create divisive influences within the Alliance by carefully measured military threats in connection with the Berlin situation. In order to meet such threats with firmness and confidence and to provide us with a greater range of military alternatives, we will need more non-nuclear strength than we have today.[41]

Thus, the driving force for major change of emphasis in NATO strategy again originated in the US. The two factors which prompted it, however – an awareness of Soviet nuclear strength and an absence of 'low-level' military capability to respond to minor provocation – clearly threatened the security and credibility of the Alliance as a whole. The new strategic posture, to become known familiarly as 'flexible response', rested on three pillars: an assured second-strike retaliatory nuclear capability based on a triad of land, sub-surface and air-launched weapons; close control of tactical nuclear weapons; and increased and more mobile conventional forces. The whole was to present the Commander-in-Chief with a flexible range of options and the ability to escalate by tight control from minimal conventional to maximum nuclear response. The President of the US was determined 'to have a wider choice than humiliation or all-out nuclear war'.[42]

Six years of Allied debate took place before the new strategy was formally adopted by the NATO Council on the recommendation of the Military Committee in 1967. It became known as 'Flexible and Appropriate Response' or more simply '14/3' from the number allocated to the original military document. Between 1961 and 1967 the air forces of NATO remained configured and deployed to meet the demands of the strategy adopted in 1954. In the early 1960s, for example, the largest NATO-wide aircraft re-equipment programme was of the Lockheed F-104 Starfighter which was adopted with a nuclear strike capability by the air forces of Belgium, Canada, Germany, Italy, Holland and Turkey, although when the nuclear posture was undertaken, all warheads remained under US control. In addition, the French Force de Frappe equipped with Mirage IVAs and the Royal Air Force's Victors and Vulcans were all operational by 1965.[43] The total tactical delivery units including missiles and tactical aircraft in Europe numbered 2,500 and the stock of warheads had doubled between 1961 and 1966. The shift of strategic emphasis to include a possible indeterminate conventional phase of conflict would, therefore, demand extensive changes in the role of allied air power.

But even before the changes could be contemplated the Alliance was to be strained by two other events: each with far-reaching political and strategic implications and each with particular significance for air power.

The first victim of the move towards a flexible response strategy was

French participation in the integrated military structure. There were several reasons for President De Gaulle's withdrawal but high on the list was his belief that NATO strategy was too heavily dominated by the US, especially in nuclear matters. Consequently, at the very time when more airspace was required for operational training, a greater area needed for reinforcement routes and base facilities, and more extended and secure communications would be essential, French territory and airspace were denied to the Alliance for regular, integrated operations. In addition, command, control and communication networks had to be reconstructed.

The second event was the slowly increasing commitment of US forces to South-East Asia. In 1965, United States Air Force Europe (USAFE) contained eighteen tactical fighter and eight tactical reconnaissance squadrons.[44] In range, payload and all-round effectiveness the F-100s, 105s and newly deployed F-4s were considerably superior to their Warsaw Pact counterparts. But three years later the numbers had slipped to seventeen tactical fighter and six tactical reconnaissance squadrons as the US turned its attention and priority to Vietnam. It was not so much the smaller numbers remaining in Europe as the identification of South-East Asia as the area where the opportunities for combat experience existed, and where 'real' command could be exercised which made events and requirements in Europe seem of secondary importance for the USAF.

The third major air power, the UK, was in the process of a major Defence Review when the 14/3 decision was finally taken. Indeed, the UK Government did not endorse the change in policy until 1970. In the short term, however, the UK was able to strengthen her conventional air power contribution to the Alliance. Partly for financial reasons and partly because the Royal Air Force had only four airfields in Germany, it was not possible to increase the numerical strength. But in 1968, responsibility for the British strategic nuclear deterrent was assumed by the Royal Navy *Polaris* fleet and the dual-capable Vulcans were committed to SACEUR in the conventional role. In the same period the Canberras in Germany were replaced by Phantoms and Buccaneers, the air defences were strengthened by the replacement of Javelins by Lightnings and, for the first time, VTOL Harriers were deployed in support of the British Army of the Rhine.

The air power of the Alliance as a whole, therefore, was not enlarged, redeployed or re-armed to match the shift in strategic posture. Indeed, one narrative on the history of Royal Air Force Germany[45] makes no mention of the strategic shift at all. But there seemed no cause for alarm, because NATO aircraft were manifestly superior to their potential opponents and there was a steady stream of crews with combat experience in Vietnam moving on to the squadrons of USAFE. By 1973 the F-111 had replaced the venerable F-100s at Upper Heyford. Its speed of Mach 2.2, its operating height range from very low to 60,000 feet, its elaborate navigation and penetration aids and its all-weather capability made it a formidable acquisition. The F-111 and F-4 had replaced seven different types of aircraft and the F-4 itself could lift 14,000 lb of ordnance and carry it three times as quickly as the earlier F-84. Moreover, the ECMs, tactics and weapons successfully employed over North Vietnam were also beginning to see service with the squadrons in Europe.

Alliance ground-to-air defences had also been improved. Medium- and high-level Nike SAMs had been deployed in 1959, followed in 1960 by low- and medium-level Hawk. The following year the NATO Council approved the creation of an integrated air defence system which was later formalised in the NATO 'Air Defence Ground Environment Improvement Plan (NADGE)' of 1963. The air defence mission was crisply summarised:

> In peace the Allied Command Europe mission is to maintain the integrity of NATO airspace and to guard against attack. In war, the role is to protect ACE by maximum destruction of the enemy air threat utilising all available weapons with maximum efficiency.[46]

By 1975 the ground weapons included twenty Hawk battalions, together with Nike, Chaparral, Bloodhound and Rapier units in a far more closely integrated early warning and control system than had been available a decade before.

Even then, however, the SAMs did not provide the extent of comprehensive area and point defence then deployed by the Warsaw Pact. Because of resource limitation, NATO surface-to-air defences were constructed as a barrier, or belt, which could, like the Maginot Line of a previous generation, be vulnerable to an enemy who was determined to outflank it and prepared to violate neutrality.

Indeed, much remained to be done to co-ordinate attack and defence across the European mainland. In the context of a short war immediately dominated by nuclear weaponry, a co-ordinated application of air power between North and South had not appeared to warrant a great deal of priority. But if an attack should be received, and if NATO's attempt to defend Allied territory as far to the East as possible should be based on conventional strength, it was essential that air power assets could be directed rapidly to any critical area and that operations could be thoroughly co-ordinated, not just between Allied air forces, but with ground forces also. There was, therefore, a need for a command structure which could provide this kind of co-ordination.

Historically, air power assets in Central Europe had been deployed under the control either of 2 Allied Tactical Air Force in the North, or 4 Tactical Allied Air Force in the South. It was believed that disparity in doctrine and procedures could inhibit the smooth transfer of command from national to NATO military authority in times of tension.[47] Consequently, on 28 June 1974, Headquarters Allied Air Forces Central Europe (AAFCE) was established at Ramstein. The commander of the supranational organisation was tasked with:

> the operational command of the assigned and earmarked air forces in the Central Region and the development of the policy required for the centralised direction of those air forces. This was to include the establishment of a common, or at least a fully compatible air doctrine and procedures region wide, improvements in interoperability and mutual support and the tactical evaluation and standardisation of training of the air forces.[48]

Therefore, if one did not look across to developments in Eastern Europe, NATO air power had cause for a certain amount of satisfaction by the mid-1970s. The disruptive effects on communications of the eviction from France had been remedied, a new generation of aircraft re-equipment was well under way, air defences were stronger and better co-ordinated than ever before, central command and control had been strengthened and, if needed, the tactical nuclear inventory was as readily available as in the days of 'tripwire'. In 1961 it had been possible to write a distinguished scholarly treatise on NATO strategy without ever mentioning tactical air power.[49] The author had not thought it necessary to make any distinction between the nuclear warheads extensively deployed on surface-to-surface launchers and their airborne counterparts. But by 1975, the conventional demands on tactical air power were far more significant. By the end of the decade they were to underwrite the fundamental credibility of the strategic posture itself.

THE CHALLENGE TO NATO AIR POWER

It is easy to forget, when the perennial assessments of NATO problems are made, that the Alliance has, since 1949, had to live with a difficulty seldom experienced by commanders at any time in military history: the assumption that the potential enemy would, in all foreseeable circumstances, have the initiative in deciding when, where and how any conflict would begin. The strategic choice is, therefore, immediately circumscribed: it must be responsive.

Therefore, any satisfaction felt about NATO air power had to be tempered by knowledge of what was happening on the other side of the hill. The enormous increase in the offensive capability of the SAF between 1967 and 1980 is fully described in Chapter 6. Between 1968 and 1976 the Warsaw Pact aircraft facing Central Europe increased by 'ten per cent in numbers . . . and three hundred per cent in delivery capability'.[50] During the same period, the defensive net of SAMs, radar and interceptors was spread more tightly across the Warsaw Pact ground forces, along their supply routes, over their forward airfields and all the way back to the Soviet heartland. At the same time, the need for allied air power to co-operate in the land battle had actually increased because of the growth in the Warsaw Pact's own conventional strength. Between 1970 and 1978 Soviet defence expenditure rose by 4 per cent a year in real terms accounting for some 11–13 per cent of the Soviet Union's gross national product.[51] Already, by 1978, it had provided in Central Europe for a 35 per cent increase in numbers of main battle tanks, a 30 per cent increase in artillery and an 83 per cent increase in armoured personnel carriers. In the eastern Atlantic it had provided for a 143 per cent growth in nuclear-powered submarine strength, a 233 per cent increase in missile armed cruiser and destroyer strength, a 56 per cent increase in frigate and escort numbers and a 29 per cent increase in fixed-wing maritime aircraft.[52] Naturally, numerical increases were accompanied by increases in quality; not yet to the level of Western equipment across the board, but rapidly closing the technological gap in many areas. The cumulative impact by 1980 was that the Alliance was outnumbered heavily on land by in-position forces and faced with potential numerical inferiority at sea in the event of swift deployment of units from Soviet home waters. All this in a period in which NATO had elected to defend itself against aggression as far as possible by conventional means.

Consequently, whereas the Allies could look with equanimity at the very limited short-range conventional threat posed by the SAF, at the considerable Western qualitative and quantitative maritime advantages and at the favourable technological balance in Central Europe when the strategic shift had been adopted by the NATO Council in 1967, the cumulative impact of Soviet military expansion during the 1970s was to erode those favourable circumstances and place even heavier demands on Western air power to redress the various deficiencies. Should deterrence fail, NATO commanders would face difficult decisions about the precise allocation of air power assets. They would obviously be determined, under overall political control, by the defensive exigencies of the moment but there would be no shortage of roles to be carried out.

In the first hours, the overall direction of COMAAFCE would be invaluable to concentrate offensive air power where it was most needed. Even without harassment from the air, ground forces could not rapidly be switched with sufficient speed or numbers even with air mobility to reinforce an area against large-scale attack. Only air power, able to intervene over 200 or more miles in some thirty minutes or less could apply lateral reinforcement in the first hours. Whether it would take the form of close air support in direct involvement in a land battle, or whether it would seek to isolate the opposition from his immediate second echelon reinforcements by battlefield interdiction, would be a decision for the day. Aircraft such as the Fairchild A-10, expressly designed for short-range air-to-ground involvement, Harrier, Jaguar and Phantom would find much to occupy them.

Increasingly, in NATO exercises, the traditional ground attack role is shared between fixed- and rotary-wing aircraft. Working closely with Allied ground forces, the helicopter armed with air-to-surface weapons can use contour-following techniques to ambush and dislocate enemy armour from the front or flank. Its ability to operate at low speed, very low level and in marginal weather conditions make it an ideal complement to the fixed-wing aircraft. Unfortunately, it possesses neither the range nor the speed to be deployed far from its potential combat area. Only the Harrier at present can combine forward, off-base deployment with rapid reaction over a wider combat radius.

The introduction of the Harrier to Royal Air Force Germany in 1970 marked not only an improvement in the quantity and quality of rapid-response air support of ground forces, it also had a very important defensive implication. The great majority of NATO airfields began to fall within range of Warsaw Pact offensive aircraft in addition to the threat from surface-to-surface missiles. The heavy dependence by NATO on its air power would surely be well understood by the Warsaw Pact, and with or even slightly ahead of a ground invasion, the air forces of the Western Alliance must be prepared to absorb and survive pre-emptive attacks on their airfields and then to respond with their own offensive riposte. The relative vulnerability of airfields to the increased Soviet offensive threat was quickly appreciated but, as always in the Alliance, possible remedies were constrained by limited resources.

Several measures were, however, taken. Aircraft such as the G-91 and the Jaguar trained in flying from and recovering to autobahns which in some cases had modified sections to accommodate aircraft. On the airfields themselves, runways were duplicated and taxiways modified to reduce dependence on one strip of concrete. New aircraft, such as the MRCA Tornado, were designed from the outset to take off and land in much shorter distances than their immediate predecessors. In addition, the June war of 1967 had demonstrated the vulnerability of unprotected aircraft in dispersal areas and NATO embarked on an extensive programme to provide hardened concrete aircraft shelters on many of the Alliance's 200 main airfields. Air-to-air defences were considerably strengthened by the entry into service of the F-15 and F-16 which, supported by older F-4s in several air forces, were considerably more formidable than any of their likely Warsaw Pact opponents. Consequently, despite their increased potential, attacks by Soviet offensive aircraft on NATO airfields would still be very costly and not necessarily as productive as Warsaw Pact planners might wish.

Conversely, Warsaw Pact air operations could be disrupted at source by counter-air missions flown by the all-weather F-111s and Vulcans, by Jaguars, Phantoms, Buccaneers and several others. Although the Warsaw Pact possessed many more military airfields than NATO, the advantages were not quite so numerous. Only a very small number of bases were 'hardened' and not even all the main bases were capable of re-arming, say, Flogger 'D's or SU-24 Fencers. One recalls the serious error made by the Luftwaffe in 1940 in failing to concentrate its attacks on those few RAF bases which could rearm Spitfires and Hurricanes. If NATO counter-air operations were designed to disrupt primarily Warsaw Pact air offensives the task would quickly fall to practical proportions. If the opposition was compelled to disperse, his problems of co-ordination, range to target and vulnerability would be seriously compounded. Certainly the battle for command of the air or its diminutive – local air superiority – whether fought against each other's airfields or in the skies above them, would be of critical importance to the outcome of the war on the ground.

On it would depend not only the ability of the Allied air forces to contribute to the land battle by direct firepower, but the ability to reinforce and resupply the in-position outnumbered ground forces. The ability to move men and weapons swiftly across a theatre, or in larger numbers from outside it, would be an essential requirement to stem a swift-moving armoured attack without recourse to nuclear weapons. The unimpeded access from North America to European airfields, harbours and railheads envisaged by the draughtsmen of 14/3 was only a cherished memory well before 1980 in the face of Soviet surface, submarine and maritime air expansion. In any future conflict the ability of the Alliance to withstand a large-scale incursion in Europe would depend very heavily on the swift arrival of reinforcements across the Atlantic. Conversely, should the Warsaw Pact ever be able to isolate the old world from the new, NATO could be faced with a very difficult choice between concession and nuclear escalation in disadvantageous circumstances dictated by the opposition.

NATO air power, therefore, has to be prepared to make an equally important contribution to maritime operations as to the defence of the transport air bridge and bridgeheads. The areas to be protected, the East and North Atlantic, the North Sea and the inshore areas, are many times greater than those of mainland Europe. Fortunately, the task was made much easier with the entry into service of the E3A Sentry Airborne Warning and Control System and by the imminent deployment of the Royal Air Force's Airborne Early Warning Nimrod. Both aircraft are capable of locating surface ships and aircraft at very long range and thus permitting either carrier-borne or land-based maritime attack engagement well outside hostile stand-off missile range. Anti-submarine warfare, as in the Second World War, would be fought by both air and naval forces. Several NATO nations, the US, the UK, Norway, Germany and the Netherlands, contribute to the Allied maritime air capability. Overall, command of the sea is no longer the prerogative of the Allied navies.

Two roles remained largely unchanged in the era of 14/3. The need remained for timely information to reach the commander about the course of the battle, the disposition of evolving threats and the impact of defensive action. In 1980, eleven air forces retained a photographic reconnaissance capability and when the role was discussed the issue was usually concerned with method rather than the utility of the role itself. Nor had the need for tactical nuclear air power disappeared. Just as the long-range manned bomber added a further flexible guarantee to the strategic deterrent power of the ICBM, so the medium-range bomber complicated the calculations of the opposing field commanders and reinforced the short-range in-theatre surface-to-surface nuclear missiles. If the appropriate Allied response should be deemed to be nuclear, then air power would offer its traditional options against a wide range of both static and mobile targets.

The best guarantee against the need for such response remained a credible deterrent posture with an equally credible conventional defensive capability to support it should deterrence fail. Consequently, in 1978, in response to the steadily increasing Soviet military strength, NATO nations pledged themselves to a 3 per cent increase in defence expenditure. But the old problems were never far away: the delicate balance between political stability, economic prosperity and defence provision. The cost of aviation fuel, for example, had almost doubled every year since 1973. In an age of general monetary inflation, costs of defence equipment had risen even faster. And, no matter how the sums were worked out, commitment to 14/3 required far more resources per unit of destruction than did the old 'bigger bang for a buck' posture of pre-1967. More weapons, more training, more joint-Service exercises, more stockpiling, better communications: these were the permanent costs of the answer devised some twenty years previously to the problem posed by growing Soviet nuclear capability.

In 1980, technology, a high degree of readiness both in Europe and among those units in the US earmarked for swift reinforcement, a strong combative and dedicated professionalism and superior operational training still encouraged the belief that the NATO air forces could discharge the role allocated to them and guarantee the success of NATO strategy.

But if the Warsaw Pact air forces could continue to reduce NATO's technical superiority, continue to increase their numerical advantages, and continue to expand their offensive capability, the ability of Western air power to discharge all the responsibilities demanded of it by NATO strategy would, inevitably, be challenged. A gap between theory and practice would open as the gap between NATO and Warsaw Pact capability began to close. Since 1949, air power had made an indispensable contribution to the security of the North Atlantic Treaty members. There was now clearly a need to look imaginatively and shrewdly ahead to ensure that a blend of technology and strategy would continue to underpin that security in the foreseeable future.

8 The Falklands Campaign

The dispute between Argentina and the United Kingdom over the Falkland Islands and its dependencies had a history as long as that of Argentina herself, but until March 1982 both sides had accepted a process of negotiation and compromise to resolve their claims. At the end of that month and despite the fact that negotiations were still in progress, the governing right-wing military Junta in Argentina took advantage of a local and minor dispute to settle its claim by force. A party of scrap-metal merchants, operating from Argentina but ironically based in the United Kingdom, landed in South Georgia to dismantle a disused whaling factory. The United Kingdom protested that the landing by this party was illegal and the Ice Patrol Ship HMS *Endurance* moved to evict its members. The Junta then despatched a force of ships and marine infantry which seized the capital of the Falklands, Port Stanley, on 2 April, a task that they quickly accomplished after a skirmish with the British garrison of only 78 Royal Marines and sailors based in and near the township. Two days later the Argentines landed a small force in South Georgia, and here too the garrison had little choice but to surrender.

The initial Argentine force in the Falklands was steadily built up over the following ten weeks or so until a garrison of about 12,300 troops with local air, artillery and other support was eventually established to hold the main settlements in East and West Falklands. International condemnation of the Argentine use of force in the Falklands was accompanied by widespread acceptance of her underlying claim to the Islands, an ambivalence that was important to Argentina in later purchasing and then transporting by air military equipment from a variety of suppliers, especially in South America and the Middle East.

From any point of view the seventy-four days' campaign that then followed was a remarkable one.[1] At the strategic level it saw Argentina, a continental power with maritime leanings, challenging a maritime

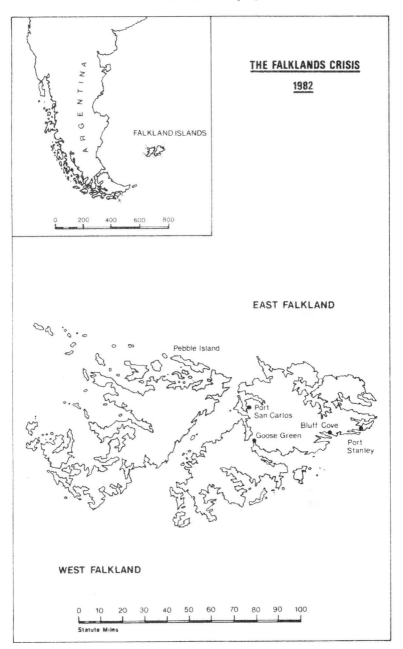

THE FALKLANDS CRISIS

1982

FALKLAND ISLANDS

EAST FALKLAND

Pebble Island

Port
San Carlos

Bluff Cove

Goose Green

Port
Stanley

WEST FALKLAND

0   10   20   30   40   50   60   70   80   90   100
Statute Miles

MAP 9   *The Falkland Islands*

power that had almost persuaded itself to adopt a continental strategy. Operationally, it was for the British a national undertaking of a kind that successive governments had declared was beyond their capabilities, while militarily it was a campaign undertaken at the extremes of one hemisphere by British forces that for nearly two decades had been almost exclusively devoted to maintaining peace at the further end of the other.

The British response to the invasion was first of all to impose a blockade by re-deploying submarines already at sea;[2] indeed, this was the only practical response that could be made until the task force, whose first elements were dispatched on the 7 and 8 April, could reach the war zone 8,000 miles away, or an average of 21 days' sailing.[3] It was correctly assessed that these nuclear-powered submarines could, because of their very low noise signature, operate in the South Atlantic at little risk from the modest Argentine anti-submarine capabilities. This blockade, which was imposed in the form of a declared Maritime Exclusion Zone of 200 nautical miles radius around a point in the middle of the Falklands, had a twofold effect. First, it was a direct and immediate response to the Argentine claim of sovereignty over the Falklands: and second, it limited the freedom of action of the Argentines in supplying their garrison on the Islands by sea.

The imposition of the MEZ could, however, do little to close the air supply route which the Argentines were already operating to Stanley airfield and to some of the other landing fields on the Islands.

There were altogether thirty-one of these fields scattered across the territory. Some were little more than a designated strip of turf in a field near a settlement or a farm; others were short stretches of beach that were uncovered only at low tide. All of them were, however, usually fit for daylight operation by light aircraft such as the Islander aircraft, while five of them were all-weather strips that could normally take a C-130 Hercules carrying a reduced load of up to 20,000 lb. Although these airstrips were such modest affairs, some of them were nevertheless vital to the new garrison; roads on the Falklands were virtually non-existent, the terrain was often totally impassable and air transport was the only feasible means of travel. Furthermore, Argentina had a sizeable fleet of transports from which aircraft could be drawn to institute an air-bridge to the Falklands and within the islands themselves. These included seven C-130s, perhaps ten Boeing 737s and five 727s of the Argentine airlines, eighteen F27 and F28s and sixteen Guarani light transports, together with a varied mixture of other smaller machines as well as over one hundred helicopters of various kinds. In the time that elapsed before the arrival in the South Atlantic of the British Task Force, both the means and the opportunity thus existed for the Argentine garrison to deploy forces widely throughout the Islands from the main logistics area at Port Stanley. At Port Stanley itself the sheltered harbour made it possible to bring substantial numbers of men and quantities of equipment ashore both from the initial invasion force of several vessels, including at least a submarine and two large amphibious landing ships, and from the follow-up force, which, between 2 and 9 April alone included two tankers and another three transport ships, as well as from several smaller vessels that ran the blockade thereafter.

An uneven but almost continuous flow of reinforcements and supplies also came in through the airport at Stanley. This was a very modest field by modern standards, with a single runway of 4,100 feet, and only one taxying strip leading from the runway to the restricted aircraft handling area which in turn had only a single small maintenance hanger. The refuelling facilities were very meagre and there were no night flying facilities. With considerable skill and ingenuity, however, the Argentines made good use of what they found at Port Stanley airfield, operating in poor weather and employing a makeshift runway lighting system so as to maintain the air-bridge by night. Inhibited only by later British air attack and naval bombardments, the Argentines continued to use the airfield to a greater or lesser extent throughout the campaign. It was reported by refugees that on at least one night for example, before the Task Force reached the area, a C-130 was landing every two hours or so, and turnrounds on the ground were taking less than thirty minutes. Using Stanley, it was estimated at the time that the C-130s could carry a payload of about 20,000 lb and probably fly 2 sorties each day. This meant a potential lift of 140 tons per day by C-130s alone, and additional lift was provided by the lighter transport aircraft. The total lift available to the Argentines was well above the likely requirements of the garrison. What the Argentines failed to do, however, was to develop the airfield or to extend its short runway, and this tends to support the view that the invasion was not the result of careful and detailed planning in advance.

Certainly there was no initial shortage of combat aircraft in the Argentine air force and navy that might have been deployed to Stanley, had the airfield been suitable. The total order of battle included seventeen Mirage III air defence aircraft, sixty-eight A4P Skyhawk and eleven A4Q Skyhawk attack aircraft, twenty-six Mirage V attack aircraft, seven Canberra B62 bombers, five naval Super-Etendards, forty-five Pucara Counter Insurgency (COIN) aircraft, perhaps three Neptunes and six S-2 Tracker aircraft for reconnaissance work, as well as various communication aircraft, twenty armed helicopters and two KC 130 air-to-air refuelling tankers.[4]

Of these substantial and by no means obsolete resources, the naval Super-Etendard with a radius of action of about 400 miles and armed with AS-39 Exocet[5] missiles emerged as the most potent weapons system in the Argentine inventory. Much more numerous however were the Mirages and A4s which, although they were armed only with conventional bombs, had a radius of action of 500 and 650 miles respectively and turned out to be just as serious a threat to the ships of the British Task Force. Opposing this varied air threat were the initial deployment of 22 Sea Harriers of the British Task Force based on the carriers *Hermes* and *Invincible*. The radius of action of the Sea Harrier in the attack role is reported to be around 300 miles, so that if the carriers approached to launch an air attack on Stanley airfield, those ships would be well within the range of any Argentine attack aircraft that might be based there.

In the air defence role, the Harrier had no look down–shoot down radar and the aircraft's pulse radar was unable to acquire low-level targets independently. Its interceptor capability, especially in marginal weather or at night, would thus be less than adequate. Low-level attack aircraft such as the Super-Etendard might therefore be able to penetrate the missile launch range before an effective counter could be deployed against them. There was also the possibility that the Argentine aircraft carrier *Veinticinco de Mayo* might head out with its escorts towards the task force under the protection of land-based air defence fighters to launch attack aircraft against the British ships, and in spite of the presence of the nuclear-powered submarines deployed in their support in the South Atlantic the level of risk might then have been very high. The scanty evidence which was available suggested, however, that the Super-Etendards might not have worked up to an operational standard on the Argentine carrier, and perhaps more significant, none of the crews of these or of the other attack aircraft had apparently been fully trained in night operations. Finally, the evidence of peacetime manoeuvres suggested that the Argentine services were not well exercised in the close co-ordination that joint operations of this kind demanded.

Thus the balance of capabilities meant that if the Argentine air force tried to operate forward from the aircraft carrier or from Port Stanley airfield, it would probably be able to do so only in daylight, and the carrier would in any case be at risk from submarine attack. On the other hand, if the British carrier group closed to a range from which it could launch Harriers against Port Stanley, it would be at risk if the Argentines did after all opt for forward deployed air, and there was also the risk from Argentine submarines. If the Argentines chose not to operate their air resources forward, they would still be left with their five very well-founded air bases in the South of the country: San Julian, Santa Cruz, Rio Gallegos, Rio Grande and Ushuaia, all of them between 400 and 430 miles from Port Stanley. Operations from these bases would mean that the Argentine combat aircraft would be at or close to their extreme radius of action when in the Falklands area, and the limited Argentine air-to-air refuelling capability would not be enough to overcome this limitation except for very small numbers of aircraft. The distance from the mainland to the Falklands also meant that response to tasking would be very slow, a useful factor as far as the British were concerned in protecting any fast-moving land operations but less of an asset for ships at sea, and even less for British ships engaged in landing operations.

Thus, although the advantage in undersea warfare lay overwhelmingly with the British, who had far more modern submarines as well as greatly superior anti-submarine capabilities, in the air the advantage was at best marginal. The only air base available to the British forces in the South Atlantic was on Ascension Island, 4,000 miles to the north of the Falklands, and there were thus no locally based attack aircraft available to take out Port Stanley airfield or to respond to any sortie by the Argentine carrier, and thus ensure air superiority.

Time was also an important factor. It was clear that the Argentines had been able to move substantial supplies to the Falklands before the blockade was imposed, and in any case aircraft and, later on, occasional supply ships were successfully running the blockade to deliver more stocks. On 11 May one supply ship was sunk by naval gunfire and on 16 May two more ships were successfully attacked by Sea Harriers. The Argentine intelligence gathering ship *Narwal* had been sunk by Sea Harriers on 9 May and three more ships were attacked and disabled in late May and early June. With continuing runs by ships but particularly by aircraft it was clear that there was little prospect of compelling an Argentine surrender by blockade, and none at all of doing so before the onset of winter in June.

Meanwhile, by 24 April the first elements of the British Task Force had arrived off South Georgia, and in appalling weather men of the Special Boat Squadron had already effected a landing and carried out a reconnaissance. On 25 April this Dependency of the Falklands was retaken after a brief action by special forces, SBS and 42 Commando, and the Argentine garrison were taken prisoner. During the action, a missile-armed helicopter attacked and disabled the Guppy class submarine *Santa Fe*, one of the four submarines of the Argentine navy, and it was later captured in Grytviken harbour.

On 30 April the blockade of the Falkland Islands was tightened by the

declaration of a Total Exclusion Zone, and early on 1 May the British
Battle Group reached a position on the edge of the Zone, 200 miles
north-east of Port Stanley, from where it could make use of the classic
potential of a carrier force to operate into rather than within the
principal area of combat. Behind the Battle Group, many other ships
were by now en route to the South Atlantic, including an Amphibious
Group as well as several of the merchant ships that were to be taken up
from trade in various roles during the course of the operation.

By the time that the British carrier force had positioned itself on the
edge of the TEZ, preparations had also been completed to employ land-
based aircraft of the Royal Air Force in the South Atlantic, and before
dawn on 1 May the first of several long-range attacks on Port Stanley
airfield by Vulcan bombers was launched from Ascension Island. This
raid, by a single aircraft carrying 21 1,000 lb bombs, was supported by a
chain of 11 Victor air-to-air refuelling tankers for its 8,000 or so miles
round flight to the Falklands and back. This flight, and the subsequent
similar ones were the longest ever made by bomber aircraft in the history
of air warfare.[6]

The stick of bombs fell across the airfield, and one bomb blew a crater
almost in the centre of the strip, the main target. That was not, however,
the most telling feature of the raid. Its significance was that the attack
could be made at all, thus serving notice on the Argentines that the
airfield and any air resources that the Argentines might seek to deploy
there were at risk from long-range air power deployed on a secure base
well outside the theatre of operations, as well as from the Harriers of the
Task Force which attacked Port Stanley airfield that same morning.

The Vulcan attack and the continuous raids by Harriers that now
began, put Stanley airfield under a bombardment that continued
throughout the remaining seven weeks of the campaign, damaging the
airfield and its facilities and causing losses among the helicopter and
Pucara light attack aircraft that were based there, as well as inhibiting
Argentine air transport activities.

For the reasons discussed, the possibility that the Argentines might
develop Port Stanley airfield had been a matter of great concern to the
British Task Force, and the fact that they did not do so was a
particularly interesting feature of the campaign. Three factors probably
influenced their decision. First, there were certain obvious physical
difficulties. To have extended the airfield at the western end would have
called for major airfield construction work, something that was beyond
the Argentine capability in the time available. At the eastern end,
however, the rocky ground is level enough to be graded to take AM3

planking, the modern equivalent of the pierced steel planking (PSP) of the Second and Korean Wars. This could have given a new total runway length of about 6,000 feet; not generous but still adequate for limited fast-jet combat aircraft, particularly if an extension to the runway had been accompanied by work to develop the aircraft servicing area and the taxying links.

Some of the construction plant that might have been used for all this work actually arrived by sea in the early stages of the campaign, but a second difficulty faced by the Argentines was that the bulk of the equipment that would have been needed was prevented from moving by the sea blockade; and even if it had been physically possible to transport the necessary plant and materials by air it would have been at the cost of other vital supplies and reinforcements. The third, and perhaps decisive factor, was that before all the airfield construction resources could be moved in, the vulnerability of the airfield to Sea Harrier and Vulcan attack had become very clear. The Argentines therefore had little choice but to confine their air activities based on the Falklands to small transports, helicopters and Pucaras, all of them aircraft that could operate from the existing facilities and from the racecourse and other nearby strips.

To the west of the TEZ, the Argentine navy, and in particular its flagship the aircraft carrier *Veinticinco de Mayo* continued to pose a potential threat to the British Task Force; but the navy engaged only in routine patrols near the Argentine coast from early April until the end of the month. At the end of April the cruiser *General Belgrano*, accompanied by two destroyers, sailed towards the TEZ posing a clear threat to the British Task Force. At 2000Z on 2 May when the *Belgrano* was closing the SW edge of the TEZ and heading towards the British units off the Falklands she was struck by two torpedoes fired by HMS *Conqueror* and sank with a loss of over 350 lives. From that time on, the Argentine fleet remained clear of British units and when the United Kingdom warned that any fleet units found more than 12 miles from the coast of Argentina would be attacked without warning, the Argentine navy, including the carrier, was even less in evidence, and the whole fleet seems to have remained in port or in coastal waters for the duration of the campaign.

Following the air attacks on Port Stanley airfield on 1 May, and a Harrier attack made on Goose Green later that day during which two light aircraft and two Pucara attack aircraft were destroyed on the ground, two ships of the Battle Group were ordered to close the East Falklands to bombard Port Stanley airfield. During this bombardment

Argentine air attacks, almost certainly supported by Neptune recce patrols flown from the Argentine mainland, were launched against units of the Fleet. One Mirage was shot down by a Sea Harrier and another by the Argentine's own anti-aircraft defences near Port Stanley. Still later that day, three Canberras attempted a bombing raid on the ships and one of these aircraft was also shot down by a Sea Harrier flying Combat Air Patrol (CAP) from the carrier HMS *Invincible*. Only minor damage was sustained by the ships of the Task Force, but an Argentine tug which later sailed into the TEZ was attacked by Sea Harriers and sunk by Sea Skua Missiles fired from a Lynx helicopter. The Total Exclusion Zone was becoming a zone of active operations, although, except for the sinking by Task Force Harriers of an Argentine tug that had been detected carrying out electronic surveillance inside the TEZ, the next few days were relatively quiet.

Meanwhile, the airfield at Ascension Island had been expanded into a major base for the support of the operations in the South Atlantic.[7] Already by these early stages of the campaign there were over 400 aircraft movements through the base each day, supported by over 700 base personnel who had deployed there from the United Kingdom. Vulcan bombers and Victor tankers were based on the Island; Nimrod surveillance sorties of more than 19 hours' duration were being flown from Ascension; Hercules transports were being used daily to drop urgent supplies to fleet units on passage, sometimes with a round flight of as much as 4,000 miles;[8] and reinforcements of Harrier aircraft were being air-ferried out to Ascension, from where 4 of them made a 9-hour flight to land on the carrier *Hermes* as she sailed south. Sea King helicopters had arrived to act as ASW patrol in case Ascension itself came under threat from the three remaining submarines that Argentina was known to possess, and other local defence measures were put in hand at Ascension to meet any possible threats, measures that included the detachment of Phantom air defence aircraft to the island on 24 May. Most of this extensive deployment to and through Ascension was made possible by the AAR Victor and Vulcan aircraft which flew in support throughout the campaign and during the consolidation phase after hostilities had ceased.[9]

On 4 May the British forces suffered their first reverse when the destroyer HMS *Sheffield* was attacked by two Super-Etendards which each fired one Exocet As-39 at low level from a range of about twenty-eight miles. *Sheffield* was hit and so badly damaged that she had to be abandoned, and although she was left afloat as a lure for any Argentine submarines that might have been in the area, six days later while she was under tow she succumbed to the heavy weather and sank. Also on 4 May, a Sea Harrier was lost attacking Goose Green airstrip, which the Argentines were consolidating into a considerable operating base for their aircraft on the Falklands; and on 6 May two Sea Harriers failed to return after they had taken off to investigate an air contact near the British fleet, at this time off the south-east of the Falklands.

A period of bad weather with fog and low cloud followed by gales heralding the oncoming winter now intervened, but the Battle Group continued its activities to interdict the Argentine air-bridge, and ships as well as aircraft were by now operating to the west of the Falklands on this mission. During a break in the weather on the afternoon of 12 May, two waves of Argentine aircraft each of four A4 Skyhawks attacked HM Ships *Brilliant* and *Glasgow* which were deployed on the gunline. Two A4s in the first wave were shot down by Seawolf missiles from HMS *Brilliant*, and a third A4 was seen to fly into the sea. Aircraft in the second wave dropped a number of bombs, one of which passed through HMS *Glasgow* without exploding.

But with the bulk of their air resources still uncommitted, the Argentine air threat from the mainland and on the Falklands remained a major concern, and further air attacks were therefore made on their base at Stanley airfield by Sea Harriers carrying 1,000 lb bombs on 14 and 15 May. During the early hours of 15 May, a highly successful raid was also carried out by Special Forces against a secondary Argentine air base that was being developed at Pebble Island. Twelve aircraft were destroyed in this attack, as well as various stores and stocks of ammunition.[10] Despite these successful attacks, however, the Argentine forces within the Falklands retained enough air assets to afford a useful airlift capability, and their garrison continued to deploy and to consolidate its positions near Stanley and in the more remote settlements, both by helicopter and by sea. Two small ships engaged in this local transport work were, however, detected and successfully attacked by Sea Harriers on 16 May for no loss.

On 20 May, Naval Gunfire Support (NGS) was laid down against shore installations ready for the next phase of the operation, and on the same day the first of the Harrier GR3s of the Royal Air Force that had arrived on the container ship *Atlantic Conveyor* and had been transferred to HMS *Hermes*, successfully attacked a fuel dump near Fox Bay, while Sea Harriers flew CAP missions.

By this time, the second week in May, a substantial British Task Force had assembled to the East of the Falklands, and further ships including the *Queen Elizabeth 2* carrying the three battalions of the 5th Infantry

Brigade were heading South from Ascension Island, while still more were being taken up from civilian use in the United Kingdom and prepared for operations in the South Atlantic. With the weather worsening as the Antarctic winter grew closer and the Argentine force on the Falklands still apparently consolidating, the need to establish at least a beachhead on the Islands as soon as possible was clear, and on 21 May the invasion began.

Fanning Head, one of the promontories at the northern end of Falkland Sound, was taken by Special Boat Section troops in advance of the main landing so as to eliminate a potential threat on the approaches, and units of the Task Force were then able to deploy into Falkland Sound. Four hours before sunrise and in clear weather, unopposed landings were made by 3 Commando Brigade and the 2nd and 3rd Battalions, the Parachute Regiment, on four beaches in the area of San Carlos Water.

The narrow inlet of San Carlos with its surrounding high ground offered a useful degree of protection to the troopships during this operation, particularly against the principal threat, that of Exocet missiles, which would not easily be able to acquire ship targets against the nearby cliffs. The geography and the fact that the landing force made very determined use of its weapons against approaching aircraft meant that the landings, involving some 10,000 troops and their equipment, were completed without loss within about four hours. Meanwhile, warships of the Task Force formed a gunline in Falkland Sound so as to intercept any attacking aircraft, and it was these ships that became the principal target for heavy and determined Argentine air attacks in three waves during the day, starting at 1120 local time, some seven hours after the first landing.

Two HM Ships, *Ardent* and *Argonaut* were severely damaged by bombs and *Ardent* later sank. *Antrim* was struck by a bomb that failed to explode, and two other ships, *Broadsword* and *Brilliant* also suffered minor damage. During these attacks the Argentine air and naval air forces lost nine Mirage aircraft and one damaged, five A4 Skyhawks and one damaged, as well as two Pucaras and a number of helicopters. Of the fourteen fixed-wing aircraft destroyed, eleven were shot down by Sea Harriers and three by ship and shore-based missiles and guns.

The day of 22 May passed relatively quietly, with the landing force consolidating ashore in the absence of any contact with enemy force on the ground and the only Argentine air reaction was a single raid by two A4s during the evening; but these aircraft did not press home their attack and one was shot down by the defences. On 23 May the Argentine air attacks were resumed in some strength when two formations, each of four A4s followed by four Mirages and then another two Mirages, launched raids against the beach-head area. Two A4s were confirmed destroyed and the other two possibly destroyed from the first wave; all four Mirages from the second wave and one of the fourth was also shot down, a total of seven confirmed and probably two more destroyed out of an attacking force of fourteen aircraft. Of these, four were kills by ship-borne missiles, one by 20mm gunfire and two by Sea Harriers firing Sidewinder missiles. Another Mirage which did not close to attack was shot down by a Sea Harrier CAP later that afternoon and on the same day Sea Harriers also attacked three helicopters in the air destroying one, and later destroying the other two on the ground. During the second raid, HMS *Antelope* was hit by a bomb that failed to explode, but it later detonated during efforts to defuse it and the ship sank.

Port Stanley was again attacked by Harriers the next day causing additional damage to the runway, and two hours later the Argentines returned to launch further air attacks on the amphibious ships of the Task Force. Five A4s attacked the San Carlos anchorage from the South, scoring one hit on the LSL *Sir Lancelot* and her sister ship *Sir Galahad* with bombs that failed to explode. A formation of Mirages then attacked and hit *Sir Lancelot* with a second bomb, which also failed to explode; but another wave of four Mirages that tried to close was intercepted by two Harriers armed with Sidewinders which shot down three of them. A final wave of mixed A4s and Mirages then came in but lost a total of five aircraft, two to ship-borne missiles and three to Rapier missiles deployed ashore. At the end of the action, *Sir Galahad* had been on fire but had brought the blaze under control and had one unexploded bomb on board, while *Sir Lancelot* was still fighting her fires and had two unexploded bombs on board.

By now San Carlos Water was the scene of intense activity as the disembarkation of equipment and stores continued, and recognising the critical phase that the whole operation had now reached the Argentine air forces returned to the attack again on 25 May. HMS *Broadsword* and HMS *Coventry* were on station about ten miles north of Falkland Sound when they were attacked by three A4 Skyhawks. HMS *Coventry* was hit by bombs and later sank with the loss of some thirty lives, while HMS *Broadsword* was hit by a bomb which passed right through the ship without exploding. One A4 was shot down. Two further A4s attacked HMS *Fearless* near San Carlos without success and both of these aircraft were shot down.

In a third attack, at around sunset on that same day, 2 Super-

Etendards attacked the Battle Group some 120 miles NE of Port Stanley. They each released an Exocet missile from 28 miles range at low level and at least one missile struck the container ship *Atlantic Conveyor*. She caught fire, lost control and had to be abandoned shortly afterwards. It seems likely that the intended targets of the attack were the aircraft carriers *Hermes* and *Invincible*, and it was fortunate that neither was hit. As it was, the loss of the *Atlantic Conveyor* was serious enough and when she finally sank some days later she took with her a large quantity of stores including tentage for the eventual garrison of the Falklands, and a number of helicopters including three Chinooks.

On 25, 26 and 27 May, further Sea Harrier attacks were made on Port Stanley airfield mainly with 1000 lb bombs, while in the land campaign advances were made across almost impassable terrain towards Douglas and Teal in the north, and Darwin and Goose Green in the south, in a two-pronged move that would eventually take the land forces to the hills just west of Port Stanley.

In these and in subsequent operations ashore, direct air support played very little part. Because the terrain was such a difficult mixture of peat-bog and trackless boulder-fields, the rate of ground movement was extremely limited. And because the terrain was so open, troops moving across it in daylight would be very exposed to Argentine defensive fire from the ground and perhaps from the air. It was therefore decided to conduct most operations by night, which increased the difficulties but sharply reduced the risks. In these circumstances, air support mainly took the form of helicopter supply and transportation work, a role which became crucial as the British troops moved eastward in worsening weather across the high and inhospitable terrain during the remainder of the campaign.

Meanwhile the Argentine air assault on the San Carlos area continued on 27 May with several attack waves during the day. During the late afternoon, two Mirages dropped bombs from medium level on land-force targets near San Carlos, but caused no damage, and two hours later a pair of A4 Skyhawks attacked the British base maintenance area, which had been set up in Ajax Bay, causing only slight damage. Two more pairs of A4s followed later, this time inflicting a number of casualties in killed and wounded. During the day one A4 was shot down and another damaged, both by gunfire from HMS *Fearless*.

Goose Green and Darwin were recaptured by 2nd Battalion, the Parachute Regiment with Harrier air support on 28 May, thus depriving the Argentine garrison of one of their four fixed-wing operating bases (Stanley, Stanley Race Course, Pebble Island and Goose Green). The next day saw further air attacks by Sea Harriers which carried out a total of three raids on Port Stanley airfield and two on the airstrips at Pebble Island. These attacks were serious blows to the Argentine air resources on the Falklands at this time. The air order of battle by now probably consisted of twenty-three Pucaras, six Aeromachis, two Skyvans, two or three Chinooks and perhaps a dozen other helicopters. Several aircraft had already been lost or damaged, particularly in the attacks on Port Stanley airfield, and the remaining force must now have found itself hard pressed to maintain any air capability at all.

Argentine air activity from the mainland was also very modest in scope at this point in operations; but what it lacked in volume it made up in character. On 29 May a C-130 Hercules transport aircraft dropped 8 bombs in a surprise attack on the tanker *British Wye* while she was en route to the Falklands from Ascension and some 600 miles from the Argentine mainland, and one bomb hit the foredeck but bounced off without exploding. This incident led to adjustments being made in the routeing followed by UK ships in the South Atlantic, and ships at South Georgia were ordered to remain at sea and to disperse when not actually engaged in transferring stores. There were also sporadic attacks on the San Carlos area during which another A4 Skyhawk was shot down by a Rapier missile, but on 30 May there was a further attack by the most threatening weapon in the Argentine air inventory – the Exocet-armed Super-Etendard. One of these aircraft, escorted by two A4s, launched a missile attack against the carrier HMS *Invincible*, but failed to hit.[11] One A4 was reported to have been shot down by a Sea Dart missile. The notable feature of this engagement was the range from the mainland at which the attack was launched, indicating that the Argentines had probably used air-to-air refuelling for the mission which, because these resources were so limited, kept down the size of the attacking force to a level at which it could not overwhelm the defences of the Carrier Group.

On 1 June a single Vulcan supported by fifteen Victor tanker sorties all launched from Ascension made a pre-dawn attack with missiles against Argentine facilities near Stanley airfield. A further and similar attack was made two days later, although on that occasion an airborne failure on the return leg caused the aircraft to divert to Rio de Janeiro. North of the Falklands Channel on this same day, an Argentine C-130 Hercules, probably engaged on a reconnaissance mission into the TEZ, was intercepted by two Sea Harriers and shot down with Sidewinder and cannon-fire.

Another period of gales followed by fog next hindered air activity, but the naval Battle Group continued to support land forces from the eastern sector of the TEZ by bombarding targets in the Port Stanley area as well as by laying down fire on Pebble Island, while on-shore work went ahead to prepare a Harrier Forward Operating Base at San Carlos. Meanwhile, 45 Commando and 3rd Battalion, the Parachute Regiment had made a fifty-mile march across extraordinarily difficult terrain in very bad weather, along the northern axis by Douglas and Teal Inlet to reach the high ground west of Port Stanley, and 42 Commando had been inserted by helicopter at night to take the key heights of Mount Kent and Mount Challenger.[12] At the same time, the first units of 5 Infantry Brigade had arrived from South Georgia after trans-shipping there, and on 1 June the 1/7 Gurkha Rifles together with some minor units disembarked in the San Carlos area. Substantial air defences were also ashore by this time, including more Rapiers, and on the whole the air threat to the forces ashore was no longer such a serious one. Out at sea there was still a considerable threat, as the attack on *Invincible* had shown, nor was there any shortage of potential targets for the Argentine air forces. By now there was a total of about 80 British ships in the South Atlantic: some 51 were in or near the Falkland TEZ, 10 were at sea between the Falklands and South Georgia, 5 were off South Georgia and 10 were on passage between Ascension Island and South Georgia.[13] But the combination of routeing, of sheer sea space available, the limited range of Argentine air power and the effectiveness of the defences, notably the Harrier in the air defence role, were all factors that combined to reduce the threat to a tolerable level in daylight hours, and at night the threat was virtually non-existent. The principal risk was that of Argentine aircraft attacking British ships that closed the Falklands in support of the troops ashore; and that risk would remain high, at least in daylight, for so long as the carrier force was compelled by that same air threat to provide air defence cover from a station well out to sea east of Port Stanley.

This same inability to ensure absolute air superiority also meant that the Argentines could still fly occasional supply runs into Port Stanley airfield and they were still able to make sporadic bombing raids on British positions on East Falkland using some of the remaining Argentine light aircraft, including the Pucaras, although very little damage was caused. The air balance changed somewhat on 6 June, when two Sea Harriers and two GR3s deployed ashore to the newly constructed Forward Operating Base at San Carlos, and from now on these aircraft were able to conduct combat air patrols as well as close air support missions from their land base, thus improving reaction time for attack missions and greatly increasing the time on station during air defence patrols over the Falklands. In the land campaign, meanwhile, the 2nd Scots Guards of 5th Infantry Brigade landed at Bluff Cove during the night of 5/6 June, thus by-passing Fitzroy bridge on the difficult track from Goose Green, and putting British troops within fifteen miles of Port Stanley itself.

Bad weather intervened again on 7 June, but on 8 June the Argentine air force took advantage of an improvement to attack HMS *Plymouth* in Falkland Sound with five Mirages using bombs, rockets and cannon. Two Mirage aircraft were destroyed and one damaged by the combined effects of Seacat missiles and 4.5″ gunfire, but *Plymouth* herself was hit and damaged by a bomb. In a later and more serious attack that day, four Mirage aircraft attacked the LSLs *Sir Galahad* and *Sir Tristram* which had sailed up the East coast of the Falklands to disembark 1st Battalion Welsh Guards at Fitzroy. *Sir Tristram* had almost completed unloading when she was hit by two bombs, which failed to explode, although fires were started. *Sir Galahad* was less fortunate and caught fire after taking hits while many troops were still on board; over one hundred casualties were sustained, and valuable equipment was lost. Both ships were abandoned. One Mirage was shot down by Sea Harriers and another damaged. Two hours later another four Mirage aircraft attacked an LCU in Choiseul Sound and scored one bomb hit on the vessel, but all four Mirages were destroyed – three by Sea Harriers, the fourth when it crashed into the sea possibly after suffering damage from debris. Argentine A4s also attacked British shore positions and sustained one aircraft lost and one damaged.

On 10 June, four Pucaras based on the Falklands bombed and strafed positions on Mount Kent, and on 11 June Sea Harriers attacked Port Stanley airfield, their likely base. Also on 11 June, units of 3 Commando Brigade were ordered to take the three main features of Mount Longdon, Mount Harriet and The Two Sisters in silent night attacks. These hill features formed part of the line to which the landing force had by now advanced after an arduous march across North Falkland, and by 0700 on 12 June all three positions had been taken by 3rd Battalion the Parachute Regiment, 45 Commando and 42 Commando against an enemy who was well dug in, supported by artillery, equipped with night vision sights and protected by anti-personnel mines. The advance of the British units had been supported by artillery and by naval gunfire by a force that included HMS *Glamorgan*, but at the end of the bombardment the ship was hit by a shore-based version of the same Exocet missile family that had posed such a threat when carried by Super-Etendard aircraft. It was later to emerge that the Argentine garrison at Port

Stanley had six of these missiles which they had installed ashore in makeshift but effective fashion for just such an opportunity.

Just before dawn on that same day, what was to be the final Vulcan bombing attack from Ascension was made on the airfield at Port Stanley. Twenty-one 1000 lb VT-fused bombs were dropped during this raid, which was supported by thirteen Victor tankers flying a total of seventeen sorties. Over the same area later on in the day, another Mirage was shot down by a Sea Harrier at high level but otherwise the day was quiet, though it was incidentally marked by the 1000th sortie flown by Harriers from HMS *Hermes* since the Task Force had left Ascension.[14]

After the success of the earlier assault on the Argentine defence positions outside Port Stanley, the British artillery was replenished by a major helicopter lift and on the night of 13 June, 5th Infantry Brigade was ordered to take the final high ground in the South. After fierce fighting the Scots Guards occupied Tumble-Down Hill and the whole brigade, Scots Guards, 1/7 Gurkha Rifles and 2nd Battalion, the Parachute Regiment, broke through. During these final thirty-six hours of the campaign, as British troops moved towards Stanley from the hills to the West, HMS *Cardiff* engaged four air contacts at 38,000 ft and destroyed one aircraft, probably a Canberra, with a Sea Dart missile; the rest of the formation dispersed when the Sea Harrier air defence readiness aircraft took off and closed to attack. Naval gunfire support continued throughout these later stages of the operations, together with ground support by Harriers including a successful attack with laser-guided bombs on a 105mm gun position, before force 10 winds, high seas and icing conditions cancelled all flying on 16 June. By then, however, these same conditions had sapped the morale of the Argentine garrison, and faced with the advancing British troops supported by extensive firepower from the sea as well as from heavy concentrations of artillery brought up by helicopter, the Argentines left their forward positions and made their way back to Port Stanley. At 0100Z on 15 June, the Argentine Commander acknowledged the hopelessness of his position and surrendered.

It had been a short but intensive conflict, and a campaign that had engaged a larger British Task Force than any other conflict since 1945. That Task Force, made up of 117[15] ships and some 25,000 men, operating 8,000 miles from its home base, had quickly defeated an Argentine garrison of over 12,000 men deployed under the protection of substantial air and maritime resources based only 400 miles away. Losses on both sides had not been low, particularly in major equipments such as aircraft and ships. Precise figures for Argentine casualties in the campaign are not available, but they include several hundred killed[16] as well as the loss of a cruiser and a submarine and the surrender of very substantial quantities of weapons and equipment. Their total air losses included 95 fixed-wing aircraft and 14 helicopters, among which were 31 A4 Skyhawks, 26 Mirage III and V and 23 Pucaras. Of these aircraft, 27 were destroyed by British air patrols, 8 were shot down by Sea Dart missiles, 4 by Sea Wolf, 5 by Sea Cat, 9 by Rapiers, 8 by small-arms and hand-held missiles, 6 were lost in accidents such as crashes during evasive manoeuvres, and 3 were destroyed by the Argentines' own anti-aircraft fire. Another 15 aircraft were found destroyed on the ground, from various causes, after the cease-fire.

British losses included 255 killed and 777 wounded; 8 Harriers were lost, 5 of them to enemy ground fire, but none in air-to-air combat, and a number of helicopters were destroyed. 12 warships were damaged; of these, 3 were sunk by bombs and a fourth sank after being bit by an Exocet missile. Of the other 8 warships damaged, 1 suffered an Exocet hit and 7 were damaged by bombs or by strafing or both. 5 other ships were damaged, 3 of them were LSLs of which 1 was later sunk; the other 2 were merchant ships, the *Atlantic Conveyor* sunk by an Exocet, and the *British Wye* damaged by one of the many unexploded bombs dropped by the Argentine air forces. This failure of Argentine bombs to explode was an interesting feature of the campaign and contrasted strongly with the success of Argentine pilots in penetrating the defences of the Task Force to bomb ships with very high accuracy. Paradoxically, several of the bomb failures were probably caused by the lack of armour on the British ships, but others resulted from the fact that the Argentine pilots were compelled to attack very low and fast by the efficiency of the defending combat air patrols. The resulting short trajectory of the bombs did not allow enough time for them to arm before impact.

For the British, the campaign was above all a highly successful exercise in maritime power. At the same time, however, the air power that was deployed by both sides not only proved formative during the conflict itself, but it was also decisive in its outcome. At the start of the campaign there had been an Argentine strength of about 360[17] aircraft of mixed quality operating almost exclusively from secure land bases, opposed by approximately 180 British aircraft afloat in the theatre, including 28 Sea Harriers of the Royal Navy and 14 Harrier GR3s of the Royal Air Force. These aircraft were backed by substantial air capabilities deployed 4,000 miles further north at Ascension Island which included long-range transport, surveillance and attack aircraft.

The initial Argentine air superiority over the Falkland Islands conditioned the concepts of the Task Force for the whole operation, and led for example to the gradual East-to-West extension of British air cover in its early stages. And it was the exploitation of the deficiencies in Argentine air capabilities by a skilful and flexible air opponent that progressively changed the overall air balance in favour of the Task Force. At least four factors, some positive and some negative, played a part in that changing balance.

First, there was the question of ship defences. The British force was dependent on two aircraft carriers for its air assets and thus for the eventual success of the whole operation, although the use of landing decks on LSDs, RFA *Engadine* (a helicopter support ship) as well as on the *Atlantic Conveyor*, spread the risk and compounded the Argentine targetting problem. These ships relied for protection from air attack on a modest Harrier air defence force backed by the ship-mounted air defences of the fleet. None of the ships in the Task Force was armoured; those that were armed, that is to say the warships, carried mainly SAMs designed for use against aircraft at medium to long range. The merchant ships had virtually no armament at all. The air defence cover available naturally included ship-borne radar, but a striking deficiency was the total absence of airborne early warning which could have gained invaluable time for defensive deployment in general, and for the launch of Harrier combat air patrols in particular.

Second, there was the question of weapons effectiveness. The Argentine air force and navy between them employed aircraft and weapons systems that ranged from the highly effective combination of Super-Etendards armed with Exocet missiles at one end of the spectrum, through ageing Mirage IIIs and Vs to obsolescent A4 Skyhawks[18] armed with conventional but often badly fused 250 and 500 kg bombs at the other. All these aircraft were able to approach at low level so that they were detected comparatively late; the Super-Etendards in pairs to launch Exocets generally outside the range of ship-borne defences, and the Mirages and A4s to make direct attacks in waves that tended to swamp those defences. The Task Force tactics were to engage with Harrier CAPs as far forward as possible, and to protect the unarmed ships with gunlines formed by warships.

A third factor was the Argentine attempt to disperse the air assets that they had deployed in the Falkland Islands themselves. Although as it turned out these were never more than a handful of Pucaras and gunship helicopters, the potential even of this modest force to attack vital elements of the Task Force, particularly during the critical landing phase, could not be ignored. But the difficulty of locating and of neutralising these aircraft on the ground in the absence of a really effective air reconnaissance capability was considerable. This ability of the Argentines to disperse on to rudimentary airstrips was thus an added and important complication for the thinly stretched air assets of the Task Force.

Fourth, and perhaps above all else, the air confrontation showed the value of an all-weather capability and the decisive effect of its absence. Not only the run-in to the Falklands by the ships of the Task Force, but the critical landing operations at San Carlos as well as the subsequent advances of the ground forces were facilitated and in most cases made possible in the first place by the lack of any Argentine night and all-weather air capability. Even so potentially vulnerable a target as the passenger liner *Canberra*, pressed into service as a troopship, was able to enter the shelter and protection of San Carlos water at lowered risk by sailing in and out during the hours of darkness.

At a more general level the campaign demonstrated three important principles for air power. First, the importance of secure air bases in the theatre of operations. Had there been such bases the British Task Force would have been able to deploy air resources such as reconnaissance aircraft, tactical maritime attack aircraft, and above all a comprehensive AEW and air defence force that could have warded off even the most determined Argentine air attack efforts. As it was, and as earlier campaigns in distant theatres had shown, there are circumstances in which carrier-borne air power can play an essential role. No less true, however, was the fact that because of a general maritime inferiority, especially in the submarine and ASW fields, the Argentine aircraft carrier *Veinticinco de Mayo*, although based in what amounted to home waters, was able to play no role whatever in the conflict, and her air wing was compelled to operate from shore bases – at considerable cost to the available range and the routeing flexibility of those air assets.

Second, the campaign showed how a single aspect of air power flexibility can produce operational effectiveness across a broad field of capabilities. In this case the key factor was air-to-air refuelling. Although expensive in terms of resources, this capability made possible vital air drops to the fleet by transport aircraft operating well beyond their normal radius of action; it facilitated the air reinforcement of an aircraft carrier at extreme range; it enabled Victor aircraft modified for the photographic and maritime reconnaissance roles to assess Argentine disposition around South Georgia before that dependency was reoccupied; it made possible the long ocean surveillance flights by maritime Nimrods; and not least, in terms of demonstrating the potential impact of long-range air power to the Argentine garrison of the Falklands, it led to the attacks by Vulcans on Port Stanley itself.

Third, the campaign was a timely reminder of the flexibility of air power at each of its three levels, tactical, operational and strategic, and many examples emerged. At the tactical level the campaign saw the Harrier in particular demonstrate the ability of air power to switch its efforts from one target array to another, from the runway at Port Stanley airfield, for example, to Argentine supply ships running the blockade or to the interception of incoming air attacks. The campaign also showed the invaluable and flexible qualities of the helicopter, not only in the attack role but more emphatically, in moving forward ground forces including artillery and their support in circumstances where effective attack without very heavy casualties would have been impossible. At the operational level air power showed its capacity to adapt to the unique circumstances of a totally unexpected theatre of operations. Nimrods, for example, were fitted at very short notice with an air-to-air refuelling capability and armed with Sidewinder and Harpoon missiles to give them respectively an air-to-air and an air-to-surface attack capability. Ageing Victor tankers were modified for the photographic reconnaissance and maritime reconnaissance roles; and Hercules transports were modified as air-to-air refuelling tankers and receivers.

Finally, at the strategic level the campaign demonstrated how the resources of air power that had been designed for war in the specific, finite, sophisticated and possibly nuclear environment of Europe and the North Atlantic could nevertheless at short notice switch the thrust of its efforts to meet the totally different circumstances of a conventional campaign for which no preparations whatever had been made, and which was fought at the far end of the opposite hemisphere.

9 Challenge and Opportunities

It was air power that opened the nuclear age, and it did so with an intensity of focus that surpassed even Douhet's exaggerated vision of the potential of air bombardment. But within a very short time new factors had begun to blur that focus, and the history of air power since 1945 is essentially a history of diffusion, a history of air power and of the strategic thought behind it moving away from an insistence on the primacy of defeating an enemy by overwhelming air attack on his homeland before his army and navy could even mobilise.

It has been a pragmatic and a piecemeal process during which five very broad categories of war and warlike confrontation have emerged: wars against guerrilla armies; a continuous and intensive confrontation, mainly in Europe; local conventional wars; aerospace surveillance; and strategic air bombardment. In each of these categories air power has played a part, and sometimes a decisive part, but at other times its influence has been less important, as the previous chapters have shown.

Guerrilla wars

That was certainly true of some of the campaigns against guerrilla armies in the many wars of this kind during the nuclear age.

During the first major campaign against guerrillas, that in French Indo-China, very modest air forces did their best to support a high-quality army, but an army that had not learned all the lessons of fighting guerrillas. And when that guerrilla army challenged the French on their own terms at Dien Bien Phu, the French belief that they had the options of defeating the attack or evacuating their fortified position by air proved to be ill-founded.

In Malaya, the British correctly assessed that their best hope of defeating the rebels lay in isolating them from their supplies and then tracking them down in the jungle. This was a long and costly process, and one that air power could do very little to shorten. Combat aircraft were used in the campaign mainly because they were available, and only transport, reconnaissance and psychological warfare aircraft and helicopters were able to play a really effective part. The most valuable contribution made by air power was in moving men and supplies rapidly from one operational area to another.

The insurrection in Algeria was conducted in circumstances that made tactical air power somewhat more useful, not only in high-speed searches across the empty terrain, but in concentrating airborne firepower on enemy units caught in the open and, more significantly, in deploying troops by helicopter to ambush and destroy guerrilla units. These local successes were not, however, enough to prevent a strategic defeat, though it is true that the defeat had as much to do with a French wish to be rid of the serious drains on her resources caused by the war in North Africa as with any military successes or failures in the field.

Comparatively massive use of air power by the US in Vietnam against the same guerrilla enemy that the French had fought in that theatre was not much more successful than those earlier efforts. Throughout the campaign in South Vietnam itself, it remained difficult and often impossible to locate enemy positions accurately because of the terrain and the weather. Because the Viet Cong on the whole held the initiative, they could often break off an attack if the reaction of the defence was proving too much for them, and melt away into the jungle.

Only when the Viet Cong attempted something like a conventional battle on American terms could air power come to grips with them and inflict heavy losses on their ground forces by employing massive air attack before the guerrillas could escape.

Against the guerrilla logistics network in southern Laos air power faced other difficulties. A comprehensive but diffuse supply network through the jungle defied all efforts to close it down completely, and enough logistic support always evaded the air interdiction campaign to allow the Viet Cong to maintain a generally offensive posture.

Air power, and even air power which can deploy the latest military technology, has not yet found the answer to a resolute guerrilla army on its own territory. Indeed it seems likely that because developments in technology have widened the gap between the relatively primitive equipment of the guerrilla and the forces seeking to destroy him, the chances of air power succeeding in this type of mission may have actually diminished. The history of the past forty years shows that when guerrillas are able to disperse into the terrain, or to conceal themselves among the indigenous population, or both, then the most effective use of air power is to transport appropriate anti-guerrilla forces from one area of ground operations to another, rather than to lay down inappropriate, often indiscriminate, ineffective and perhaps even counterproductive, firepower.

Conventional confrontation

Above that level of war against guerrillas and insurgents, there has been since 1945 an intense and continuous military confrontation between the superpowers, notably in Europe, that has been not only the driving force for many of the air concepts that have emerged but also for much of the worldwide air systems procurement that has taken place over those same four decades.

As far as the West is concerned, those concepts and that procurement have a twofold bias which could have the effect of distorting any attempts to transpose air power thinking to any other type of conflict. The first source of bias is the unbroken assumption that the strategy of the West is defensive and reactive. To give only one example of the result of this in terms of concepts, to achieve any rational objectives in Europe the forces of the Warsaw Pact must occupy ground, and to deny them that ground the NATO Alliance has the option of employing firepower rather than using countervailing and expensive ground forces. Most of the firepower employed would be delivered by air and it is the air weapon that makes it possible for the defence to concentrate intense and flexible firepower rapidly at any point along a very extensive front.

Warsaw Pact air power, on the other hand, is not driven by the imperative to concentrate firepower in order to redress imbalances of force on the ground. There is therefore far more scope in the Warsaw Pact armoury for the relatively short-range, light-payload characteristics of the helicopter, thus releasing the fixed-wing components of that air power to undertake penetration missions.

The second source of bias is that, paradoxically enough, within the defensive strategy of the West, air power is virtually the only offensive arm. Only air power is explicitly equipped to penetrate to objectives on the territory of the potential opponent and to destroy them, and the result is an emphasis on the offensive aspects of air power that is entirely appropriate for example in Europe, but may not always be so fitting in other circumstances.

Conventional war

The detailed roles of air power that are implied in that kind of intense but static confrontation between the super powers are dealt with later, but meanwhile the weapons deployed have been actually engaged in several lesser though still very major conflicts, notably in Korea, in the Arab–Israeli Wars, in the air campaigns fought by the US over Laos and North Vietnam and in the Falklands.

These conventional wars hold many lessons for the employment of air power, and three need to be stressed here. First, the wars on the whole have again confirmed the very high effectiveness of the air weapon when properly applied. Second, they have shown that the proper application of offensive air power is against targets that are beyond the reach or the capacity of other weapons systems.

This means, for example, that for so long as ground forces are capable of dealing with their direct opponents, they should continue to do so and that if a very high local mobility of firepower is called for it is probably best provided by organic helicopters. Fixed-wing aircraft should, in those circumstances, be directing their theatre efforts against more profitable target arrays such as the enemy air infrastructure of airfields and other facilities so that our own air power can seize and maintain the air initiative, and against interdiction targets.

A third and crucial lesson from these conventional wars is that of the high lethality of anti-aircraft defences. Those defences form a direct threat to air operations, but at least equally serious is the indirect threat. Means have been found to reduce the risks to aircraft, and other means will no doubt emerge in the future. But these countermeasures will always absorb scarce resources and thus tend to deflect air effort away from the primary targets. Simply to reduce the vulnerability of air weapons systems is not enough; that reduction must be matched by the maintenance of the level of primary effort, or at the least there must be a carefully calculated balance between the one and the other.

Surveillance

Aerospace surveillance, that is to say surveillance and monitoring both by satellite and by aircraft, has proved to be a vital factor not only in stabilising the direct confrontation between the super powers, but in monitoring developments in peripheral areas. Strategic systems on both sides of the super power confrontation are continuously verified by satellite, while the progress of, for example, the Arab–Israeli War of 1973 was closely followed by Soviet satellites, and during the Iran–Iraq war of 1980/81 US AWACS aircraft were deployed to Saudi Arabia to provide surveillance of the disputed region.

The unspectacular and often covert nature of aerospace surveillance conceals a continuing and crucial politico-military influence by air power that extends well beyond its immediate operational roles.

Strategic air power

Finally, but by no means least in these four categories of air power development, there is strategic air bombardment. This was once the mainstream of Western air power doctrine, since all other missions including that of air superiority were at one time held to be merely supportive; they were designed to gain time for the strategic air offensive to take full effect, or in some other way to facilitate its success.

At Hiroshima and Nagasaki the doctrine of strategic air bombard-ment seemed to be fully vindicated, but within only six years the Korean War showed not only that the US strategic bombing resources were inadequate for the magnitude of the task that theory seemed to indicate, but they were also totally inappropriate to that type of peripheral conflict. Thus the whole strategy with which the Second World War had ended was undermined.

Following that, the development of highly effective SAMs dealt a tactical blow to the strategic bomber, and the emergence of nuclear-armed intercontinental ballistic missiles dealt a blow at the strategic and conceptual level from which the manned bomber has never fully recovered – at least in the superpower context.

Outside that context, however, strategic bombing has remained a viable concept. Although the Americans, for example, referred to their 'Linebacker' attacks on the Hanoi and Haiphong areas as interdiction raids, they were explicitly designed to force the North Vietnamese back to the conference table; that is to say to undermine the will of the enemy to continue the war. Strategic bombing has therefore already shown its potential in wars other than global. Misleading impressions to the contrary have their origin in the assumption that the term 'strategic' in air power concepts refers only to the superpower confrontation. Its meaning is much wider than that, and the future will certainly see the use of strategic air power within discrete theatres of war.

FUTURE CHALLENGES

Speculation about the future place of air power must be a cloth woven of many different threads. Important among them are the changing geopolitical climate in which air power must operate; the extent to which the resources of air power might be made available when other priorities are competing; and the technical and operational problems of actually bringing effective air power to bear in crisis or combat situations.

As far as the first two are concerned, at least some of the likely principal factors can be suggested before a more detailed analysis of the operational roles of air power is offered.

Geopolitical shifts

Militarily, there seems little doubt that one of the principal developments of the past three decades has been the shift of military decision back to the battlefield; the resulting emphasis on conventional and guerrilla warfare has been described in earlier chapters. Politically there have been equally fundamental changes.

Until well into the nuclear age, events in the international field were guided almost exclusively by a handful of relatively powerful nations, a fact recognised explicitly, for example, in the existence of the Security Council of the UN. Not only that, but the gap between the nations which wielded modern weapons and those that did not, itself a phenomenon several centuries old, had still not been closed. The really powerful armouries in the world were, until perhaps as late as 1960, still in the hands of five or six nations.

At the same time, the confrontation between the Soviet Union and the US was a relatively uncomplicated one in which spheres of influence, tacit as well as explicit, could not only be identified but were, on the whole, respected.

Since the 1960s that world picture has been radically changed by at least four factors. First, the process of de-colonisation initially accelerated, and then ran its full course, but whereas most of the nations of what is sometimes referred to as the Third World were once joined, however loosely, by a common anti-imperialist drive, that single ambition has now been replaced by growing nationalisms with varied objectives, many of them incompatible. The potential for dispute among the smaller nations has thus greatly increased.

Second, it is widely asserted that there is a growing pressure on key resources in the world such as oil and certain ores, resources which in general exist in significant quantities in the nations of the Third World. Those same nations, though often small and sometimes relatively poor, are now able to deploy sophisticated and highly effective weapons to support their national policies. Interestingly enough, that deployment of modern weapons, even if only for prestige or other non-military reasons, seems to reduce some of the moral objections to intervention by an external power using similarly advanced equipment. The effect of all this is that intense local conflicts are not only possible but very likely, and smaller nations are thus likely to be more vulnerable in the future, and their resources may well be at increasing risk.

Third, the clear spheres of superpower interests have meanwhile been eroded. The end of monolithic Communism was one cause; the involvement of the superpowers in disputes arising from local rather than global animosities was another; the growth of quite new sources of influence such as the OPEC group and perhaps Islam, represent a third factor. Much of the world has slipped out of the grasp of the super-powers.

Fourth, one of the principal lessons of the nuclear age, and quite contrary to the widespread belief in its early years, is that even major conventional conflicts do not necessarily lead to global war.

All this suggests not only that small wars will be at least as numerous in the future as they have been in the past, but that support and intervention in those conflicts by external powers will be perceived to be more necessary, believed to be less risky and will perhaps be thought more acceptable as instruments of national policy.

Already we have seen armed interventions on a very small scale by Belgium, France, Germany and the US. All of them, with the exception of the US landing in the Iranian desert, received widespread approval, and even that expedition would have been seen in quite a different light had it succeeded. Activity on a much larger scale by Cuba in Angola and by the Soviet Union in Afghanistan brought protests but little more, and the pattern for the future seems already to be firmly established. To the objection that this is an over-pessimistic assessment of the future politico-military scene, it must be said that it is at least a better outlook than one of global war.

So far as the West is concerned all this will pose a considerable dilemma. Resources available for defence are likely to remain, as always in peacetime democracies, severely constrained; and yet it may well become essential to sustain at least the full strength of the present defences in, for example, Europe, and at the same time to maintain a capability for intervention outside the present area of superpower confrontation.

If only because of the distances that are involved in simultaneous commitments of this kind, the potential for speedy reaction and for flexibility that is offered by air power seems certain to be engaged. This could be air power engaged in reconnaissance and surveillance, or it could involve air transport resources to move ground or other forces quickly into a crisis area, or it could mean the use of air power in its more direct form to lay down firepower in an effort to redress or to forestall a threatened or actual local imbalance of other forces.

Other arms will no doubt have a part to play, and land force elements, however modest, are virtually certain to be engaged. Their obvious advantage is that they can hold ground, although an army presence tends to take on a permanent appearance that may be inappropriate and it usually introduces complex problems of support and logistics.

Naval forces can provide an over-the-horizon presence for lengthy periods, and aircraft carriers have proved themselves to be particularly valuable in many crises and in several wars. It is also the case that almost all areas of concern for the future are littoral states, or at the very least are within range of seaborne air power; indeed some of them are readily accessible to air power only if it is based at sea. In exercising sea-based air power in these circumstances, however, there are three difficulties. The first is that, depending on its deployment at the time, a naval force can take days or even weeks to reach the area of a sudden crisis. The second difficulty is that a permanent out-of-area naval presence by any of the NATO powers can only be at the expense of the Alliance defences themselves. And the third is that to maintain a naval force on distant station will usually imply a very extensive infrastructure of support so as to be able to absorb the demands of time on passage, maintenance and general turnover of men and equipment.

Air power has the advantage that it can deploy over very long ranges with great rapidity and yet be at high readiness to return or to redeploy. It can provide a presence that will indicate to a potential aggressor an intention to globalise the crisis, or it can be used to deliver the countervailing firepower that is likely to be called for in actual operations. Finally, and unlike sea or land power, air power can exert a very high military leverage while committing very few personnel to combat.

It is true that airfields will be needed in or near the seat of the crisis, and that this can imply over-flying rights and the presence of allies in the theatre concerned. But this is entirely consistent with the variety of local nationalisms that seem to be emerging, and there are few countries today that do not possess modern and comprehensive civil airports. Furthermore, international airports can be the scene of routine military as well as civil movements, and air forces can operate from their often rural locations without necessarily arousing local hostility or even local attention.

The air arm thus seems ideally suited to deploy power or presence in the kind of circumstances that can be foreseen, provided only that the implied resources are available and that the operational concepts are valid.

Resources

Air power is not and never has been merely a matter of air strength. Behind the frontline of any effective air force there must be a comprehensive infrastructure of support, including the skills of maintenance and repair as well as training for the multiplicity of ground and air skills that are essential to an operational front line. That in turn will almost invariably depend upon the character of the nation itself, on whether it has the kind of skills that are essential to operational effectiveness. That in turn will almost invariably depend upon the character of the nation itself, on whether it has the depth of skills that are demanded and on whether those skills are in the right sectors. If they are in the wrong sectors, if the nation does not have a certain air-mindedness, its ability to project air power will either be low or it will depend on the imported skills of a nation that is air-minded, and its air power will lack depth and resilience. Above all therefore, like warfare itself, air power is about people.

It is also about the ability and the willingness of a nation to meet the budgetary and opportunity cost of air power. The latter is largely a question of national defence policy, but the budgetary cost is an aspect that must concern professional airmen themselves since it is their advice that largely determines the efficiency with which the resources devoted to air power are employed.

The room for manoeuvre is, it must be admitted, somewhat limited. Over the past twenty to thirty years the real cost of all military equipment has been rising at an average rate of about 6 per cent per year, which, with an approximately constant procurement budget like that of the United Kingdom means either that the age of in-service equipment must rise, or that the size of the inventory must shrink. The most disturbing aspect of this factor is that it impinges more deeply on aircraft procurement than on most other types of military equipment. For example, the average annual rise in real cost between the Centurion tank and its successor the Chieftain was 2.9 per cent; the rate of increase in the case of the Leander class frigate and its successor the Type 22 was 6.4 per cent; but the rate for the Hunter aircraft and its replacement the Jaguar was 7.1 per cent. The effect of this is that, in very round figures, the modern tank costs twice as much as its predecessor, and the frigate three times as much but the aircraft costs four times as much, all in real terms.[1] Even more disturbing is the suggestion in a recent US study that not only are costs increasing at these high rates, but that the rates themselves are increasing.[2]

One answer to this cost-spiral has been to capitalise on the inherent flexibility of aircraft and design multi-role systems, but there are three problems. The first is that roles are becoming increasingly specialised, and the possibilities for flexibility are therefore diminishing. The second is the realisation that multi-role also means multi-risk and compounded attrition. In the days of very large air forces this was not crucial, but at a time when so much combat potential is being concentrated into comparatively few airframes, the risks and therefore the reluctance of commanders to commit their resources to the less vital roles, while understandable, is inhibiting to the wider potential of air power.

The third problem approach is that because multi-role systems tend to represent a move towards ever more resource-intensive solutions, unit costs rise, numbers shrink and the difficulties of risk and of compound attrition multiply.

The answer is not to reverse the whole trend by procuring high numbers of very cheap weapons systems because, quite apart from the extra cost of very much larger numbers of expensive operators such as aircrew, the systems would not survive the demands of modern intensive war. Far more promising is an approach that examines whether present concepts should be pursued or whether the improvements in operational performance that accrue from further resource investment have become so marginal that it is better to search for other concepts altogether, and this is the basis of the analysis of current air power roles that now follows. Each of the nine principal roles is examined, and where possible and appropriate, suggestions for a way forward are made.

Usually any improvement in military capabilities demands some kind of technological improvement, and an interesting dilemma of two possible approaches arises. The scientists can be asked to suggest possibilities, in the hope that the military man can make something useful out of them; but that is bound to be a random business. On the other hand the military man can decide what it is he wants and perhaps how he wants it done, and then demand solutions from technology. But if that approach were universally successful it would by now be possible to detect submarines in deep oceans, and a solution to the IFF problem would by now have been found. The only realistic way forward is a mix of the operational and the technological.

The pattern of progress in the development of air power has usually been only incremental; technological breakthroughs are extremely rare, indeed in the whole history of air warfare there have been only two: radar and nuclear weapons. Ever since the first aircraft flew, itself the result of fusing the science of aerodynamics with a practical lightweight internal combustion engine, progress has depended essentially on a process of synergistic technology, the marriage of one or more technologies to produce a new capability. It is of course true that these new capabilities can themselves represent a military breakthrough either because of their pervasive impact on a wide field of military capabilities – as in the case of the jet engine or micro-electronics – or because of their revolutionary influence on a broad spectrum of military activities – as in the case of satellites; and indeed the significance of this process is that it has by no means come to an end.

At a level below that of revolutionary military change synergistic technology can have almost equally striking results. One example was the development and construction of the B-29 bomber during the Second World War. By amalgamating the incremental progress that had by that time been made across a very wide range of technologies, an aircraft was produced that represented a remarkable leap forward in strategic aircraft design. The Thor missile was another example of the same process. By combining proven propulsion, guidance and warhead technology, an entirely new weapons system was designed, built and tested within a year. More recently the Cruise Missile, although by no means a new concept, has emerged as a promising weapons system as the result of fusing advanced propulsion, guidance and control technologies into a small but long-range vehicle.

Any discussion of future possibilities should therefore seek out new applications and new partnerships for existing or emerging technologies rather than leap into the realms of speculative technological break-through which, by definition, cannot be foreseen.

AIR POWER ROLES

Air transport

Because it deals with the rapid movement of military resources, often over very long distances, air transport is one of the most enduring and pervasive of all air power roles. It has played a major part in virtually all the wars of the past four decades. For many years it has also been the bridge upon which the NATO Alliance depends for rapid transatlantic reinforcement; and it was an important factor in, for example, the Soviet and the US resupply efforts during the Middle East war of 1973. For the future it may well be the case that the ability of air transport – strategic and tactical – to deliver the very varied resources of modern war will be at least as important as the ability of air power to deliver firepower directly on to targets.

The aircraft that will be used for the air transport role in the future will probably look much like those of today, but two comments can be offered. First, there is a huge untapped military potential in the civil air fleets of most nations, and it would be surprising in view of the high cost of dedicated military systems if that potential is not engaged more fully in the future. There is nothing new in the principle, and some nations such as Israel and Korea already have airliners that have been modified to take bulk military loads, while the USAF has a Civil Reserve Air Fleet, and the whole airline of the Soviet Union, Aeroflot, is actually available as a reserve of the SAF.

Aircraft manufacturers have identified further possibilities, and for example Boeing have a scheme in which a very lightweight air-to-air refuelling rig can be built into airliners so that in a crisis all that is needed is to take out the seats and put in collapsible fuel tanks. More developments can be expected, and it may be that airliners will be adapted for the surveillance role or even as cruise missile platforms. This would be a logical progression. Progress in microelectronics is now making it possible, both physically and in terms of low costs, to put into missiles the kind of capability that formerly could be accommodated only in an aircraft. That transfer of complexity into the missile should make it increasingly possible to reduce the demand for complexity in the launching platform, and in some cases make it possible to use civil aircraft modified only by the addition of modules.

Next, there is the whole question of aircraft fuel, and the increasing concern about the high consumption of petroleum products implied in all aircraft operations, but particularly in transports. As far as petroleum is concerned, oil will not suddenly stop flowing; it will become increasingly expensive, thus giving a budgetary rather than a conceptual problem, and making it economical to use resources such as oil-bearing shale that have so far not been tapped.

The eventual shortage of oil will affect the three modes of transport – sea, land and air – in different ways. In theory at least all land transport could be undertaken by electricity – using, for example, a static power source fed along power lines. In theory, nearly all ships could eventually use nuclear power – as many do now. Aircraft can use neither of those sources. They must rely on a portable source of fuel, which obviously cannot be electric and which, because of the size and the weight of the plant implied, is unlikely to be nuclear except perhaps in the very long-term future.

For the medium-term, there are three options. The first is to widen the specification of aircraft fuel so that more of the crude oil can be used, a development that seems certain to be adopted. The second is to develop synthetic liquid hydrocarbons, a proven technique and one that could, with the application of advanced technologies to exploit the unprofitable and therefore untapped resources of coal, provide a further source of aircraft fuel.

The third option is to develop alternatives such as liquid hydrogen. Although for given energy content liquid hydrogen weighs a great deal less than kerosene, it has four times the volume and it will therefore take up extra space and potential payload. Another disadvantage is that liquid hydrogen boils at $-253°$ C and it therefore has to be kept in specially refrigerated systems that add weight, complexity and expense to the aircraft. Finally, the hydrogen has to be extracted, probably by electrolysis from water, which on the one hand is an unlimited source, but on the other hand depends upon some other form of energy before the liquid hydrogen can be produced.

Perhaps the most important factor, however, is that in the whole question of future fuels for aircraft, the way seems certain to be led by the civil sector. If there are to be changes, they will be felt first in the market-sensitive civil air transport sector, and in a slow change in the huge infrastructure of airports and of conventional fuel and support facilities that at present exist all over the world. The interests of the military sector will be best served, not by military research and development, but by keeping up with the state of the art so that if and when changes become necessary, the special needs of the military sector can be taken fully into account.

The second role of air power dealt with here is that of the control of the sea in its two aspects of antisubmarine warfare, and the tactical air support of maritime operations, usually abbreviated to ASW and TASMO respectively.

Tactical warfare at sea

Because ships offer such a high contrast against the surface of the sea, there is no particular difficulty about finding ships at sea by using high-level reconnaissance aircraft or satellites. The problem is the tactical application of air power at sea in the face of the very high effectiveness of the latest ship-borne air defences, and the solution almost certainly lies in the use of stand-off weapons of some kind. But even stand-off missiles can be intercepted by ship-borne systems, and one possible way ahead may be a missile that combines two or more of the basic approach modes; ballistic, surface-skimming and sub-surface.

Whether the missile-carrying aircraft in this role should be land-based or sea-based raises the question of the future place of the aircraft carrier, and although carrier-based aircraft can be employed in many other roles such as, for example, strike on targets ashore, this will be a convenient point at which to discuss the role of the carrier.

As is the case with all other weapons systems, aircraft carriers can be justified if they meet three conditions: first, that they are consistent with national strategic commitments and requirements; second, that the resource cost is tolerable; and third, that the system is operationally viable. Cost and vulnerability can to a great extent be reduced by employing short take-off and landing aircraft and adapted merchant ships; but then the operational effectiveness will also be sharply reduced because although the ships will provide useful dispersal operating platforms they will have very serious deficiencies as operating platforms, while the penalty for short-deck performance in the aircraft will be loss of range and lift. As far as conventional aircraft carriers are concerned it will be useful to discuss the question of viability in two parts: first in the circumstances of global war, and second in those of lesser wars and confrontations.

In global war it seems certain that aircraft carriers, being large and high-contrast targets, would be very vulnerable to a wide variety of air, surface and sub-surface weapons and that they would be unlikely to survive the initial stages of such a conflict. They can play a valuable part in deterring global war and they would be able to launch some nuclear strike elements in the very early stages of it. But other systems, such as submarines offer a better second-strike capability, and purely in terms of a global war aircraft carriers seem a doubtful investment.

In lesser wars and confrontations, on the other hand, aircraft carriers have often proved to be not only the best, but sometimes the only, means of deploying a flexible military presence with a strong potential for offensive action; but there are several difficulties.

To maintain a single carrier on a distant station can imply a total carrier force of as many as three such ships in order to allow for time on maintenance, in refit and on passage. If the distant station is an unmistakable military commitment, then there may be other and less expensive methods of deploying a presence or a capability in the area. If, however, there are several possible deployment areas for the carrier, its relatively low mobility may mean that it is unable to meet the demands of a rapid redeployment.

Quite apart from that, the operation of aircraft carriers demands on the one hand a complex and expensive logistics and training organisation to put it to sea, and on the other hand it calls for extensive support and self-defence efforts to sustain and protect it once it is there. It is true that the result can be theoretically a balanced force; but it is one in which the inherent vulnerabilities of all surface ships can mean that the carrier group is thrown on to the defensive. The aircraft carrier then becomes merely a part of the protective element of its own group rather than a secure base for offensive action.

The classic situation for the effective deployment of aircraft carriers against land targets is one in which the carriers operate from an area of absolute or relative sanctuary. Absolute sanctuary implies either that the enemy has no anti-ship weapons, or that the carrier-borne aircraft can strike their primary target from outside the effective range of his weapons. Because of the wide and growing proliferation of highly effective weapons such as anti-ship missiles that can be operated by semi-skilled crews belonging to even the least developed nations, absolute security for the future seems more likely to depend on a stand-off posture than on assumptions about the total absence of effective opposition.

Relative security is possible when the enemy capabilities against the carrier force are so modest that the carrier task force can neutralise them with little deviation from the primary attack role. Failing that, relative security may be achieved by a progressive attrition of the enemy capabilities, defensive and offensive, as the carrier task force approaches strike range against the primary target. This is clearly a more demanding concept of operations and one that will usually call for much more complex resources.

All these operational and resource factors must be weighed against the demands of national strategy, since if the aircraft carrier concept is adopted by any nation other than the superpowers, it could lead to a distortion not only in the maritime frontline but in the national defence effort as a whole. Aircraft carriers are ultimately about strategic priorities, and if all questions of prestige and the momentum of history can be ignored, then the decision on whether to sustain a carrier programme should depend on how vital to a nation is the ability to deploy that kind of force in the constrained circumstances to which it is appropriate.

Antisubmarine warfare

Antisubmarine warfare poses precisely the opposite problem to that seen in surface warfare. If a submarine can be located, it can be sunk without very much difficulty. The problem is to find the submarine in the first place, particularly in deep oceans.

A great deal of work in ASW has been done over the years by the West and by the Soviet Union, but nothing has yet emerged that makes the oceans transparent, and there is nothing to suggest that a breakthrough of that kind is imminent. What can be said is that the West is about seven years ahead of the Soviet Union in the ability to find, identify, locate and destroy submarines.

Although it may well be that a really significant improvement in ASW would be more to the advantage of the Soviet Union than to the West, because the West depends so heavily on the Polaris and Trident concepts, the West still needs to pursue solutions so as to maintain a safe lead in the whole state of the art. One important element in that state of the art is the quick reaction, and the long range and endurance on station, of shore-based maritime patrol aircraft, which can be expected to provide a valuable contribution in antisubmarine warfare well into the future.

One future development is likely to be the provision of self-defence anti-aircraft missiles for submarines. Experiments in the US have already demonstrated that a submerged submarine can detect and locate nearby aircraft, and the carriage of a small SAM platform in the submarine that could be released to the surface once hostile aircraft were detected, seems to be a logical next step. In that case ASW aircraft might be compelled to abandon their present over-flying tactics, and to lay sonars and dispatch their weapons from stand-off ranges. This would greatly complicate the solution of the tactical problem, and it would afford the submarine a far higher chance of escape once detected.

Strategic air bombardment

The importance of the strategic bomber in the development of air power has already been mentioned, and it is worth stressing again here that strategic air bombardment does not necessarily mean the bombardment of one superpower by another. But even in that context of global war and of global deterrence the concept of the manned strategic bomber still has a place.

The ICBMs which largely replaced the strategic bomber are now so numerous, and so varied in their mode of deployment, that a total defence against them either by interception at the target end of their trajectory or by direct attack on them at the launching end is out of the question; indeed this is the rationale for the theories of nuclear deterrence. And although it can be argued that in terms of the mutual strategic over-kill potential which undoubtedly exists actual numbers of weapons deployed would have little relevance in war-fighting, numbers are important in terms of perceptions and perhaps above all in terms of arms limitation agreements.

The viability of strategic systems, and thus the balance between the opposing armouries, is affected by technological developments: systems become obsolete. New accuracies in warhead deliveries have, for example, already brought into question the supposed invulnerability of many existing fixed silos, and this is turn led in 1980 to the US plans for the MX system which was to be an armoury of ICBMs deployed on an extensive but closed rail system that would on the one hand ensure survival but would on the other hand facilitate verification. Other shifts in the overall balance are likely to be caused by future advances in technology, and although there is so far no sign of any breakthrough that might neutralise submarine-launched systems, even this possibility cannot be ignored.

One form of insurance against future changes in the balance lies in diversification, and it is at this conceptual level that air-breathing systems and particularly the manned bomber have a place. Below that level of strategic concepts the manned bomber offers valuable operational qualities. A force of bombers can be brought to ostentatious alert so as to signal political will; it can be flown off to be held on airborne alert, or to be dispersed for survival; it can be launched, and then diverted or recalled. In short, the bomber is a platform, not a weapon, and it can therefore play a highly flexible role in nuclear deterrence or it can even revert if required to the conventional role.

In seeking to evade or defeat enemy anti-aircraft defences, future strategic bombers could use one of the two basic options. First, there is the concept of penetrating enemy airspace at low or ultra-low level so as to fly under the lobes of his air defence radars. This is not, however, a complete solution. It is a tactic that can evade some, or even most, of the enemy radars so that in a relatively restricted theatre of operations the opportunities for the enemy ground-based radar network to detect the intruder will be only fleeting. This will be particularly so if the area of penetration has been close enough to friendly territory to allow the use of anti-radar weapons such as drones to permit the use of stand-off electronic jamming. Some opportunities for engagement may, even so, remain to the defence, but the intruder can be equipped to detect the radar lobes that he has penetrated and to take self-defence electronic measures to confuse the local defence picture.

This whole process can, however, itself give the defence a useful indication of the position and progress of the intruder, so that eventually an intelligence picture can be built up with a coherence that will improve as the penetration deepens. Not only that, but the time available to the defence to mount a response is then increased, and the difficulties for the attack begin to rise.

Some alleviation can be sought by tactical routeing. Since the enemy cannot blanket the whole of his territory with low-level radars, and since the radars that he has deployed can be plotted by means of satellite electronic reconnaissance, this is a relatively straightforward process. Against that, however, must be weighed the increasing use of airborne warning and control aircraft that can give a coherent real-time picture of the lower airspace over a very wide area. Using such a picture, air defence aircraft can be directed into the areas likely to be traversed by the low-flying intruder to destroy it using look-down radar and weapons.

If the deep penetration attacks implied by the strategic air mission are carried out at low level they will demand a high degree of defence suppression and other support, and even that degree may not be enough to give them secure flight all the way to the target. All that can be said is that some residual attack capability to penetrate in the low-level mode will compel the defence to invest wholly disproportionate resources in countervailing systems; but although that may be an economic bonus it can hardly be termed a decisive military advantage.

The second option will be to penetrate enemy airspace at very high level, that is to say at a height well above 60,000 feet. At that kind of altitude it might be possible to fight a way through to the target. Electronic countermeasures have now been developed to a point where a great deal of the edge has been taken off high-altitude SAMs, and there are two other possibilities for the future.

First, there is the prospect of anti-missile missiles. In order to reach extreme altitudes, a SAM must be of a substantial size, and it will take perhaps up to a full minute to reach its target. This would be enough time for the high-flying bomber to detect the missile soon after launch, to track it and then to destroy it with a relatively small downward-firing interceptor missile. The emergence of self-protection missiles of this kind for aircraft in many roles now seems not only technically feasible but militarily essential and inevitable.

A second promising avenue for developments is the use of the destructive power of high-energy laser beams. Claims have already been made that lasers have inflicted damage on titanium panels and on the seeker head of an air-to-air missile. If two problems – one the difficulty of very high precision aiming, and the other of overcoming the attenuation of laser beams in the earth's atmosphere – can be overcome, then this developing technology could offer a very significant improvement in airborne weapons.

Because beams of this kind travel with the speed of light, tracking and 'lead' problems are greatly simplified. An aircraft crossing a laser beam at a speed of Mach 2 and a range of 1 mile, for example, will travel only $\frac{1}{8}$ inch in the 6 millionths of a second between laser firing and laser impact. The difficulty is to keep the beam steady on the same very restricted area for long enough to inflict damage, and to construct some kind of damage-recording systems so that the operator knows when the weapon is free to switch to another target.

The atmospheric attenuation of laser beams seems to be an insurmountable problem for effective generation at low and medium altitudes; but at extreme altitudes the problem hardly arises, and for that reason a laser self-defence weapon for very high-flying aircraft seems to be a distinct future possibility. Such a development would tend to shift the whole balance between attack on, and the defence of, very high-flying aircraft.

The other development in this new field of directed energy weapons is the research that is being carried out both in the US and in the Soviet Union, but mainly in the latter, into particle beam weapons. Research so far suggests that charged particle beams will not be effective weapons in space because of beam dispersion. Within the earth's atmosphere, on the other hand, their range is likely to be limited by geo-magnetic deflection and by attenuation of the beam as the result of ionising collisions with atmospheric atoms.

What is more, these weapons would also suffer from the same aiming and pointing problems as high-energy lasers, and although there are conflicting opinions within the scientific community about the viability of particle beam weapons, these difficulties and the limitations that might appear during their development seem to make them a doubtful area for decisive progress.

One other possibility for strategic bombers is that of an aircraft that penetrates enemy defences without being detected at all. Such an aircraft would fly at ultra-high-level, and using some of the new structural materials now available it could be designed to give such a small radar echo that it would pass unnoticed by present-day radars designed to detect conventional aircraft. It could have engines with a very low IR signature and no perceptible noise, and its skin could be treated with materials that diffuse any reflections, thus making it for all practical purposes an invisible aircraft.

The difficulty is that although such an aircraft might be able to evade present-day detection techniques using, for example, radar, there is little doubt that those techniques could be refined in the future to detect and to acquire those smaller signatures. What cannot be assessed is whether the expense of securing an advantage for the high-flying aircraft by this means could be justified by the length of time that the concept might remain viable.

Taken together, however, there are signs of an awakening interest in the very high-flying bomber, and technological progress in several fields is beginning to show solutions to many of the problems of aircraft vulnerability at those heights.

Reconnaissance, surveillance and control

Reconnaissance, surveillance and control is an area of air power activity in which the use of satellites as well as aircraft is now well advanced. There are, however, two difficulties with satellites. First, for a satellite to give continuous information it must be geo-stationary. This implies an orbit of about 35,000 km above the earth – a distance from which it may not be possible to acquire targets with any useful definition. If technology could make effective definition available then the whole concept of reconnaissance, of real-time intelligence and of precision attack against mobile target arrays would be revolutionised.

Second, the alternative to geo-stationary satellites is a satellite system with a much lower orbit; but because these satellites are not geo-synchronous, continous cover is available only from a whole series of satellites each with a limited scanning time over an area of interest such as Western Europe. This is adequate for strategic reconnaissance, but the number of satellites implied for tactical use would make it an enormously expensive project. It is, however, a possibility, and with advanced radar developments such as synthetic aperature techniques an all-weather high definition tactical surveillance system could be available.

Meanwhile there is a continuing need in some circumstances for tactical reconnaissance by means such as aircraft, but here the effectiveness of modern air defences has already led to efforts to find other solutions. One answer, the use of airborne sensors in aircraft flying at middle altitudes over friendly territory and scanning across into hostile areas, will be discussed later as part of the tactical use of air power. Another answer is the use of drones. Although drones are inherently vulnerable to enemy defences, in the case of limited roles and for short penetrations of hostile airspace the level of risk can be justified by the valuable results obtained from relatively inexpensive systems.

Drones do away with the need for a crew support system, and, because they carry lightweight sensors rather than heavy weapons, they can be built to have insignificant radar response characteristics together with low noise and heat emissions, and all at a comparatively modest cost. Synergistic technology involving high-density electronics, new airframe materials and low-emission engines can therefore be expected to produce entirely new platforms in this role, and some progress is already being made.

It is worth mentioning in passing that similar vehicles can be fitted with warheads and operated in the defence suppression mode. Such drones could, for example, loiter over a heavily defended area and attack an air defence target once a specific emission was identified on the ground. If the signal were cut off in reaction to the approach of the drone, then the drone could be programmed to re-cycle, orbit and await the next transmission. These interruptions in the defence surveillance would of course themselves represent a success for the attack.

Other airborne surveillance systems, including those such as AWACS with control facilities, are a comparatively recent development and one in which there are both urgent demands for improvements as well as broad potentials for satisfying them. One challenge will be that reliance on a limited number of airborne surveillance and control vehicles will make it increasingly attractive for the enemy to develop counter-systems to destroy them.

One possible means by which this could be done would be to employ aircraft with long-range air-to-air missiles, thus giving the defence the problem of stationing a combat air patrol of interceptors at long range round each AWACS aircraft. This would be very expensive in resources. A better defence for AWACS might be to rely upon on-board defences, including the kind of system discussed earlier to disrupt or to destroy incoming missiles.

Close air support

In low-intensity warfare, or in other circumstances in which ground forces are not covered by comprehensive air defences, attack on them by fixed-wing aircraft able to deliver intense, accurate and flexible fire-power can produce devastating effects without committing resources permanently to that sector. Modern conventional armies, however, will generally include effective air defences, and the operational problem then takes on two aspects. For as long as ground formations can deal with the enemy to their immediate front, they should be allowed to do so, assisted, as far as resources will allow, by armed helicopters organic to the ground forces. Meanwhile fixed-wing air should be used against targets that are beyond the reach of army organic weapons. Fixed-wing air support should be called in only when an enemy breakthrough is developing, or when it has actually taken place.

In the case of a breakthrough there are two important considerations. First, sizeable concentrations of enemy armour and support arms are implied, almost certainly calling for the use of area munitions. The concept of acquiring and targeting individual targets with fixed-wing air power may thus be an unnecessary refinement.

Second, modern air defences generally imply a mix of systems which, to be effective, must be tactically deployed so that the weaknesses of some elements are covered by the strengths of others. During the kind of rapid advance implied in an armoured breakout some of the tactical cohesion of such a system is lost, and therefore the advance must either be restricted to a steady pace, thus sacrificing much of the advantage gained, or an increased vulnerability to air attack must be accepted. This means that the circumstances demanding the most urgent intervention of air power will be the same circumstances that make its intervention most effective and least costly.

The air power employed can be fixed-wing or helicopter, but quite apart from questions of relative costs and vulnerabilities, helicopters have two fundamental disadvantages. They are, above all, aircraft with limited range and payload characteristics and they do not have the mobility to create rapid concentrations of firepower at widely separated points in a conflict. They are also, generally speaking, unsuited to penetration missions, and they therefore lack the flexibility to switch for example from the close air support role to that of interdiction or offensive counter-air.

In some circumstances the helicopter can be a valuable asset, as it is for example to the Warsaw Pact in the Central Region of Europe. Because the Warsaw Pact holds the initiative and can therefore foresee with some clarity the likely areas of intensive combat, their forces would be able to assemble helicopters in large numbers just behind the battle area, knowing that those helicopters would have the range and the logistic support to sustain them in the battle.

The air arm of NATO, on the other hand, must be able to concentrate its firepower at almost any point along the whole border between East and West, and in order to overcome the numerical superiority of the Warsaw Pact ground forces it will need to concentrate that firepower from across the whole region and perhaps even from outside it. Helicopters do not have that kind of range with the payloads that would be needed, and the helicopter thus has a significance for the Warsaw Pact that it does not have and cannot have for the Alliance.

Air superiority

Next the discussion will deal with the mission of air superiority in its sub-missions of air defence and offensive counter-air. Classically, air superiority was only a means by which freedom of action was gained so that bomber forces could achieve their primary aim. But once the bomber offensive became outdated, at least in the superpower confrontation, and once attention focused on a likely short war rather than a long war of attrition, then not only the notion of air superiority but even the use of the term itself lost its currency. Air superiority was replaced by expressions such as 'local air superiority', 'favourable air situation', or even by the phrase a 'tolerable air situation'. The era when air power advocates could say, as Seversky did in 1955, that 'either one controls the entire air ocean clear around the globe or one controls nothing', has gone.

Certainly there will still be a pressing need to prevent the enemy from gaining the initiative in the air, even if only locally, and air defence is certain to be a continuing role. It is also clear that it is bound to have two aspects: air combat and air interception. Air combat is the use of highly manoeuvrable aircraft to engage enemy tactical aircraft penetrating our own airspace, particularly in the area of the ground battle, probably supported by AWACS aircraft operating in the rear.

These AWACS aircraft will have a role in identifying enemy air activity in what is bound to be a highly confused situation, to monitoring the assembly of enemy air formations and their progress towards the combat area, and then directing our own aircraft into that area to intercept them. It seems on the whole to be very unlikely, however, that an AWACS aircraft could actually control the combat that then ensues. It is much more likely that, once committed, air defence aircraft will need to act autonomously using the local judgement of the aircrew.

Air defence

In order to exercise that judgement and, for example, to identify their targets, the air combat aircraft will need to approach to visual ranges, and in the close engagements that are then likely to follow, a highly manoeuvrable aircraft will be needed. Manoeuvrability will allow the air defence aircraft to gain an advantageous firing position; it will make it possible to seize a final attack position in close combat; and it will enable air defence aircraft to accelerate and to manoeuvre out of difficulties. The air defence aircraft in this air superiority role must therefore have a high degree of aerodynamic agility and high Specific Excess Power.

Agile air-to-air missiles will be a valuable armament along with cannon, but they must be regarded as an additional degree of overall agility rather than a substitute for agility in the aircraft itself. Only the maximum agility in the whole weapons system, aircraft and missile, is likely to be a sufficient response to a similar combination in the opponent.

The question of aircraft identification will be important, and IFF seems certain to play a part over the next few years. But in its present form it can never be the complete answer. The present difficulty for NATO is to devise something that is effective but robust, and acceptable to all the nations of the Alliance yet inaccessible to the Warsaw Pact even in combat conditions. IFF is therefore likely to remain unreliable both in the positive and in the negative sense, and it should not be regarded as more than an aid to identification in confused circumstances. For the longer-term future, experiments are now being made with laser for IFF purposes against ground targets. The reflected laser beam can be used to identify the pattern of vibration from particular vehicle types, in the same way that the vibration of ships at sea can be analysed for the purposes of recognition. It seems at least possible that this use of lasers could also be extended to airborne air defence.

Interception

Air interception, as distinct from air combat, is a role calling for quite different characteristics since it implies the interception of an air attack fairly well out from the target.

Because in the future each attacking enemy aircraft is likely to carry a salvo of stand-off missiles, it will be necessary in those circumstances to take out the aircraft rather than to intercept the missile after launch. It seems likely, therefore, that air defences will be drawn further out as the range of stand-off missiles is increased, and this implies an increased need for air-to-air refuelling so that interceptors can hold their stations for longer periods at extended ranges. Ultimately, however, air defences can expect to have to intercept incoming missiles – technically an entirely feasible operation.

Offensive counter-air

A particularly important aspect of the air superiority mission, because at its most successful it can neutralise substantial enemy air elements in a single attack, is offensive counter-air; that is to say direct air attack on the enemy air infrastructure and in particular on his airfields.

New aircraft weapons are being developed specifically for use against the most vulnerable feature of airfields, the concrete operating surfaces, with a mix of concrete-breaking munitions and small sub-munitions that make the work of airfield repair hazardous and therefore very slow.

The concept is likely to remain valid well into the future but there will come a time when the terminal defences of airfields begin to divert into defence suppression measures an unacceptably large proportion of attacking air effort, and there will then be a need for new tactics and new weapons. One mode of attack could employ unmanned aircraft on the lines of the cruise missile; but there are serious disadvantages. An automatic weapon of this kind has the fatal weakness that it can be programmed to deal only with foreseen operational circumstances. If the enemy can surprise the system, and there will be many options open to him, then the automatic system can often be disabled. With nuclear armed automatic systems this may not be decisive, because even if only a small number of them manage to penetrate the enemy defences they will be enough to inflict great damage. With the conventional warheads that are being assumed in the present discussion, however, this is not the case; the attacker could not be sure that enough missiles would reach the target to inflict the sustained level of destruction that would be necessary to render airfields unfit for use.

One other possibility is that of remotely controlled weapons, but here the problem is that they move after launch out of the airspace in which the controller can apply his judgement to the safe progress of the device, and progressively deeper into the airspace in which the enemy can increasingly apply his judgement to its destruction. In order to survive in these circumstances, the missile must have systems that can measure and transmit all the relevant human perceptions in one direction, and then receive and implement all the appropriate human manipulative skills in the other; and they must do so despite the efforts of an equally skilled opponent to interrupt the whole process from a tactical position very much closer to the missile.

Both types of system, remote and automatic, suffer from one other fundamental weakness. They are bound to be complex machines and the enemy may be able to disable not only key elements in the control mechanisms, but elements on which the system was relying to detect and to rectify any combat damage or unserviceability. In those circumstances the missile will enter a technically self-destructive spiral.

The most promising way forward with air-breathing systems will be to employ a manned aircraft for all but the attack phase of the mission, with a crew able to improvise in order to overcome operational degradation and above all able to use their tactical skills to counter enemy defences. Automatic or even remotely-controlled weapons would then be released from outside the perimeter of the enemy terminal defences, and since the weapons could be relatively small and designed in such a way that they offered signatures to the defence that were modest in amplitude and limited in variety, the defence would be presented with an entirely new level of threat.

Apart from air-breathing systems, there is the possibility of using conventionally-armed ballistic missiles, which, because they would bring to bear on the target a combination of kinetic and chemical energy and because they could be given an adequate degree of accuracy – perhaps even by means of some form of terminal guidance, would inflict a high degree of damage on airfields. It might also be possible to use a mix of weapons systems. Ballistic missiles could, for example, be employed to dilute the enemy air defences so as to open the way for conventional air attack, and thus free more of the available fixed-wing resources for targets better matched to their characteristics, notably time-sensitive targets in a fast-moving ground war. It should not be forgotten that it will not be enough to win the air battle: both the air and the ground battle are vital.

Resilience of air infrastructure

Finally, in considering the question of air superiority, there is the need to protect one's own air assets against enemy attempts to seize the initiative. There will always be the strong possibility that enemy air elements will not only escape offensive counter-air but will evade interception by defending aircraft, and a high level both of local AA defence and of resilience under attack will be essential. The expense of substantial point defences is justified by the importance of the target, but as anti-aircraft defences become even more efficient and more comprehensive with the use of missiles, guns and perhaps even barrage balloons against low-flying aircraft, stand-off attacks can be expected using missiles or other unmanned vehicles to penetrate the dense terminal defence envelope.

Resilience implies the survival of operational aircraft and other weapons systems, as well as the facilities to launch them. Aircraft and their communication centres can be protected against all but the heaviest weapons by housing them in reinforced concrete shelters.

Far more vulnerable, however, are the airfield operating surfaces, and in efforts to reduce that vulnerability there are broadly two options. The first is to develop and procure aircraft with a vertical take-off and landing capability so that the necessity for long runways is avoided altogether. But there are technical difficulties in combining this attribute with other important military qualities such as supersonic characteristics and high range and payloads; it is even a challenging problem to fit twin engines in such an aircraft because of the fine tolerances demanded in the hovering mode. Nevertheless there is a sound case for VTOL (vertical take-off and landing), or its derivative STOVL (short take-off and vertical landing) near the ground combat zone where the short range of such aircraft when fully loaded is not important, but where their quick reaction could be vital.

A second option is to construct aircraft that can operate from very short operating surfaces of, say, up to 500 m in length instead of the contemporary runways of between 2,000 and 3,000 m. A design capability such as that means not only that various 500 m strips on a damaged airfield can be used, but small civilian fields and even motorway strips can be brought into service both to disperse aircraft for survival and to recover them in emergency. One innovative way forward for airfield design may be to design them on an annular layout with a conventional runway for day-to-day training and practice, but a network of interconnected strips outside the main perimeter for use in war. Such a dispersed operating layout would present a very difficult target for air attack, yet all the peacetime infrastructure would still be available in war.

Progress in aerodynamics, and in aircraft design generally which is making combat aircraft more agile is also making it possible to reduce the take-off and landing runs of modern aircraft, and the process of improvement can be expected to continue as new technological and other advances are combined to enhance performance.

At the same time, however, some aircraft such as strategic transports, air-to-air refuelling tankers and large AWACS aircraft seem likely to have to rely in the future on airfields very much like those of today. Thus while it may be possible to dispense with runways in the forward areas and to use short strips further behind the combat zone, airfields well back from the front will still be vulnerable to some air threat and will therefore need active defences.

Interdiction

Closely linked to the other operations in support of the ground battle is
the role of interdiction, that is to say the disruption of enemy military
resources – combat and support, en route to the ground battle but
before they can reach it. It is a role with two aspects; attack on the
resources themselves, and attack on their means of transportation –
especially road and rail targets, and the experience of the last forty years
of air warfare teaches two important lessons about it.

The first is that if interdiction against traffic routes is applied too far to
the rear, then the enemy will usually have enough flexibility in depth to
absorb the breaks in the logistic flow that air attack is causing, and he
will often have enough lateral flexibility to be able to re-route his
logistics around any key features of the system that have been destroyed.
The most effective area for the application of air interdiction is therefore
relatively close to the battle area, say between 2 km and 50 km behind it.

Second, if the enemy has the initiative on the ground, then successful
interdiction will cause him to reduce the level of the conflict to one that
matches the volume of logistics managing to evade the interdiction
campaign. Since interdiction will very rarely result in the total isolation
of the battlefield, this means that the enemy will reduce the intensity of
his activity, or postpone it until enough logistic support has arrived to
sustain further activity. Air interdiction in these circumstances can thus
never be decisive. It can be decisive only if ground forces can impose on
the enemy a higher level of consumption in combat than in evading the
air interdiction. Success therefore rests on holding the initiative on the
ground, even if only temporarily, as well as in the air, and this in turn postulates the closest possible co-ordination between land and air activity.

As far as the destruction of combat reserves is concerned, there is the
problem of actually locating the targets in order to attack them. The
targets are likely to be on the move, they will be covered by a dense and
comprehensive umbrella of anti-aircraft defence systems and they must
be destroyed or delayed in large numbers if they are not to reach the
battle area.

For the future, the effectiveness of the enemy mobile organic air
defences can be expected to continue to improve, and as in the case of
offensive counter-air operations the effect of this must be to absorb more
of the resources of the air attack and thus to divert them from the
primary mission.

Two answers have so far emerged. One is the use of ground-based
systems to neutralise at least some of the air defences, though there is
something unnecessarily complex about a concept that depends on

ground systems to locate and neutralise other ground systems so as to open a way for air attack. The other answer is for attacking aircraft to operate outside the enemy air defences, and here three sets of technologies are being combined to produce a new concept of stand-off attack.

In the first area of technology, radar, developments in millimetre wave radars, which give high resolution, a better resistance to jamming and a lower probability of being intercepted, are showing great promise for guidance systems. Together with developments in sideways-looking radar, and in particular in synthetic aperture radar – which is a means of increasing the resolution of targets by means of a high-speed signal processing system so as to combine successive pulse returns gathered along the track of an aircraft in flight, these areas of research are providing entirely new surveillance and targeting capabilities.

Second, there are developments in sub-munition guidance, using again mm wave radar as well as infra-red sensors, and sophisticated electronics to make the sub-munition or sub-missile 'smart', that is to say capable of seeking out its own target.

Third, there are improvements in warhead capabilities, in particular the use of self-forging fragments, which is an advanced method of directing the explosive force of the sub-munition warhead so precisely that it causes the copper element of the warhead to forge itself at great velocity into solid slugs which then strike the armour with enough force to tear through it.

These developments are together producing concepts such as the American Assault Breaker programme, which will be able to deliver a mix of sub-munitions at ranges of up to 150 or more kilometres, well beyond that needed for battlefield interdiction. At present the missiles used in Assault Breaker are ground-launched and guided by an airborne radar, but an obvious next step will be to put the missiles as well as the radar into the air. With the kind of ranges that will be available, the aircraft will be able to operate well back from the battle area and thus within the protection of our own air defences.

This is almost certainly the way that air power should now be developing in order to overcome the problems posed by intensive and highly efficient air defences in any area of modern ground conflict. Using stand-off techniques to degrade the enemy defences and to begin the process of disruption throughout his second echelons, perhaps followed by the use of conventional fixed-wing aircraft to lay down the intense concentrations of firepower that only they can provide, offers a flexible and effective combination that will pose entirely new problems for large-scale attacking ground forces.

Another and very important benefit would be that the long-range surveillance and targeting implied in a concept of this kind would obviate the need for most, and perhaps all, of the tactical reconnaissance missions. Targets in the enemy rear that were less time-sensitive could be covered by other means such as satellite photography or satellites designed to detect radar or other characteristic emissions. And since tactical reconnaissance at present demands not only advanced aircraft that could be employed in combat roles, but also expensive support facilities, the total savings in air resources might be very considerable.

Command, control and communications

No discussion of the roles of air power would be complete without some mention of the machinery of command, control and communications (C^3) that is essential to its successful application. To a degree that does not apply to other arms of war, aircraft are on the one hand extremely mobile platforms with a high potential for independent operation, and on the other hand they are very flexible vehicles that can co-ordinate or concentrate their efforts with great precision. To operate successfully at these two extremes, as well as at any point between them, aircraft require centralised control and delegated execution, but above all they demand a highly effective system of C^3.

It is a wide field and one in which the range of options is changing so rapidly that comment cannot deal with specifics and is therefore best confined to principles. Indeed, that rapidity of change is itself one of the present difficulties. Complex systems can become obsolescent before they are brought into service, and C^3 is a particular area in which the excellent may not only be the enemy of the adequate, but in which rapid technological progress may be a factor that actually hinders the introduction of effective systems because something better always seems to lie just ahead.

The first comment here is that any belief that advanced data processing and other capabilities will replace decision making is misplaced. Warfare is about people and about the judgements that affect them. The new systems are only aids to decision making, and final judgments will always rest with commanders at the various levels. Second, new C^3 systems seem very unlikely to save manpower. On the contrary they are usually manpower-intensive as well as capital-intensive. In the whole question of C^3 there is a clear need for care in making assumptions, and the best way forward is to seek those avenues for short-term progress that are most likely to be compatible with longer-term solutions.

Third, in selecting those solutions, two things need to be borne in mind. The systems must be operationally robust; that is to say, they must be so designed that in the face of the inevitable attempts to disrupt them they will not collapse, but rather fall away in a manner that can be controlled, a process that has been called 'elegant degradation'.

Electronic warfare

It was suggested earlier that electronics have a pervasive impact on a wide range of military capabilities. Both in attack and in defence, the functions of intelligence, surveillance, detection, identification, acquisition, engagement and assessment in modern warfare all depend to a greater or lesser extent on electronics. This is particularly true of air operations.

At the technical level, the impossibility of fitting a practical level of armour to aircraft leads to an inherent mechanical vulnerability that must be countered in other ways. At the same time, effective self-defence weapons can be installed only at the cost of primary payload, and such weapons also raise difficulties of engagement geometry that can be solved only by a degree of manoeuvrability that is inconsistent with heavy conventional weapon loads. Aircraft thus rely upon tactics such as ultra-low-level high speed flight, and above all upon electronic measures for their survival.

They also rely on electronics to a large extent in their primary roles, but principally in order to bring the aircraft into position for weapons release. Progress in electronic systems that can then deliver the released weapon with high assurance on to the target has so far been remarkably slow, although developments in this area would bring valuable and perhaps decisive advantages. It is clear that one reason for the high cost of current aircraft is that so many capabilities – for peace as well as for war – are built into them. The ability to reach a release point with extreme accuracy in the face of very capable enemy defences is only one of them. The need to carry all the other capabilities of the aircraft, including the crew and the support systems for the crew, up to that final point, leads to a very expensive upward spiral of capabilities and thus vulnerabilities. By designing weapons that could be directed on to the target with only two capabilities, those of being able to find the target and then to kill it, the spiral of high resource investment and shrinking inventories would be at least partly reversed.

At the tactical level, the high contrast of airborne platforms and their very limited scope for physical concealment, together afford valuable opportunities to the electronic systems of the defence which in turn must be deflected as far as possible by countermeasures in the attack. At the operational level, the three dimensional quality of air warfare combined with the very high mobility of the platforms, make the factors of time and space central, and the need for control – in its widest sense – imperative.

All this has led to what is virtually a new branch of warfare. Electronics have on the one hand made possible new tactics and new flexibilities in the exercise of air power, but on the other hand they have introduced the potential for very high levels of attrition. Since the form of air power that seems most appropriate to the future challenges facing the West deal essentially with intervention, initiative and thus with the offensive, it will be vital to its success that investment in the broader aspects of electronic warfare is recognised as being at least as important as investment in primary weapons systems. In almost all operational circumstances, any serious imbalance in electronics is likely to negate the effectiveness of the air arm. Short-term economies in electronics particularly are likely to lead to a whole cycle of mismatched capabilities, and thus to a pattern of operational inadequacy or worse.

Future warfare, almost regardless of its intensity, will thus demand capabilities to jam whatever opposing systems can be jammed, to apply deception where deception can be practised, and to destroy any electronic warfare targets that are vulnerable to destruction. The challenge will be to accomplish all this without an undue diversion away from primary operational roles.

CONCLUSION

Except for the closing stages of the Second World War, and in one or two isolated instances since then, the history of air warfare has been characterised by a divergence between theory and practice. Before the Second World War, and in the early years of that war, it was a divergence caused very largely by a lack of resources, but also by military conservatism on the one hand and by the inability of contemporary technology to close the gaps on the other. The imperatives of that war removed most of these obstacles, so that by its closing stages all the claims that had been made for air power by its advocates seemed to have been vindicated.

During the nuclear age that followed, and with which this book has been concerned, the divergence of practice from theory has been of a quite different kind. The unbroken assumption of a military threat from the Soviet Union and her allies has meant that the resources with which to maintain air power in the West have, on the whole, been available, and to the extent that air power has at times played a key part in nuclear deterrence and that no global war has taken place, theory and practice have run close together.

But partly because of an emphasis on that independent, strategic and in a narrow sense negative role, air power has often been out of phase with the positive military demands that have been put upon it by the characteristics of wars that have been fought at very much lower levels. Theatre conventional war in Korea for example found Western air power equipped only for a limited strategic offensive, while the colonial wars saw air power engaged in largely nugatory effort because it was air power that happened to be available rather than because it was a weapon appropriate to the tasks it was called upon to perform. But in wars where air power was specifically prepared for the type of operations in which it took part, notably in the Arab–Israeli conflicts, eventually over North Vietnam and to some extent in the Falklands campaign, air power did have a decisive effect.

Although colonial wars are now a thing of the past, conflicts in regions that experienced colonisation as well as in other areas peripheral to the superpower confrontation seem to be more rather than less likely to occur in the future, and the possibility of major conventional wars on the scale of Korea or Vietnam or of expeditions like that seen in the Falklands, can by no means be ruled out. To an extent never before seen therefore, Western military power may be called upon to invoke what is best called lateral mobility; that is to say the capacity to deploy military resources rapidly and at short notice at decisive points in a band of potential crisis areas stretching right around the globe.

Air power offers the capability to deploy a military presence or the capacity for military intervention with the speed of reaction that those future challenges seem certain to demand. Air power also has the potential flexibility to meet the variable nature of those demands, whether they require the high mobility of direct firepower, the rapid establishment of logistic support for other arms or the swift deployment of other arms into crisis areas.

Thus far in the development of air power, lateral mobility can be seen almost as a by-product of the fundamental insistence of air power theory on the primacy of the strategic, deep penetration role. That insistence has now been muted by the emergence of new capabilities in anti-aircraft defences and by the proliferation of long-range nuclear missiles, but it has not yet been replaced by a sufficient emphasis on the lateral mobility that future strategic circumstances seem certain to demand.

Below that strategic capability for rapid deployment, air power offers a unique capacity for concentrating military effort at the theatre or operational level of warfare. It is, however, a power of concentration which, combined with the potential of air power for ubiquitous operation, leads to a central difficulty that has repeatedly inhibited the successful application of air power – a political reluctance to employ it. Worse even than that, the history of air power shows many examples of attempts to compromise by applying political gradualism to a weapon that depends for much of its effectiveness on the characteristics of surprise, concentration and shock action.

The result has sometimes been to undermine the effectiveness of air attack not only by inducing in the defence a psychological resilience that deprived air power of much of its impact, but also by encouraging and facilitating active defence measures that were too often able to match any subsequent escalation of offensive air action. Air power was thus trapped between the need to increase its efforts in order even to maintain a constant level of military pressure, and political constraints that prevented any increase in that pressure from reaching decisive levels.

Political gradualism is a restraint with which air power must learn to live; but air power itself can make an important contribution in mitigating the effects of that restraint and perhaps in removing some of the grounds for its necessity. Political restraint springs from four factors: a proper humanitarian concern for non-combatants; an unwillingness to provoke reprisals; a wish to contain conflict at the minimum appropriate level; and, overlying all three, a concern that the lack of discrimination often seen in past air power operations might itself break those restraints and lead to unintended and perhaps even counterproductive results.

Political assessment of the likely results of defined military action will remain a matter of political judgement, but as far as air power is concerned the answer to the dilemma must be tactical precision. This in turn will depend upon sound Intelligence and on the accurate physical application of air power. The Intelligence aspect is beyond the scope of the present discussion, although it should be said in passing that surveillance from the air and from space has already revolutionised many aspects of intelligence-gathering.

As to the application of air power at this third, tactical, level, it is one of the most serious criticisms of air power in the nuclear age that so little progress has been made in procuring weapons that have the kind of precision demanded by contemporary circumstances. It is a failure that can be traced to several factors, including an earlier conviction that nuclear weapons had made precision unnecessary, and to some extent to the belief that in conventional operations a lack of precision could be discounted by sheer weight of application; that is to say, by mass. Yet the growing effectiveness of anti-aircraft weapons has led to the diversion of extensive resources to counter them, at the expense of the primary air attack role, and the rising cost, in real terms, of combat aircraft in the face of fairly constant defence budgets together mean that the trend is emphatically away from numbers and away from mass attack.

Against that tendency towards more complex, expensive but fewer aircraft, the number of targets that air power may be called upon to engage is likely to remain very large, especially, but not only, in the likely circumstances of armoured warfare in the Central Region of Europe. That challenge, together with the continuing improvement in the effectiveness of relatively simple and very numerous ground-based anti-aircraft weapons, means that the number of attacking aircraft put at risk must be reduced while at the same time more ground targets are engaged. The solution to that dilemma must lie in tactics that hold aircraft outside the most effective defences yet permit the use of multiple, highly accurate and flexible weapons. A change from the past emphasis on platform performance and on to weapon performance therefore seems not only inevitable but imperative.

The means with which to effect this shift, to escape the spiral of high cost but low numbers and at the same time to bring revolutionary improvements in weapon effectiveness, are now available in the potential of electronics. That change, together with shifts in concepts at the tactical, operational and strategic levels will make it possible for Western air power to develop an even more powerful capability than it has at present to deploy and to concentrate military effort with the precision, and above all with the selectivity, that future circumstances will demand. Properly applied, air power could be a ubiquitous arm of the first hour, and thus escape the need to be employed as a weapon of last resort.

Notes and References

CHAPTER 1: THE DOMINANT FACTOR

1. Except where specified the term 'nuclear' is used generally in this chapter to denote either fusion or fission weapons; non-nuclear weapons are referred to as 'conventional'.
2. Lord Tedder, 'Air Power in War', Lees Knowles lectures (London: Hodder & Stoughton, 1947).
3. Churchill quoted in Eugene M. Emme (ed.), *The Impact of Air Power: National Security and World Politics* (New York: Van Nostrand, 1959).
4. Montgomery quoted in Emme, op. cit., p. 442.
5. Quote from Brigadier General A. F. Hurley, *Billy Mitchell: Crusader for Air Power* (Indiana University Press, 1975) p. 142.
6. H. G. Wells *War in the Air* (London: George Bell and Sons, 1908).
7. Emme, op. cit., p. 136.
8. Ibid., p. 305.
9. Captain C. J. Burke, 'Aeroplanes of Today and their use in War', *Journal of the Royal United Services Institution*, May 1911.
10. *Air Power and Warfare, Proceedings of the Eighth Military History Symposium* (USAF, 1978) p. 23.
11. Headquarters Royal Flying Corps Memo, 22 September 1966. Quoted in full in Hyam, *Military Intellectuals in Britain 1918–39* (New Brunswick: Rutgers, 1966) pp. 253–6.
12. Ibid.
13. Air Staff memorandum to AOC Central Area and AOC Inland Area, 19 July 1923.
14. Cabinet Paper 332: CAB 24/27, 1929.
15. Conversations with author, 1978.
16. ACTS, *Air Force, Part 1*, 'Air Warfare', 1 March 1936, p. 14, quoted by R. F. Futrell in *Ideas, Concepts, Doctrine: A History of Basic Thinking in the United States Air Force, 1907–1964* (Alabama: Air University Maxwell Air Force Base, 1974).
17. ACTS, *Air Force, Part 1*, 'Air Warfare', 1 February 1938, p. 1.
18. A comprehensive analysis of the various influences on national air power before 1939 is given in R. J. Overy, *The Air War 1939–45* (London: Europa Press, 1980).
19. Conversations with author.
20. Overy, op. cit., p. 29.

21. Alexander Boyd, *The Soviet Air Force since 1918* (London: Macdonald & Jane's, 1977) pp. 180–2.
22. Ibid.
23. Royal Air Force Air Historical Branch Digest of 83 Group Operational Reports, pp. 88–9.
24. S. W. Roskill, *The War at Sea*, vol. 1 (London: HMSO, 1954) p. 500.
25. B. H. Liddell-Hart, *History of the Second World War* (London: Cassell, 1970) p. 390.
26. N. G. Frankland, 'The Bombing Offensive against Germany'; Harris, 'The Bomber Offensive'; Verrier, 'The Bomber Offensive'; Webster, 'The Strategic Air Offensive against Germany 1939–1945'; Hastings, 'Bomber Command'.
27. RAF Staff College Records, Lecture by Wing Commander F. J. W. Mellhuish on 'Air Armament – Training and Development', Andover, 11 May 1939.
28. H. D. Hall, *History of the Second World War, North American Supply* (London: HMSO, 1955) p. 424.
29. Analysed in full in P. M. Smith, *The Air Force Plans for Peace, 1943–1945* (Baltimore: Johns Hopkins Press, 1970).
30. Quoted by Lieutenant Colonel D. MacIsaac in Wilson Center Paper no. 8, *The Air Force and Strategic Thought 1945–51* (Wilson Center, 21 June 1979).
31. Memo for Chiefs of Staff, 28 May 1945. Quoted by J. T. Greenwood in *Air Power and Warfare* (USAFA, 1978) p. 219.
32. Third Report to Secretary for War, 12 November 1945. Quoted in Emme, op. cit., p. 311.
33. Emme, op. cit., p. 305.
34. Greenwood, op. cit., p. 218.
35. Ibid., p. 228.
36. MacIsaac, op. cit., pp. 39–40.
37. See Chapter 7 below.
38. Greenwood, op. cit., p. 237.

CHAPTER 2: AIR POWER IN KOREA

1. General Mathew B. Ridgway, *The Korean War* (New York: Doubleday, 1967).
2. For a discussion on this shortage, see Chapter 2.
3. Ridgway, op. cit., p. 148.
4. Apart from the USAF, and air units of the US Navy and the US Marine Corps, there was an operational squadron each from the RAAF and the SAAF, as well as transport aircraft of the Royal Hellenic Air Force and the Royal Thai Air Force, Sunderland flying-boats of the Royal Air Force, and aircraft of the Royal Navy and of the Royal Australian Navy.
5. CG FEAF to COS USAF, 10 September 1950, quoted in R. F. Futrell, *The United States Air Force in Korea* (New York: Duell, Sloan and Pearce, 1961) p. 55.

6. JCS 1259/27, quoted in Futrell, op. cit., p. 46, which also gives details of the inadequate steps taken.
7. Futrell, op. cit., p. 55.
8. FEAF report on the Korean War, 20 March 1954, p. 130, quoted in Futrell, op. cit.
9. The North Korean Air Force seems to have had a total of 132 combat aircraft; apart from the IL-10s, it had seventy Yak-3 and Yak-7Bs, twenty-two Yak-12 transports and eight PO-2 trainers. These were all obsolescent, but none the less valuable, aircraft for conventional roles. Futrell, op. cit., pp. 19, 20.
10. Futrell, op. cit., p. 96.
11. With considerable success then as later. They were the only aircraft that could operate from South Korea's inadequate airfields. By 6 August, six squadrons had been converted to F-51s, and 145 more F-51s were recalled from the Air National Guard. As General Timberlake said at the time, 'one squadron of Mustangs adequately supported [inside the Pusan perimeter] is equivalent to four F-80s based on Kyushu'. This was not only because of the higher sortie rate, but the Mustangs could carry napalm which was highly effective against tanks and infantry. The jet aircraft had no wing racks for bombs, and being based in Japan they could neither react quickly to tasking nor remain long in the battle area on cab-rank. See Futrell, op. cit., pp. 81, 83, 90, 91 and 104.
12. Ridgway, op. cit., p. 25.
13. Without conspicuous success in the case of the B-29s. In an extraordinary attack on 16 August along the north bank of the River Baktong forming part of the Pusan perimeter, ninety-eight Superfortresses covered a 27 square mile area with nearly 1,000 tons of bombs in a carpet-bombing operation. There was never any evidence that even a single North Korean soldier had been killed. See Futrell, op. cit., p. 131.
14. Major General W. B. Kean, Commander of 25 Division, said: 'The close air support sorties flown by the Fifth Air Force again saved this Division, as they have many times before.' Quoted in Futrell, op. cit., p. 134.
15. Futrell, op. cit., p. 185.
16. 5th Air Force was the tactical air formation of FEAF; the B-29s were controlled by FEAF Bomber Command.
17. Futrell, op. cit., p. 122.
18. Ibid., p. 124.
19. Ibid., p. 164.
20. Ibid., p. 147.
21. Ibid., p. 126.
22. 'Since the start of operations in Korea, the problem of night attack on moving targets has obviously been one of our greatest weaknesses', said General Vandenberg in September 1950, quoted in Futrell, op. cit., p. 129.
23. *Aerospace Historian*, Summer/Fall 1970, p. 137.
24. Futrell, op. cit., p. 195.
25. Ibid., p. 159.
26. Ibid., p. 166.
27. Ibid., p. 205. On 25 October, for example, FEAF Combat Cargo Command airlifted 1,767 tons of supplies to Korea, 90 per cent of it to North Korea and

the bulk of that being made up of rations and fuel for the 8th Army.
28. Ibid., p. 209.
29. Ibid., p. 211.
30. USS *Leyte* had arrived from the Mediterranean on 3 October. Cagle and Manson, *The Sea War in Korea* (USNI, 1957) p. 226.
31. Ibid., p. 222.
32. Futrell, op. cit., p. 216.
33. It was not merely a shortage of aircraft, but also a lack of skilled interpreters. The RF-80 Squadron could not operate at full potential for this reason. Futrell, op. cit., p. 212.
34. Ibid., p. 217.
35. Ibid., p. 224.
36. During 2 December, for example, forty to sixty tactical aircraft constantly circled the two US Marine regiments. Cagle and Manson, op. cit., p. 173.
37. Futrell, op. cit., p. 240.
38. Ibid., p. 240.
39. Cagle and Manson, op. cit., p. 186.
40. See David Rees, *Korea, the Limited War* (New York: St Martins, 1964) p. 167.
41. Futrell op. cit., p. 227.
42. Ridgway, op. cit., pp. 146–7. There was always the possibility of enemy attack on the UNC air bases, but worse than that, the B-29 strategic bombers based on some of those airfields would be at risk. That fact led the JCS to deny MacArthur's request for the return of two bomber groups to the theatre on 5 December 1950. See Futrell, op. cit., p. 356. Nor was the risk entirely illusory; in mid-June, PO-2 bi-plane trainers made a series of nuisance raids over UN targets, and one attacking aircraft managed to destroy one Sabre and damaged eight others, four of them seriously. Ibid., p. 280.
43. Their appearance in action was delayed by the need to recover the aircraft from the effects of salt spray corrosion sustained on passage.
44. The attacks are described in Futrell, op. cit., pp. 292–5. The US Navy also employed guided missiles in at least one series of operations. On 28 August, pilotless Hellcats (F6-F5s) of Second World War vintage were loaded with high explosives, launched from USS *Boxer* and flown to their targets by means of a television guidance system. Several scored hits on the targets. Cagle and Manson, op. cit., p. 58.
45. Futrell, op. cit., p. 292.
46. Ibid., p. 347.
47. Ibid., p. 349.
48. Ibid., p. 380.
49. Ibid., pp. 308–10. ·
50. Ibid., p. 405 *et seq.*
51. 'Operation Strangle' briefing, quoted in ibid., p. 407.
52. Press release quoted in ibid., p. 413.
53. FEAF Int. Summary of 28 December 1951, quoted in ibid., p. 413.
54. There are several hints of this in Futrell, ibid. Cagle and Manson, op. cit. is more explicit, and quotes the Commander of Air Group 5 on USS *Essex* as saying that 'maintaining the morale of his pilots was one of his toughest

jobs'. The Air Group had gone through two sets of aircraft between 22 August and 30 November 1951; they had lost 27 aircraft and 11 pilots. Ibid., p. 253.

55. Futrell, op. cit., p. 418.
56. All quoted in ibid., p. 434.
57. Article by General Weyland, 'The Air Campaigns in Korea' published in Stewart, *Air Power, the Decisive Force in Korea* (1957), reprinted in Emme (ed.), *The Impact of Air Power: National Security and World Politics* (New York: Van Nostrand, 1959).
58. Futrell, op. cit., p. 482.
59. Ibid., p. 526.
60. Ibid., p. 526.
61. Ibid., pp. 572–5.
62. Ibid., p. 598. This rate was held down only by avoiding the lower altitudes on which anti-aircraft fire was most effective, and by attacking the less well-defended targets.
63. Ibid., p. 581.
64. History of FEAF January–June 1953, and FEAF Report II, paraphrased in Futrell, op. cit., p. 653.
65. Ibid., p. 653.
66. Between 24 and 28 aircraft were normally engaged in each attack.
67. Cagle and Manson, op. cit., pp. 460–7.
68. Futrell, op. cit., p. 626.
69. General Mark Clark, *From the Danube to the Yalu* (Westport, Conn.: Greenwood, 1974) p. 252.
70. Rees, op. cit., p. 420.
71. In June, 8908 close air support sorties were flown. Futrell, op. cit., p. 631.
72. The six were all in 'sensitive areas'.
73. Futrell, op. cit., pp. 638–9.
74. I.e., the equivalent of 20 Wings, or between a third and a quarter of the number of USAF wings that existed, all told, in 1950.
75. Rees, op. cit., Appendix c; Futrell, op. cit., pp. 644–6; Cagle and Manson, op. cit., Appendix X.
76. Because Korea was a peninsula around which UNC forces held total air and sea superiority, carriers were however a most valuable source of air power, particularly when airfields were so scarce. Their success in the campaign led the Eisenhower administration to authorise six Forrestal Class carriers and the first nuclear carrier, the *Enterprise*, which were commissioned at the rate of one a year from 1955 to 1961. The USN maintained 15 attack carriers during the 1960s.
77. 'Air Power and World Strategy, Especially in the Far East'. *The Annals*, May 1955.
78. Quoted in Futrell, op. cit., p. 644.
79. In Soviet Total War I, issued by the House Committee on UN–American Activities, September 1956. Reprinted in Emme, op. cit., p. 673.
80. 'Air Power and World Strategy', Sir John Slessor, *Foreign Affairs*, October 1954.

CHAPTER 3: AIR POWER IN COLONIAL WARS

1. Keeping 70,000 Japanese troops under arms in order to do so. E. J. Hammer, *The Struggle for Indo-China 1940–55* (Standard University Press, 1966).
2. Ex Luftwaffe JU-52s.
3. German Fieseler Storchs, built under licence.
4. Bernard B. Fall, *Street Without Joy – Insurgency in Indo-China 1946–63*, rev. edn (Harrisburg, PA: Stackpole, 1965).
5. Quite extensive fighting had taken place before this, and for example as early as March 1946 a force of 1,400 rebels at Takhek on the River Mekong in Laos. The assault was supported by artillery as well as by the JU-52s and four Spitfires. The bombs and cannon of the Spitfires broke the enemy resistance at a critical stage of the battle leading to the dispersal of the rebel force and the capture of 150 prisoners. General L. M. Chassin, *Aviation Indochine* (Paris: Amiot Dumont, 1954) pp. 59–60.
6. Ibid., p. 62.
7. Ibid., p. 64.
8. Ibid., p. 66.
9. Joseph Buttinger, *Vietnam: A Dragon Embattled* (New York: Praeger, 1967).
10. By 1950 it contained divisional formations, though it is true that they were much weaker than conventional divisions.
11. See, for example, a letter by the Commander of a Moroccan battalion to Commander GATAC Nord thanking him for twenty-one months of offensive and transport air support. Chassin, op. cit., pp. 81–2.
12. Fall, *Street Without Joy*.
13. 'French Air in Indo-China' *Aviation and Marine International Magazine*, December 1973.
14. Chassin, op. cit., pp. 83–5.
15. Compared with 3,690 hours in July, 3,834 in August and 4,489 in September 1950. Two Kingcobras and several Criquets had been lost. Ibid., p. 86.
16. Which dropped 50 tons of ammunition to the beleaguered troops.
17. They also evacuated 120 wounded. Chassin, op. cit., p. 100.
18. Chassin, op. cit., pp. 93–4 and Robert B. Asprey, *War in the Shadows* (London: Macdonald & Jane's, 1976) p. 764.
19. The rainy season in Northern Indo-China lasts from April till September. In 1953 and 1954 rains were heavier and earlier than usual.
20. With a loss of one Hellcat, one Kingcobra and two Criquets. Chassin, op. cit., p. 101.
21. Asprey, op. cit., p. 765; Chassin, op. cit., p. 104.
22. For a description of these fortifications see Fall, *Street Without Joy*, p. 173.
23. Asprey, op. cit., p. 767.
24. This was the last operation in which the old JU-52s were used. By now C-47s were arriving in Indo-China in large numbers. Fall, *Street Without Joy*, p. 45.
25. Chassin, op. cit., p. 119.
26. General Chassin uses this expression, but after Hoa Binh it seems to have been replaced by the term 'Base Aero-Terreste'. See Asprey, op. cit., p. 781. See Fall's comments in *Street Without Joy*, p. 57.

27. Fall, *Street Without Joy*, p. 74. Na San is 190 km by air from Hanoi. The entire operation was mounted and sustained by air, and up to 84 Dakotas were landing each day on the airstrip. Some of the difficulties of operating into the airstrip and of bombing the surrounding area in bad weather and in the face of increasingly effective Viet Minh anti-aircraft fire are described in Chassin, op. cit., p. 146. Dakotas, for example, would make up to a dozen runs on the same axis at heights down to 600 feet. Fighter escort to suppress the AA fire was essential, but it was not very effective against the accurate, mobile and well camouflaged Viet Minh AA guns. As a result, flak jackets were issued to French aircrews, and armour plate was fitted to the cabins of aircraft such as the C-47. Ibid., p. 150.

28. Bernard B. Fall, *Hell in a Very Small Place* (London: Pall Mall, 1967) p. 24.

29. Fall, *Street Without Joy*, pp. 75–7 and 79. All available civil transport aircraft in Indo-China were requisitioned for this operation to supplement the military transports available which included the whole force of about 100 C-47 aircraft.

30. Normally the three French air transport groups reckoned to fly 2,400 hours a month. After Na San the figure rose to 3,600, and with the new base in the Plaine de Jarres it rose to 4,180 hours in March and 4,480 in April. French fighters flew 1,840 sorties, while bombers flew 390 hours and liaison aircraft 1,800 during this same month of April 1953. Chassin, op. cit., pp. 162–4.

31. Bernard B. Fall, *The Two Vietnams* (London: Pall Mall, 1963) p. 122.

32. The total flying hours for August 1953 amounted to 9,060 hours, of which 3,860 had been flown by Dakotas. Chassin, op. cit., p. 198.

33. See the discussions in Fall's *Hell in a Very Small Place*, Chapter 2, and in *Street Without Joy*, p. 308. The latter makes mention of Nevarre's own statement in his book 'Agonie de l'Indochine' that 'I have always claimed for myself the entire responsibility for the operational decisions leading to the battle of Dien Bien Phu', and later, 'Laos could not be defended by a war of movement . . . thus another method had to be used; that . . . of hedgehog systems or fortified camps . . . It (this solution) would not prevent light enemy detachments from roaming through the countryside, but, leaving in our hands essential points, would prevent an (outright) invasion . . .'

34. Chassin, op. cit., p. 206.

35. For comparison, the Viet Minh combat strength when the battle began on 13 March was 49,500 men. Fall, *Hell in a Very Small Place*, p. 133 and Appendix D. Reinforcements arrived on both sides during the battle.

36. The other was at strongpoint Isabelle, 5 km south of Dien Bien Phu.

37. Jules Roy, *Battle of Dien Bien Phu* (London: Faber, 1965) p. 143.

38. According to French estimates, the Communists finally had in position at Dien Bien Phu at least forty-eight 105 mm howitzers, forty-eight 75 mm guns, forty-eight 120 mm mortars with at least as many recoilles rifles as well as some Soviet multi-tube rocket launchers. All told the Viet Minh had at least 200 guns above 57 mm calibre; the French had at the most sixty, and only about forty a week after the start of the battle. Fall's *Hell in a Very Small Place*, p. 127 and *Street Without Joy*, p. 316.

39. Fall, *Hell in a Very Small Place*, p. 130, and Appendix C. Some extra effort was available from C-119 Boxcars which dropped six-ton loads of napalm.

40. See Chapter 2 of this book dealing with Korea. The American Air Force could not accept that their efforts in Korea, particularly in the interdiction role, had been ineffective, indeed they were claiming at this time that air power had been the decisive factor in the Korean war. They seem to have given no warning of the difficulties that the small French Air Force might face. See Fall, *Hell in a Very Small Place*, p. 129 *et seq.*
41. Chassin, op. cit., p. 208.
42. From private sources. The French official records are not yet available for examination, but this visit and the advice that followed it seem to have played a more important part in the fall of Dien Bien Phu than has so far been recognised.
43. Fall, *Street Without Joy*, p. 259.
44. Another 101 were taken out by helicopter. Fall, *Hell in a Very Small Place*, p. 168.
45. Ibid., p. 176.
46. Including Aigle Azur, Air Vietnam, Air Outre-Mer and several others.
47. Fall, *Hell in a Very Small Place*, p. 241.
48. There is a useful discussion of this aspect in Fall, ibid., Chapter 4. According to the figures given there, Dien Bien Phu lacked 34,000 tons of combat engineering equipment, or 12,000 C-47 transport loads.
49. French pilot losses alone in Indo-China were 650 killed and missing in action, a total that does not include the 70 or so civilian crew members killed. Fall, *Street Without Joy*, p. 260.
50. 26 Battalions in June 1950. The strengths at the start of the campaign had been 9,000 police and 10 Bns. Details are in the Annual Reports on the Federation of Malaya, issued by the then Colonial Office.
51. Figure quoted from various sources including an unpublished Royal Air Force History dated June 1970.
52. 4 Sqns of the RAF reinforced by RAAF and RNZAF aircraft.
53. As Air Commodore Warcup points out several times in the *Rand Symposium on The Malayan Emergency*, A. H. Peterson *et al.* (eds), June 1963. See for example p. 76.
54. The maximum number of terrorists killed in a single air strike was 22 when on 21 February 1956 for the first time in the whole campaign a camp was struck whilst actually occupied by CTs. No. 1 (RAAF) Squadron for example, dropped 17,500 tons of bombs between 1950 and 1958 – over half the tonnage dropped during the entire campaign, but were credited with killing only 16 terrorists. *Rand Symposium* (Malaya), p. 60. Malaya–Colonial Office Report 1956, p. 443.
55. If a bomb missed the target by only 100 yards, its effects could be totally absorbed by the dense jungle.
56. Air Commodore Warcup, *Rand Symposium* (Malaya) p. 49.
57. In 1956 it was less than a quarter of what it had been in 1951 – *Rand Symposium* (Malaya), p. 70.
58. Ibid., p. 55.
59. For comparison, during one of the heaviest USAAF raids on Berlin in the Second World War, on 3 February 1945, 2,022 tons of HE and 244 tons of incendiaries were dropped. During the Korean War, a total of 386,000 tons of bombs had been dropped, and 313,600 RPs and 166,853,100 rounds

of ammunition discharged. Futrell, *The United States Air Force in Korea* (New York: Duell, Sloan and Pearce, 1961) p. 645.

60. Unpublished figures from Royal Air Force sources.
61. Details from AHB (History of Campaigns, p. 72).
62. General Clutterbuck, *The Long, Long War* (London: Cassell, 1967) p. 160–1. Compare this with the US technique in Vietnam.
63. Never more than a total of 41 light and medium manned helicopters, including one RN Squadron, No. 348. Unpublished RAF sources.
64. Unpublished RAF sources.
65. Even the occasional reinforcements from Bomber Command had the primary aim of proving the routes, and the flights continued long after the Malayan Emergency was over.
66. The precise features of the barriers varied with the terrain, but in particularly vulnerable areas it could consist of two complex fences 25 feet apart, with an electric fence between them, ground radar and booby traps of all kinds. The difficulty was that without constant patrolling the barriers were useless, and in mid-1958 no fewer than 80,000 troops were tied down in patrolling these barriers. *Rand Symposium, on The Algerian Emergency*, A. H. Peterson *et al.* (eds), July 1963, pp. 7, 8, 11, 13 and 63.
67. Ibid., p. 16.
68. More than 30 airfields were built in the 250 km strip between the coast and the Sahara, and in the eastern Sahara 200 runways were built ready for light aircraft by 1959. Ibid., p. 23.
69. *Guerilla Warfare and Airpower in Algeria 1954–1960* (Air War College, Maxwell, 1965) p. 111, where a full discussion of the command and control arrangements can be found.
70. The T-6s alone carried out more than half the firepower missions flown during 1959, 14,255 sorties not including their extensive reconnaissance efforts. Ibid., p. 63.
71. Details are in *Rand Symposium* (Algeria), p. 21, and some details of the units involved as well as of the numerous other aircraft types are in *Air Britain Digest*, May–June 1975, p. 71.
72. In 1957 the helicopters flew 56,000 combat hours, and in 1959 66,000 hours. See Asprey, op. cit., p. 1004.
73. On 1 January 1959 the French had about 500,000 men in Algeria of which 35,284 were air force personnel. *Rand Symposium* (Algeria), p. 22. The casualties were given by de Gaulle himself at a press conference at the end of 1958 – see Asprey, op. cit., p. 1002. Aircraft losses seem to have been high. Twenty-two aircraft of all types were shot down by rebel fire in 1959 alone – see *Guerilla Warfare and Airpower in Algeria 1954–1960*, p. 64 and the references given there.
74. Air reconnaissance played a vital part in this and, for example, in the month of November 1959, 3,220 reconnaissance and 110 photo-recce sorties were flown resulting in 24 guerilla groups and 19 guerilla convoys being located by these means. Interestingly enough, although the Vampire jets had only a limited endurance, their very high speed meant that they could make rapid searches of huge areas of the flat Sahara.
75. *Rand Symposium* (Algeria), p. 22.
76. There is a full discussion of the command and control system, and its variations, in the *Rand Symposium* (Algeria).

77. There were 3 Tactical Air Commands in Algeria divided into 12 zones each of which corresponded to a divisional area of responsibility, and each zone was further divided into 72 regimental sectors. Sectors were typically 250 square miles covering a population of 100,000 or more. There was a JOC in each Corps and Zone area, and an Air Directing Post to direct tactical air operations in each Sector. Command in the field was exercised by a group commander and an air commander in the same aircraft, or on the ground together, or one airborne and the other on the ground. If the ground commander was not airborne, the air commander would frequently assume direction of the ground troops to take advantage of terrain features or enemy dispositions that he was able to see from a vantage point. Conversely, on unplanned missions, the ground commander would assume control of the supporting aircraft.

78. *Rand Symposium* (Algeria), p. 50.

79. O'Ballance, 'The Algerian Insurrection', the *Rand Symposium* (Algeria) and Asprey, op. cit. There are conflicting figures but those given here seem to be about right.

80. The techniques are well described by MRAF Sir John Slessor in *The Central Blue* (London: Cassell, 1956).

81. Made by Venoms and Shackletons as well as by Sea Venoms and Sea Hawks from HMS *Bulwark* which was then in the Persian Gulf.

82. The squadron was withdrawn from anti-Mau Mau operations in Kenya to take part in this operation.

83. In the words of an unpublished RAF History.

84. The intended target was the High Commissioner himself who was injured by the grenade thrown.

85. Including 45 Royal Marine Commando and 3 Battalion The Parachute Regiment.

86. In the Defence White Paper published 22 February 1966.

87. Between May and October, 59 loyal Africans had been murdered by the terrorists.

88. Later two Meteor PR-10s were also added for photo-reconnaissance work.

89. These and other operational facts are from an unpublished RAF History of the campaign.

90. See General Frank Kitson's book *Gangs and Counter-Gangs* (London: Barrie and Rockliff, 1960) for a full account of these operations.

91. General Erskine's remarks are quoted in an unpublished RAF History. He made the comments when he addressed a RAF audience before he left Nairobi in April 1955, but recent conversations with officers who were on his staff in Kenya make it clear that none of them shared his assessment, even at the time.

CHAPTER 4: THE AIR WAR IN SOUTH-EAST ASIA

1. General William Momyer, *Airpower in Three Wars* (USAFA, 1978) p. 11.
2. Ibid., p. 271.
3. Ibid., pp. 18–19.
4. These controversial attacks and their genesis are the subject of the book by

William Shawcross, *Sideshow: Kissinger, Nixon and the Destruction of Cambodia* (London: Deutsch, 1979).

5. Momyer, op. cit., p. 33.
6. See Colonel Ray L. Bowers, 'Airlift and Airmobility in Vietnam', *Air University Review*, November–December 1974.
7. Ibid.
8. Ibid.
9. Ibid.
10. Helicopter losses to all causes in March 1971 are shown in Department of Defence figures as 124, against an average monthly loss for the whole year of 42 – Dept of Defence OASD Comptroller Director for Information Operations – dated 6 May 1974.
11. Momyer, op. cit., p. 324.
12. Figures calculated from 'Military Airlift in South-East Asia', *Air Force Magazine* October 1972. (Standard tons have been used.)
13. Momyer, op. cit., p. 271, 2nd Division became 7th Air Force on 1 April 1966.
14. Colonel Ray L. Bowers in *Air Power and Warfare, Proceedings of the Eighth Military History Symposium* (USAFA, 1978) Chapter VI.
15. Momyer, op. cit., p. 278.
16. And later at U-Tapao in Thailand.
17. By September 1967, the entire B-52 fleet was modified to this standard. Later, some of the B-52s operated from U-Tapao in Thailand. John Greenwood in *The Vietnam War* (London: Salamander Books, 1979) p. 198.
18. Momyer, op. cit., p. 285.
19. One of them, the 173 Airborne Brigade, made the only parachute assault of the war. Ibid., p. 296.
20. Ibid., p. 303.
21. Ibid., p. 305, and Major C. E. Watts, 'Aerial Resupply for Khe San', *Military Review*, December 1972, pp. 79–88.
22. Momyer, op. cit., p. 310.
23. See Capt. Moyers S. Shaw, US Marine Corps. *History of the Battle of Khe San* (US Marine Corps, 1969).
24. Greenwood, op. cit., pp. 201–2. For details of the tactics used, see 'AOK Air Power over Vietnam' *Aerospace Historian*, March 1972, p. 2. Bernard Nally in his chapter of *The Vietnam War* states that the total weight of bombs dropped in the whole siege was 1,000,000 short tons thus making it, he says, the most heavily bombed target in the history of Warfare. See p. 162. Nally also claims that 53,000 tons of napalm were used in the four-week period ending in mid-February, p. 158.
25. USAF tactical squadrons were flying operational missions within 72 to 96 hours after they were alerted in the US. General Clay, quoted in 'The Air War in Vietnam', *Air Force Magazine*, September 1972.
26. Momyer, op. cit., p. 175.
27. Momyer deals with these problems in detail. See his Chapters II and III.
28. Ibid., p. 95.
29. See J. J. Holst (ed.) *Beyond Nuclear Deterrence* (Allison and Morris), 'Precision Guidance for NATO; Justification and Constraints', p. 212 *et seq*. The logic was that it was wasteful to use a $3000 bomb to destroy a

$1000 truck, ignoring the point that spending ten $1000 bombs on the same target was even worse.

30. An estimated 90 per cent of all trucks destroyed and damaged were hit at night.
31. Momyer, op. cit., p. 223. About 65 per cent of all aircraft shot down over North Vietnam were lost to AA fire.
32. Ibid., pp. 137–49.
33. Ibid., pp. 123–5.
34. See ibid., for a detailed discussion.
35. Ibid.
36. Details from ibid., and from Greenwood, op. cit.
37. Quoted in several sources for example in Admiral U. S. G. Sharp, *Strategy for Defeat* (Novato, CA: Presidio Press, 1978) p. 255.
38. For a discussion of this, see General Westmoreland, *A Soldier Reports* (New York: Doubleday, 1976) pp. 417–23.
39. Sharp, op. cit., p. 271.
40. Westmoreland, op. cit., p. 413.
41. The figures do not include the losses sustained by the Australian, New Zealand, Korean, Phillipino, Thai or South Vietnamese forces. Total losses for the whole period of the US involvement were probably about 55,000 dead.
42. Including all non-combat losses sustained in connection with the war. All figures from Dept of Defence OASD (Comptroller) Director for Information Operations, 6 May 1974.
43. Charles E. Myers, combat pilot in the Second World War, and one-time Director of Air Warfare in the Office of the Deputy Under Secretary of Defense for Tactical Warfare Programs, in an article 'Deep-Strike Interdiction' in *Proceedings*, Nov. 1980.

CHAPTER 5: AIR POWER IN THE MIDDLE EAST

1. This claim is confidently and reliably made by Brigadier N. T. Bagnall in an unpublished thesis, 'The Israeli Experience, A Study of Quality', written at the University of Oxford in 1973. His conclusion was based on extensive conversations with Israeli officers before the outbreak of the October War.
2. Egyptian Mig-21 pilots were limited to five hours training per month and the aircraft was not cleared for aerobatics. Mig-19 pilots had similar restrictions on flying time but were also impeded by technical problems involving engine fires. As a result, many Mig-19s were grounded for six months before the June War. The two Mig-17 squadrons were theoretically converted to the air-to-ground role but realistic exercises were only practised three times a year. (Conversation between author and Egyptian participants.)
3. Revised training procedures included up to ten practice air defence scrambles from one squadron in one day; pilots flew a minimum of four air-to-ground sorties a month using live ammunition for 60 per cent of them; new ranges were built including one whose position was frequently changed to improve and test target identification and navigation accuracy; aircraft vulnerability to the Hawk system during target acquisition was reduced

almost exactly to the Hawk's assessed engagement time of 22 seconds. (Ibid.)

4. Figures given by Major General Shlomo Gazit, Director of Intelligence Branch IDF to an International Symposium in Tel Aviv in October 1975. Reproduced in Williams (ed.), *Military Aspects of the Israeli–Arab Conflict* (Tel Aviv, 1975: University Publishing Project, p. 190. Batteries of SAM-2 missiles would normally comprise six static launch platforms with reload capability, SAM-3s just four. SAM-6 units carry three missiles in launch array on a tracked vehicle but require additional transport for reloads. Consequently, the term 'battery' could denote three, four or six missiles depending on the type.

5. Herzog, *War of Atonement* (London: Weidenfeld & Nicolson, 1975) p. 252. General Herzog suggests that 'the 2 main influences' on EAF thinking were the trauma of 1967 and Soviet training which itself reflected Soviet lack of combat experience.

6. Comment made to Shlomo Aronson during interview on 11 October 1974 in Tel Aviv. Summarised in Aronson, *Conflict and Bargaining in the Middle East* (Baltimore: Johns Hopkins Press, 1978) p. 163.

7. There is a little doubt about the exact order of battle or 'orbat' of the Syrian Air Force because the IISS Military Balance for 1972/73, published earlier in the year, intimated that some of the Sukhoi-7 fighter bombers were 'in storage'. Even if all were brought forward to the line, it is highly unlikely that all were serviceable in October.

8. Only the TU-16s could have reached the Israeli heartland and the EAF believed that they would not have survived the missions. There was, however, no practical reason why Syrian Mig-17s or SU-7s should not have attacked military targets more widely in Israel. There is no evidence yet to explain any decision not to do so.

9. Egyptian sources concede three aircraft destroyed in hardened shelters, all because doors were left open. Direct hits by 1,000 and 3,000 lb bombs had no effect. (Author conversation.)

10. *Aviation Week and Space Technology*, 7 July 1975, p. 15. Interview by AWST reporter with commander of the Egyptian Air Defence Force.

11. A reference to comments made to *Le Monde* 18 October 1973 and quoted in Golan, *Yom Kippur and After* (Cambridge University Press, 1977) p. 86. Golan comprehensively analyses the diplomatic activity associated with the Soviet airlift.

12. Report of the Special Sub-Committee on the Middle East of the Committee on Armed Services of the House of Representatives, 13 December 1973, p. 4. Foxbat would continue to present a problem to the IAF until the arrival of the F-15 Eagle in 1979. Foxbat was too quick for the Phantom and too high for the Hawk SAM and there seems no reason to doubt reports of its presence over the battle area in October 1973. The opportunity for 'combat trials' would certainly be valuable to the USSR and its presence would also illustrate confidence in its invulnerability at the time.

13. Comments made in response to questions during the Tel Aviv Symposium referred to in note 4 above. Proceedings, p. 256. In the same session, General Elazar explained what he believed the major contribution of air power should be to the land battle:

the primary goal of the Air Force is to secure the skies throughout the country above the combat forces. This need not be an airtight defence, but it must prevent systematic and effective destruction. I see the Air Force's main role in the support of ground forces in interdiction – to achieve destruction of the enemy's military infrastructure, cause havoc among troop movements and, in one word, to paralyse the enemy forces. Even before 1973, I considered the subject of close air support the last priority task of the Air Force. I always believed that ground forces, secure from the enemy's air activity, should defeat enemy ground forces unaided. The October War reconfirmed my belief that close air support is costly in casualties, and that there is no positive ratio between relatively great losses and limited results.

Proceedings, page 249.

14. Egyptian sources are adamant that Foxbat was not the only reconnaissance interloper, but that on 14 October and again on 16 October a USAF SR-71 'covered the whole of Egypt, at a height of 27,000 metres at exactly 2,880 km/hour. No component of our air defences could have engaged it.' (Author conversations.) It has not been possible to verify this report, but if true, and the source is reliable, it indicates that the USAF was very confident in its assessment of the maximum altitude of the SAM-2.
15. In an interview given to Al Ahram after the war, quoted by Major General D. K. Palit in a paper given to an International Symposium on the October War held in Cairo, October 1975. Ramadan/M/CO/061, p. 6.
16. Israeli sources were not unanimous in explaining the breach of the SAM defences. General Peled stated it had been achieved by air attack, while Generals Elazar and Sharon claimed that ground forces were responsible. The author received firm Egyptian assurance that General Sharon's forces did, in fact, do the damage.
17. The Israeli concession of just three aircraft lost in air-to-air combat is scorned by Egyptian pilots. One EAF Wing alone claims very confidently to have shot down 22 Israeli planes throughout the conflict. (Author conversations.)
18. Palit, *Return to Sinai* (Salisbury, Wilts: Compton Russell, 1974) pp. 154–5. General Palit's analysis is corroborated by various reliable Western military sources.
19. At certain times the Egyptian defences operated 'guns tight' to permit maximum interceptor activity. This procedure may well have been the most successful but at the obvious cost of neutralising the ground-to-air component.
20. Gazit, op. cit., p. 189.

CHAPTER 6: SOVIET AIR POWER 1945–80

1. International Institute for Strategic Studies, *The Military Balance 1979* (London) pp. 9–10.
2. Alexander Boya, *The Soviet Air Force since 1918* (London: Macdonald & Jane's, 1977) p. 111.

3. V. D. Sokolovsky, *Military Strategy, Soviet Doctrine and Concepts* (London: Pall Mall, 1963) p. 158.
4. Ibid., p. 130.
5. Ibid., p. 158.
6. I. V. Timokhovich, *The Operational Art of the Soviet Air Force in the Great Patriotic War* (Moscow, 1976) pp. 8–9.
7. J. Alexander, *Russian Aircraft since 1940* (London: Putnam, 1975) p. 18.
8. Asher Lee, *The Soviet Air Force* (London: Duckworth, 1961) p. 72.
9. Ibid., p. 80.
10. Ibid., p. 114.
11. Quoted in T. W. Wolfe, *Soviet Power and Europe, 1945–1970* (Baltimore: Johns Hopkins Press, 1970) p. 63.
12. Ibid., p. 63.
13. Boyd, op. cit., p. 212.
14. A. Yakovlev, *The Aim of a Lifetime* (Moscow: Progress Press, 1972).
15. Alexander, op. cit., p. 208.
16. Boyd, op. cit., p. 243. The letters PVO stand for *Protivovozdushnaya oborona*.
17. The Long Range Air Force is frequently referred to by the initials DA standing for *Dal'nyaya aviatsiya* which was reconstituted in April 1946 after spending two years as the 18th Air Army, part of the tactical air organisation which in turn had followed the ADD (*aviatsia dalnego deistvia*) which had been created by Stalin in 1942. Lee succinctly summarises the evolution from ADD to DA and the aircraft are comprehensively described by Boyd, op. cit.
18. Sokolovsky, op. cit., p. 131.
19. Lee, op. cit., p. 128.
20. N. Khrushchev, *Khrushchev Remembers* (London: André Deutsch, 1974) p. 39.
21. 'Bison' was the NATO codename allocated to the Molot. The allocation of names was based on a simple principle of the initial letter indicating the major role of the aircraft, e.g., B for bomber, F for fighter, C for cargo etc. A monosyllabic word, e.g., 'Bear' indicated a piston or turbo-prop aircraft while a two-syllable codename such as 'Bison' indicated jet propulsion.
22. Khrushchev, op. cit., p. 40.
23. R. F. Futrell, *Ideas, Concepts and Doctrine in USAF 1907—64* (Air University Maxwell, 1974) pp. 167–71.
24. Khrushchev, op. cit., p. 43.
25. Article in *Red Star*, Moscow, 31 August 1955 on 'Strategic Aviation'.
26. Colonel General of Aviation Nikitin, *Soviet Aviation in Military Thought 2–49*, p. 62 quoted in R. L. Garthoff, *Soviet Strategy in the Nuclear Age* (Atlantic, 1958) p. 173.
27. As reported in *Pravda*, Moscow, 20 February 1956.
28. Khrushchev, op. cit., p. 540.
29. Ibid., p. 39.
30. As quoted in *Pravda*, 15 January 1960.
31. F. Gibney (ed.), *The Penkovsky Papers* (London: Collins, 1965) p. 169.
32. Ibid., p. 173.
33. Khrushchev, op. cit., p. 52.

34. Gibney, op. cit., p. 157.
35. Ibid., p. 247.
36. Ibid., p. 244.
37. Ibid., p. 245.
38. Wolfe, *Soviet Power and Europe*, pp. 134–5.
39. *Military Strategy* was published by the Military Publishing House of the Ministry of Defence in Moscow in September 1962 in an edition of twenty thousand copies. In the introduction to the first English language translation R. L. Garthoff observes 'it is described in the introduction as the first comprehensive book on strategy published in the Soviet Union since General Sbechin's *Strategy* appeared in 1926. While this is true, there have been a number of other important works in this field in recent years; the Soviet comment therefore underlines the particular importance accorded to this volume.'
40. Garthoff, introduction to Sokolovsky, p. vii.
41. Sokolovsky, op. cit., p. 14.
42. Ibid., p. 195.
43. Ibid., p. 182.
44. Ibid., pp. 182–3 and Gibney, op. cit., p. 173.
45. As reported in *Red Star*, 23 March 1957.
46. Sokolovsky, op. cit., p. 221.
47. Ibid., p. 60.
48. Ibid., p. 158.
49. Colonel V. Kolechitsky, *Military Thought 10/55*, as quoted in Garthoff op. cit., pp. 188–9.
50. Sokolovsky, op. cit., p. 193.
51. Ibid.
52. In Western analyses of the developments in Soviet aircraft production, the expression 'first generation' is applied to those of the Mig-15 era, the 'second generation' are those which generally appeared in the mid-1950s and the 'third generation' are those such as SU-17, Mig-23 and SU-19 which entered squadron service in the late 1960s and early 1970s.
53. Yakovlev, op. cit., p. 327.
54. Sokolovsky, op. cit., p. 78.
55. Gibney, op. cit., pp. 265–6.
56. Sokolovsky, op. cit., p. 281.
57. Ibid., p. 283.
58. R. L. Garthoff, *Soviet Military Policy* (London: Faber & Faber, 1966) p. 120.
59. Wolfe, *Soviet Power and Europe*, p. 169.
60. Sokolovsky, op. cit., p. 232.
61. Ibid., p. 233.
62. Biryuzov, *Lessons of the Beginning Period*, p. 44. *Military Thought 8/64*, quoted in J. D. Douglass Jr, *Soviet Military Strategy in Europe* (London: Pergamon, 1980) p. 94.
63. Sokolovsky, op. cit., p. 224.
64. Ibid., p. 232.
65. Ibid., p. 194.
66. Ibid., p. 32.

67. Khrushchev, op. cit., p. 42.
68. Ibid., p. 254.
69. Gurov, *Economics and War 1965*, quoted in Douglass, op. cit., p. 177.
70. Ibid.
71. Sokolovsky, op. cit., p. 158.
72. Khrushchev, op. cit., p. 37.
73. Sokolovsky, op. cit., p. 229.
74. Ibid., p. 292.
75. Kruchinin, *Contemporary Strategic Theory October 1963*, quoted in Douglass, op. cit., p. 106.
76. Sokolovsky, op. cit., p. 234.
77. Confusion occasionally arises because 'Bear' is referred to variously as TU-20 and TU-95. TU-95, according to Alexander, was the Tupolev OKB designation or what was to become, once in operational service, designated TU-20.
78. Sokolovsky, op. cit., pp. 107-9.
79. Ibid., p. 107.
80. Wolfe, *Soviet Power and Europe*, p. 139.
81. T. W. Wolfe, 'The Military Dimension in the making of Soviet Foreign and Defence Policy', statement to the United States House of Representatives Sub-Committee, 11 October 1977, pp. 35-40.
82. Sokolovsky, op. cit., p. 282.
83. These increases may be plotted from the London source of the annual Military Balance published by the International Institute for Strategic Studies, or in the collective statistical comparisons of J. M. Collins in *American and Soviet Military Trends* (Georgetown, 1978).
84. J. H. Hanson, 'Development of Soviet Aviation Support' in *International Defence Review*, 5/1980, p. 683.
85. Ibid.
86. See for example the annual survey by J. W. R. Taylor which occurs in the March edition of *Air Force Magazine*.
87. These details on the Flogger family are largely culled from the article in *Air International*, London, August 1980, pp. 70-87, under the general editing of W. Green and G. Swanborough.
88. Samorukov, 'Combat Operations', *Military Thought* 8/67, p. 32, quoted in Douglass, op. cit., p. 113.
89. Colonel I. Andrushkevich, 'Combat against Tanks in Modern Operations', *Military Thought* 4/69, p. 40.
90. Quoted without date by J. W. R. Taylor in 'Gallery of Soviet Aerospace Weapons', *Air Force Magazine*, March 1980, p. 131.
91. *Daily Telegraph*, 25 August 1980.
92. Wolfe, *Soviet Power and Europe*, pp. 451-2.
93. Hanson, op. cit., p. 683.
94. Taylor, op. cit., p. 121.
95. Extract from 'United States Fiscal Year 1979', Department of Defence annual report quoted by Taylor, ibid., p. 121.
96. See Chapter 9 below for explanation of origin of the posture and its implications for NATO and Warsaw Pact air power.
97. As quoted in *Red Star*, 21 July 1967.

98. *Defence in the 1980s*, Cmnd 7826–1 (London: HMSO, 1980).

99. Zheltov, 'Methodological problems of military theory in practice, by the Lenin Political Military Academy in 1969', quoted by Douglass, op. cit., p. 191.

100. *The Economist*, 24 June 1967.

101. See the comprehensive summary by Captain J. E. Moore in Erickson and Feuchtwanger (eds), *Soviet Military Power and Performance* (London: Macmillan, 1979).

102. See Chapter 7 above for a full account of the operations.

103. W. Schneider Jr, 'Soviet Military Airlift', article in *Air Force Magazine*, March 1980.

104. Ibid.

105. I. Sidelnikov, 'Peaceful Co-existence and the People's Security', *Red Star*, Moscow, 14 August 1973.

106. V. M. Kulish, *Military Power and International Relations 1972*, translated in *Selected Soviet Military Writings 1970–5* in the USAF 'Soviet Military Thought' series, no. 11, p. 30.

107. Ibid., p. 32.

108. N. A. Lomov (ed.) *The Revolution in Military Affairs* (Moscow, 1973) translated by USAF 'Soviet Military Thought' series, no. 3, p. 6.

109. A major Soviet publication, recommended to all officers was V. V. Druzhinin and D. S. Kontorov, *Concept, Algorithm, Decision* published in Moscow in 1972 and translated as no. 6 in the USAF 'Soviet Military Thought' series. During 1980 three excellent articles on developments in Soviet command and control were 'Command and Control and the Soviet Military System' in *Defence Attaché* and 'Soviet Command Technology' in *Jane's Defence Review* 1/1980, both by John Erickson, and 'Soviet C³' by N. Polmar in *Air Force Magazine*, June 1980.

110. This is an important theme in the Druzhinin publication.

111. Colonel V. A. Uryzhnikov, 'In a complex situation', *Red Star*, 7 January 1977, translated in *Soviet Press, Selected Translations* distributed by the USAF, p. 97.

CHAPTER 7: AIR POWER IN NATO

1. Ismay, *NATO, the First Five Years 1949–1954* (Paris, 1955) p. 4.

2. JCS 1725/1, 1 May 1947 quoted in T. H. Etzold and J. L. Gaddis (eds) *Containment, Documents on American Policy and Strategy 1945–50* (New York: Columbia, 1978) p. 302.

3. R. F. Futrell, *Ideas, Concepts Doctrine: A History of Basic Thinking in the United States Air Force 1907–1964* (Alabama: Air University Maxwell Air Force Base, 1974) p. 109.

4. *Forrestal Diaries, Inner History of the Cold War* ed. Millis (London: Cassell, 1952) p. 313.

5. Etzold and Gaddis JCS 1725/1 paras 10, 11 and 14.

6. Lieutenant Colonel H. Borowski USAF, *Military Affairs*, October 1980, p. 108.

7. *Forrestal* Diaries, op. cit., p. 489.
8. Beaufré, *NATO and Europe* (London: Faber & Faber, 1967).
9. JCS 1844/13, para. 3.
10. Ibid., para. 10.
11. JCS 1952/1, 21 December 1948, para. 32a.
12. Harman Report, para. 3 in Etzold and Gaddis, op. cit., p. 361.
13. Ibid.
14. Ibid., para. 12.
15. Ibid., para. 13.
16. Ibid., para. 18.
17. Defence Committee of NATO DC6/1, 1 December 1949 para. 5. Etzold and Gaddis, op. cit., p. 337.
18. Ibid., paras 7a, 7c.
19. M. Gowing, *Independence and Deterrence*, vols 1 and 2 London: (Macmillan, 1974).
20. Ibid., vol. 1, p. 183.
21. Ibid., p. 185.
22. Marshal of the Royal Air Force Sir John Slessor, address to the Royal Institute of International Affairs, March 1953.
23. R. N. Rosecrance, *Defence of the Realm* (New York: Columbia, 1968) p. 160.
24. Interview in *Saturday Evening Post*, 13 October 1949, quoted by Futrell, op. cit., p. 140.
25. DC6/1, op. cit., para. 5c.
26. Ismay, op. cit., p. 102.
27. Joint Senate Committee on Foreign Relations and Armed Services 1951, quoted in R. E. Osgood, *The Entangling Alliance* (University of Chicago Press, 1962).
28. Ismay, op. cit., p. 47.
29. Futrell, op. cit., p. 142.
30. Ibid.
31. Ismay, op. cit., p. 101.
32. Beaufré, op. cit., p. 51.
33. Rosecrance, op. cit., Chapter 5.
34. Quoted in Osgood, op. cit., p. 103.
35. Ismay, op. cit., p. 104.
36. Beaufré, op. cit., p. 51.
37. Osgood, op. cit., p. 109.
38. United Kingdom Defence White Paper 1955, Cmnd 9391 paras 19 and 22.
39. Air Commodore J. H. Knoop, *NATO's Fifteen Nations*, April/May 1971, p. 70.
40. General Maxwell D. Taylor, *The Uncertain Trumpet* (New York: Harper & Row, 1960) p. 145.
41. Quoted by W. W. Kaufman, 'The McNamara Strategy' in Head and Rokke (eds), *American Defence Policy* (Baltimore: Johns Hopkins Press, 1973) p. 73.
42. Ibid.
43. Institute for Strategic Studies, *Military Balance 1965–6*.
44. Ibid.

45. Air Chief Marshal Sir David Lee, *The RAF in Germany 1945–1978* (Air Historical Branch, 1979).
46. Knoop, op. cit., p. 72.
47. Address by General Richard Ellis to the Royal United Services Institution London, 25 February 1976.
48. Ibid.
49. In his *Entangling Alliance*, Robert Osgood makes no mention of tactical air power.
50. Ellis, RUSI, op. cit.
51. United Kingdom Defence White Paper Cmnd 7826–1, April 1980, page 5.
52. Cmnd 7474, February 1979, pp. 6–7.

CHAPTER 8: THE FALKLANDS CAMPAIGN

1. The account of the campaign given here relies on UK material; no Argentine sources have been consulted.
2. Up to four nuclear-powered and one diesel-powered boat were on patrol in the South Atlantic during the hostilities.
3. The nucleus of this force was 3 Commando Brigade, Royal Marines. On 1 April they had been at seven days' notice to move with one Commando (battalion) on leave and elements of another on jungle training in Borneo. The Brigade mobilised and sailed in five days.
4. The Argentine Air Force Commander was later to claim that only 80 of his aircraft had taken part in the campaign; the rest were unsuited to the type of operations called for. BBC News Monitoring Service 9 July 1982.
5. There are basically two versions of the Exocet; the AM-39 air-to-surface model, and the AM-38 surface-to-surface. The Argentine Navy had both.
6. The airborne time for these Vulcans was about 15§ hours.
7. The base built up to a strength of over 700 personnel. By the end of the operation about 5,600 personnel and 7,500 short tons of stores had been flown into Ascension, an airlift that absorbed over 17,000 flying hours by RAF C-130s and VC10s.
8. Hercules were regularly remaining airborne for as much as 25 hours at a time; one sortie was airborne for over 28 hours. Fifty-three long-range air drops were flown during the campaign. The Nimrods flew about 150 sorties from Ascension Island.
9. Up to 24 June, the Victor tankers had flown 573 sorties involving 3,225 hours; 635 fuel transfers had been undertaken of which only nine had been unsuccessful for one reason or another. Later in the operation, Vulcans and C-130 Hercules were converted to the AAR role to augment resources.
10. Patrols of the Special Air Service and the Special Boat Squadron were landed in East and West Falklands three weeks before the main landings to gather intelligence for this and other engagements.
11. During the campaign, three air-launched Exocets were successfully countered by the ships against which they were targetted.
12. 80 Sea Kings and Wessex helicopters were by now available for this and other operations ashore.

13. During this campaign, 54 ships, 16 of them tankers, were requisitioned from trade to operate alongside the 21 Royal Fleet Auxiliary ships involved, and no fewer than 19 of the ships taken up from trade were fitted with helicopter operating platforms for the operation.
14. About 1,500 Sea Harrier and over 150 Harrier GR3 sorties were flown altogether.
15. Made up of 42 Warships, 21 RFAs and 54 ships taken up from trade, the latter totalling 673,000 gross tons. They carried over 100,000 tons of freight, 9,000 personnel and 95 assorted aircraft during the campaign.
16. Mainly in the cruiser *General Belgrano*.
17. These figures include helicopters.
18. The original version of the A4 Skyhawk first flew in 1954, the Mirage III and V prototype in 1956.

CHAPTER 9: CHALLENGE AND OPPORTUNITIES

1. 'Budgeting for Defence', Sir Arthur Hockaday, 2nd PUS MOD, at the RUSI, 15 November 1978.
2. 'Defense Facts of Life', Franklin C. Spinney, 5 December 1980, which contains much else of interest in this field.

Select Bibliography and Further Reading

Air War College, Maxwell, *Guerilla Warfare and Airpower in Algeria, 1954–60* (1965).

Alexander, A. J., *Decision Making in Soviet Weapons Procurement*, Adelphi Paper 147/8 (London: IISS, 1978).

Alexander, J., *Russian Aircraft since 1940* (London: Putnam, 1975).

Aronson, Shlomo, *Conflict and Bargaining in the Middle East, An Israeli Perspective* (Baltimore: Johns Hopkins Press, 1978).

Asprey, Robert B., *War in the Shadows* (London: Macdonald & Jane's, 1976).

Bagnall, Brigadier N. T., 'The Israeli Experience, A Study of Quality', unpublished thesis, University of Oxford, 1973.

Beaufré, *NATO and Europe* (London: Faber & Faber, 1967).

Berman, R. P., *Soviet Air Power in Transition* (Washington: Brookings, 1978).

Boyd, A., *The Soviet Air Force since 1918* (London: Macdonald & Jane's, 1977).

Buchan, *NATO in the 1960s* (London: Weidenfeld & Nicolson, 1960).

Cagle and Manson, *The Sea War in Korea* (USNI, 1957).

Chassin, General L. M., *Aviation Indochine* (Paris: Amiot Dumont, 1954).

Clutterbuck, General Richard L., *The Long, Long War* (London: Cassell, 1967).

Collier, *The History of Air Power* (Book Club Edition, 1974).

Collins, J. M., *American and Soviet Military Trends* (Georgetown, 1978).

Coulton, T. J., *Commissars, Commanders and Civil Authority* (Cambridge, Mass.: Harvard University Press, 1979).

Douglass, J. D. Jr, *Soviet Military Strategy in Europe* (London: Pergamon, 1980).

Druzhinin, V. V. and Kontorov, D. S., *Concept, Algorithm, Decision* (Moscow, 1972).

Emme, Eugene M. (ed.), *The Impact of Air Power: National Security and World Politics* (New York: Van Nostrand, 1959).

Erickson, J., *Command and Control under Soviet Military System* (Defence Attache, 1980).

Erickson, J., 'Soviet Command Technology', *Jane's Defence Review*, 1/1980.

Erickson, J., 'Whither Soviet Air Power?', unpublished paper, Edinburgh, 1978.

Erickson and Feuchtwanger (eds), *Soviet Military Power and Performance* (London: Macmillan, 1979).

Etzold and Gaddis (eds), *Containment, Documents on American Policy and Strategy 1945–50* (New York: Columbia, 1978).

279

Fall, Bernard B., *Hell in a Very Small Place* (London: Pall Mall, 1967).
Fall, Bernard B., *Street Without Joy – Insurgency in Indo-China 1946–63*, rev. edn (Harrisburg, PA: Stackpole, 1965).
Fall, Bernard B., *The Two Vietnams* (London: Pall Mall, 1963).
Fall, Bernard B., *Vietnam Witness* (London: Pall Mall, 1966).
Feuchtwanger and Mason (eds), *Air Power in the Next Generation* (London: Macmillan, 1979).
Foreign Languages Publishing House, *Contribution to the History of Dien Bien Phu, Vietnamese Studies* (Hanoi, 1965).
Futrell, R. F., *Ideas, Concepts and Doctrine: A History of Basic Thinking in the United States Air Force 1907–64* (USAF, 1974).
Futrell, R. F., *The United States Air Force in Korea* (New York: Duell, Sloan and Pearce, 1961).
Gardner (ed.), *The Korean War* (Chicago: Quadrangle Books, 1972).
Garthoff, R. L., *Soviet Military Policy* (London: Faber & Faber, 1966).
Garthoff, R. L., *Soviet Strategy in the Nuclear Age* (Atlantic, 1958).
Gibney, F. (ed.), *The Penkovsky Papers*, Oleg Penkovsky (London: Collins, 1965).
Golan, *Yom Kippur and After: The Soviet Union and the Middle East Crisis* (Cambridge University Press, 1977).
Gowing, M., *Independence and Deterrence*, vols 1 and 2 (London: Macmillan, 1974).
Greenwood, John in *The Vietnam War* (London: Salamander Books, 1979).
Groom, *British Thinking about Nuclear Weapons* (London: Pinter, 1974).
Hahn and Pfaltzgraff (eds), *Atlantic Community and Crisis* (Oxford: Pergamon Press, 1979).
Hansen, J. H., 'Development of Soviet Aviation Support', *International Defence Review*, 5/1980.
Head and Rokke, *NATO 1955, American Defence Policy*, 3rd edn (Baltimore: Johns Hopkins Press, 1973).
Hemsley, Colonel J., 'Soviet Command and Control', unpublished Defence Fellowship Paper, Edinburgh University, 1980.
Herzog, *War of Atonement* (London: Weidenfeld & Nicolson, 1975).
Higham, *Air Power: A Concise History* (London: Macdonald, 1972).
Higham and Kipp (eds), *Soviet Aviation and Air Power* (London: Brassey's, 1978).
Historical Branch, USMC, *The Battle for Khe San* (1969).
HMSO, *Defence in the 1980s*, Cmnd 7826-1 (London, 1980).
Howard and Hunter, *Israel and the Arab World*, Adelphi Paper No. 41 (London: IISS, 1967).
Ismay, *NATO, The First Five Years* (Paris, 1955).
Khruschev, N., *Khruschev Remembers* (London: André Deutsch, 1974).
Kilmarx, Robert A., *A History of Soviet Air Power* (London: Faber & Faber, 1962).
Kissinger, *The Troubled Partnership* (New York: Praeger, 1975).
Kitson, General Frank, *Gangs and Counter-Gangs* (London: Barrie and Rockliff, 1960).
Knorr (ed.), *NATO and American Security* (Princeton University Press, 1959).
Kohler, Gouré and Harvey, *The Soviet Union and the October War, Implications for Detente* (Miami: CAIS, 1974).

Kozlov, S. N., *The Officers' Handbook* (Moscow, 1971).

Lee, Asher, *The Soviet Air Force* (London: Duckworth, 1961).

Liddell-Hart, B. H., *History of the Second World War* (London: Cassell, 1970).

Littaner and Uphoff, *The Air War in Indo China* (Cornell University Press, 1972).

Lomov, N. A. (ed.), *The Revolution in Military Affairs* (Moscow, 1973).

MacIsaac, Colonel D., *Strategic Bombing in World War II* (New York: Garland, 1976).

MacIsaac, Colonel D., *The Air Force and Strategic Thought 1945–51*, Paper No. 8 (Wilson Center, 1979).

Mason, R. A., *Warsaw Pact Air Forces in Air Power, The World's Air Forces*, (London: Orbis, 1980).

Momyer, General William W., *Air Power in Three Wars* (USAF, 1978).

Monroe and Farrar-Hockley, *The Arab–Israeli War October 1973*, Adelphi Paper no. 111 (London: IISS, 1975).

Montross and Canzona, *US Marine Operations in Korea* (US Government Printing Office, 1957).

Morris, James, *Farewell The Trumpets* (London: Faber & Faber, 1966).

O'Ballance, *No Victor, No Vanquished* (London: Barrie and Jenkins, 1979).

Odgers, *Across the Parallel* (London: Heinemann, 1953).

Office of Air Force History, *Air Power and the Fight for Khe San* (Washington, 1973).

Osgood, R. E., *NATO, The Entangling Alliance* (University of Chicago Press, 1962).

Overy, R. J., *The Air War 1939–45* (London: Europa, 1980).

Palit, *Return to Sinai, Arab–Israeli War 1973* (Salisbury, Wilts: Compton Russell, 1974).

Petersen, P. A., *Soviet Air Power and the Pursuit of Non-Military Options*, Studies in Communist Affairs, Vol. III (USAF, 1979).

Polmar, N., 'Soviet Command, Control and Communication', *Air Force Magazine*, June 1980.

Rand Symposium on the Role of Air Power in Counter Insurgency and Unconventional Warfare: The Algerian Emergency, A. H. Peterson, G. C. Reihnhardt, E. E. Conger (eds), July 1963. RM/3653/TR.

Rand Symposium on the Role of Air Power in Counter Insurgency and Unconventional Warfare: The Malayan Emergency, A. H. Peterson, G. C. Reihnhardt, E. E. Conger (eds), June 1963. RM/3651/TR.

Rand Symposium, 'The Philippine Huk Campaign', Memorandum RM3652-PR, 1963.

Rees, David, *Korea, the Limited War* (New York: St Martin's Press, 1964).

Ridgway, General Mathew B., *The Korean War* (New York: Doubleday, 1967).

Rosecrance, R. N., *Defence of the Realm* (New York: Columbia, 1968).

Roy, Jules, *The Battle of Dien Bien Phu* (London: Faber & Faber, 1965).

Royal United Services Institution Seminar Papers, 'Lessons from the Arab–Israeli War', January 1974.

Savkin, V. Y. E., *Operational Art and Tactics* (Moscow, 1972).

Schneider, W. Jr., 'Soviet Military Airlift', *Air Force Magazine*, March 1980.

Schutze, *European Defence Co-operation and NATO* (Paris: Atlantic Institute, 1969).

Sharp, Admiral U. S. G., *Strategy for Defeat* (Novato, CA: Presidio Press, 1978).

Shawcross, William, *Sideshow: Kissinger, Nixon and the Destruction of Cambodia* (London: André Deutsch, 1979).

Slessor, Sir John, *The Central Blue* (London: Cassell, 1956).

Slessor, Sir John, *The Great Deterrent* (London: Cassell, 1957).

Smith, P. M., *The Air Force Plans for Peace* (Baltimore: Johns Hopkins Press, 1970).

Sokolovsky, V. D., *Military Strategy, Soviet Doctrine and Concepts* (London: Pall Mall, 1963).

Spielman, K. F., *Analysing Soviet Strategic Arms Decisions* (Boulder, Col.: Westview, 1978).

Stewart, *Air Power, the Decisive Force in Korea* (Nastrand, 1957).

Sunday Times Inside Team, *The Yom Kippur War* (London: André Deutsch, 1975).

Symposium Papers on October 1973 War (University of Cairo, 1975). Ramadan/M/CO/061.

Taylor, J. W. R., 'Gallery of Soviet Aerospace Weapons', *Air Force Magazine*, March 1980.

'The Flogger Family', *Air International*, August 1980.

Timokhovich, I. V., *The Operational Art of the Soviet Air Force in the Great Patriotic War* (Moscow, 1976).

Tokaev, G. A., *Stalin Means War* (London: Weidenfeld & Nicolson, 1951).

Trevenen, James, *The Royal Air Force, The Past Thirty Years* (London: Macdonald & Jane's, 1976).

Tunner, General William H., *Aerospace Historian*, Summer/Fall 1970, pp. 135–7.

USAF 'Soviet Military Thought' series, no. 11, *Selected Soviet Military Writings 1970–75*.

USAFA, *Air Power and Warfare, Proceedings of the Eighth Military History Symposium* (1978).

Van Creveld, *Military Lessons of the Yom Kippur War: Historical Perspectives* (Georgetown: CSIS, 1975).

Vandenberg, *Air Power in the Korean War*. Reprinted in Emme (ed.), *The Impact of Air Power: National Security and World Politics* (New York: Van Nostrand, 1959).

van Haute, André, *Pritmill History of the French Air Force, Vol. II* (Shepperton, Middx: Ian Allan, 1975).

Vasil'yev, B. A., *Long Range Missile Equipped* (Moscow, 1972), trans. DGIS, Ottawa.

Von Karman, *The Wind and Beyond* (Boston, Mass.: Little, Brown, 1967).

Ware, L. B., *The Handbook of the Arab–Israeli Conflict* (Air University, USAF, 1978).

Westmoreland, General, *A Soldier Reports* (New York: Doubleday, 1976).

Weyland, *The Air Campaigns in Korea*. Reprinted in Emme (ed.), *The Impact of Air Power: National Security and World Politics* (New York: Van Nostrand, 1959).

Whiting, K. R., *Soviet Airpower 1917–76* (Air University, USAF, 1976).

Williams (ed.), *Military Aspects of the Israeli–Arab Conflict*, Tel Aviv Symposium (Tel Aviv: University Publishing Project, 1975).

Wolfe, T. W., *Soviet Power and Europe 1945–1970* (Baltimore: Johns Hopkins Press, 1970).

Wolfe, T. W., *Worldwide Soviet Military Strategy and Policy* (Chicago: Rand, 1973).

Wolfe, T. W., 'The Military Dimension in the Making of Soviet and Defence Policy', statement to the United States House of Representatives Sub-Committee 1977.

Yakovlev, A., *The Aim of a Lifetime* (Moscow: Progress Press, 1972).

IISS Military Balance and Strategic Survey Papers 1967–75.

Interavia.

International Defence Review.

Journals of the Royal United Services Institution 1948–1980.

NATO's Fifteen Nations.

Royal Air Force Quarterly, 1948–1980.

Index

23555730R00175

Printed in Great Britain
by Amazon